Clearing
the Way

Clearing
the Way

DECONCENTRATING THE POOR

IN URBAN AMERICA

Edward G. Goetz

THE URBAN INSTITUTE PRESS
Washington, D.C.

To my mother

THE URBAN INSTITUTE PRESS
2100 M Street, N.W.
Washington, D.C. 20037

Library of Congress Cataloging in Publication Data

Goetz, Edward G. (Edward Glenn), 1957–
    Clearing the way: deconcentrating the poor in urban America / Edward G. Goetz.
        p. cm.
Includes bibliographical references and index.
    ISBN 0-87766-712-8 (pbk.: alk. paper)
    1. Poor—Housing—Minnesota—Minneapolis Metropolitan Area. 2. Poor—Housing—Minnesota—Saint Paul Metropolitan Area. 3. Urban poor—Housing—United States. 4. Low-income housing—Government policy—United States. 5. Urban policy—United States. I. Title: Deconcentrating the poor in urban America. II. Title.
    HD7287.96.U62M675 2003
    363.5'56'09776579—dc21

                                                                2003004782

Printed in the United States of America
Cover photos courtesy of the Center for Urban and Regional Affairs of the University of Minnesota

THE URBAN INSTITUTE is a nonprofit policy research and educational organization established in Washington, D.C., in 1968. Its staff investigates the social, economic, and governance problems confronting the nation and evaluates the public and private means to alleviate them. The Institute disseminates its research findings through publications, its web site, the media, seminars, and forums.

Through work that ranges from broad conceptual studies to administrative and technical assistance, Institute researchers contribute to the stock of knowledge available to guide decisionmaking in the public interest.

Conclusions or opinions expressed in Institute publications are those of the authors and do not necessarily reflect the views of officers or trustees of the Institute, advisory groups, or any organizations that provide financial support to the Institute.

Contents

Acknowledgments

This book is the result of several different research efforts over the past decade. Mara Sidney, now on the political science faculty at Rutgers-Newark, and I were studying community development in Minnesota during the early 1990s when we first noticed how the deconcentration discourse was affecting neighborhood politics. Alan Arthur provided me with the opportunity to see how the deconcentration argument affected affordable housing at the neighborhood level. About the same time, Joan Pearson, then the director of the Saint Paul Tenant's Union, got me interested in the way the war on drugs was playing out in Saint Paul. As my interest grew, Joan and other affordable-housing advocates, such as Caty Royce of the Community Stabilization Project, were helpful in drawing out the connections among deconcentration, the war on drugs, and the demolition of affordable housing. Also, I would like to thank the dozens of local neighborhood activists and community development officials throughout Minneapolis and Saint Paul who agreed to be interviewed during this period.

Several people read parts of the book (whether they knew it at the time or not) and provided helpful feedback, including Joan Pearson, Tim Thompson of Minneapolis Legal Aid, Elvin Wyly of the University of British Columbia, and George Galster of Wayne State University. Because portions of this book have been published as journal articles, I am indebted to several anonymous reviewers for helping me to hone my arguments. I would especially like to thank Judith Martin of the University of Minnesota's Urban Studies program, and Myron Orfield, both of whom read the full manuscript and provided me with their reactions. Rick Custer and Suellen Wenz at the Urban Institute Press also made significant contributions to this project.

A good portion of the book is based on my research on the implementation of the *Hollman* consent decree in Minneapolis. Tom Fulton of the Family Housing Fund and Kit Hadley, then-commissioner of the Minnesota Housing Finance Agency, made decisions in 1999 to fund that research. Their interest in finding out how this experiment in deconcentration was turning out and how it was affecting the families involved, and their understanding that *Hollman* was a central issue for the entire region, were important elements in ensuring that the study was completed. The Minneapolis Public Housing Authority (MPHA) granted full access to a wide range of information necessary to do the study; without its cooperation the study would have been significantly compromised. Tim Thompson was extremely helpful before and during the *Hollman* research, as was Tom Streitz (first as a Legal Aid attorney and then as an MPHA official). Officials with the Minneapolis NAACP, the Minneapolis HUD office, and the Metropolitan Council were also involved in shaping the research design and providing information along the way. Naturally, the arguments I make in this book do not necessarily reflect their views or the views of their agencies. Several research assistants lent their abilities to the *Hollman* work, including Lori Mardock, Elfric Porte, Chris Dettling, Kathy Ember, Yang Zhang, and Li Luan. Molly McCartney and Jeff Matson created maps, and the Minnesota Center for Survey Research conducted the in-person interviews with hundreds of *Hollman* families that gave their time to relate their stories. The Center for Urban and Regional Affairs at the University of Minnesota also provided support for the *Hollman* research, and Tom Scott and Mike Greco in particular were instrumental in facilitating the research and its dissemination.

I was sustained in this endeavor, as in all my endeavors, by my wife, Susan, and my daughters, Hanne, Mary, and Greta.

Edward G. Goetz
Minneapolis, Minnesota
March 2003

1

Introduction

*We know that poverty by itself doesn't cause urban problems. It's the concentration
. . . that eventually strangles those neighborhoods economically, making it impossible
for residents to have access to jobs, good schools, health care, transportation. These
are living conditions that can, and too often do, foster hopelessness, despair, and
antisocial behavior.*

——Minneapolis Mayor Sharon Sayles Belton, 1995

*If this concentration in Minneapolis continues at the same rate in the next 10 years
as it has in the last 10 years, it will be to the proportion that you have today in
Detroit and East Saint Louis—overwhelmingly people of color and certainly an
over-concentration of drugs and crime.*

——Matt Little, president of the Minneapolis NAACP, 1995

By 9 A.M., the protesters who had stood between the bulldozer and the two-story townhomes had already been arrested and taken away. The more than 300 units of low-cost public housing stood largely vacant, virtually in the shadow of downtown Minneapolis—about a mile from the city's financial and cultural heart. More than 600 other public housing units had already been demolished at the site over the previous three years. Some dated back to 1939; all were the product of previous urban revitalization efforts. By the 1990s, however, these homes showed the wear of 50 years, with structural problems made worse by shifting soil underneath. The neighborhood had become the city's most highly concentrated pocket of poverty, with more than 70 percent of the population living below the federal poverty level, and a median income one-third that of the city as a whole. Many residents lived in constant fear of crime and complained about the declining quality of their apartments and the neighborhood. Yet, on a warm June morning in 1999, the remaining protesters stood behind the construction fence, holding their signs and watching as the bulldozer began to tear through the homes. The prevailing question that day was whether the city was indeed clearing the way for the previous residents to have a chance at a better life or merely clearing the way for a new, more affluent class of residents to occupy this prime parcel of real estate.

The United States is in the middle of a large and coordinated effort to "deconcentrate" its urban poor. As the country's most recent antipoverty strategy, deconcentration raises a number of public policy controversies, ranging from the federal government's culpability in prevailing patterns of racial and class-based residential segregation to the proper role of public authority in shaping residential communities for both the poor and nonpoor. This book examines the premises underlying the deconcentration of poverty, along with its potential effects and political dynamics. While events occurring in cities across the country are discussed to a certain extent, we will focus primarily on a case study of the Minneapolis–Saint Paul metropolitan area.

Concentration of Poverty

The current policy initiative comes from the reality that poverty in America is becoming highly spatially concentrated. The number of neighborhoods in which a majority or near majority of residents live below the federal poverty level has increased dramatically over the past three decades. Unemployment rates in these communities are extremely high. Chances for a productive work life, and even the existence of positive role models in this respect, are relatively rare. Such intense concentration of disadvantage is not restricted, moreover, to our largest and oldest cities, but occurs in cities all over the country.

Various explanations exist for how this growing concentration of poverty came about. Some experts point to a history of racial discrimination and segregation in housing markets, while others point to economic shifts over the past three decades. Evidence shows that the mobility choices of the nonpoor (both black and white) have been a factor. Many have argued that the geographic distribution of subsidized housing in the United States has significantly contributed to concentrated poverty. No one, not even the federal government anymore, contests that in many cities public housing has been systematically placed in the poorest neighborhoods and in neighborhoods with the highest percentage of minority residents. Other publicly subsidized housing developments have also tended to be geographically concentrated in central cities and their more disadvantaged neighborhoods. This concentration of subsidized units has anchored poor and, increasingly, minority residents in these neighborhoods. Home-ownership subsidies, on the other hand, which were targeted to a more affluent and white population, were strictly directed to suburban areas for more than 25 years, facilitating the flow of white middle-class residents out of neighborhoods that were receiving public housing and its housing "cousins."[1]

Further, little argument exists about the results of this extreme concentration of poverty. It produces a range of social problems whose whole is greater than the sum of its parts. For example, school delinquency, school dropout, teenage pregnancy, out-of-wedlock childbirth, violent crime, and drug abuse rates are all greater in these communities than would be predicted by a linear extrapolation of poverty effects. Something about the extreme concentration of disadvantage begets even more community and individual dysfunction. The explanation for such dysfunction is a combination of loosely connected hypotheses that, taken together, can be called the neighborhood-effects arguments. They provide slightly different accounts of the causes behind the effects about which they all agree—that neighborhood environment is critical in determining individuals' opportunities and experiences.

Concerns about the concentration of poverty, therefore, focus on the dysfunctional aspects of poor communities and on the barriers these produce for families trying to make their way out of poverty. However, there are larger fears as well. Concentrated poverty not only affects individual families, but also produces aggregate community effects. Crime rates increase, rates of private investment and economic life (at least legally sanctioned economic activity) decline, and the communities themselves become dysfunctional. Furthermore, residents fear the spread of this blight—its gradual, or not-so-gradual, diffusion throughout larger sections of a city. In Minneapolis, concerned citizens tend to point to the example most geographically proximate—Detroit. Efforts at deconcentrating the poor in Minneapolis stem, to a great extent, from what can be called "the Detroit Scenario." Detroit typifies a city overcome with neighborhoods of high poverty where the middle class has fled to relatively safe and secure havens of racial and class exclusivity. The city is wracked by high property-tax rates on ever-devaluing property, generating insufficient resources to fund essential city services and the elevated level of public and social services necessary to support an impoverished populace. Its schools are underfunded and inadequate, and its streets unsafe as drugs and crime have taken over whole communities. All the while, an affluent ring of suburbs, whose residents benefit from low tax rates because their communities lack a dependent population in need of public and social services, surround the city.

Deconcentration through Dispersal of Subsidized Housing

Given this analysis of urban problems, policymakers have responded with programs designed to deconcentrate the poor through a greater dispersal of subsidized-housing residents. In practice, this has meant five different, though related, policy initiatives. First is the shifting of housing subsidies from project-based assistance (in which the subsidy is tied to a particular unit that is fixed in space—typically in lower-income neighborhoods) to tenant-based subsidies (in the form of vouchers that allow greater locational choice by families). Second is the federal government's attempt to refine tenant-based subsidies to facilitate the greatest possible dispersal of assisted families. Third is an effort, begun in 1990 and made permanent in 1998, to introduce a greater mix of incomes into existing subsidized public housing developments. Fourth is a small-to-modest effort at dispersing project-based subsidies into neighborhoods and communities that previously had little or none. Fifth is the government's largest effort aimed at demolishing or revitalizing extreme concentrations of public housing, scattering the previous residents with household-based subsidies and converting the project sites into mixed-use, mixed-income developments. Each initiative is present in Minneapolis and the Twin Cities region.

The Shift from Project-Based to Tenant-Based Subsidies

Since the mid-1970s, federal housing budgets have shifted away from funding the construction of new housing units or the rehabilitation of existing units to assisting families through vouchers. Furthermore, existing unit-based subsidies have actually been converted to household-based subsidies. This process typically involves either the demolition of housing units and the provision of household-based subsidies to the families in them, or the conversion of subsidized projects to market rate apartments (also accompanied by tenant-based assistance to the families residing there).

At the same time, the tenant-based subsidies themselves have changed. Section 8 certificates, the original form of tenant-based assistance, were gradually replaced by vouchers during the 1980s and 1990s. Finally, in 1998, Congress merged vouchers and certificates into a single form of assistance—the Section 8 Housing Choice Voucher. The current voucher allows families to rent units above the fair market rent (FMR) as long as they pay the difference between the government-established FMR limit and the actual rent. This provision enables Section 8 families to expand their housing search to previously unaffordable neighborhoods.

Refinement of Tenant-Based Assistance

Since the late 1980s, Congress and the U.S. Department of Housing and Urban Development (HUD) have tried to increase the "portability" of Section 8 assistance—that is, the ability of a household given Section 8 in one city to use it in a neighboring community. This policy allows those who receive their assistance from central-city jurisdictions to search suburban areas, thus facilitating a greater spread of assisted households.

Income Mixing in Public Housing

In 1990, Congress authorized a demonstration aimed at exploring the feasibility of introducing a wider mix of incomes into existing public housing projects. Then in 1998, Congress permanently changed the public housing program to require greater income diversity. The experience of the demonstration program is confined to a few cities, while the broader public housing reforms are too recent to have produced any measurable effects. Nevertheless, these initiatives signal a course change in public housing policy based on the deconcentration-of-poverty argument.

Scattered-Site Subsidized Housing

Tenant-based assistance has been instrumental in creating new "mobility" programs in cities around the country. In these programs, families are given vouchers that must be used in neighborhoods of low poverty (or in some cases, with low minority populations). In addition, families are given relocation counseling and assistance, and local agencies aggressively recruit property owners to expand the pool of potential relocation sites.

Not only have Congress and HUD introduced these first four policy initiatives through conventional means (i.e., legislation and the creation of new programs), but HUD has also been able to thread these initiatives into the negotiated settlements of several lawsuits filed against the agency in cities across the country over the past 20 years. In several of these negotiated settlements (consent decrees) in cases alleging discrimination in the planning and operation of the public housing program, HUD has "agreed," as a remedy to the complaints, to various combinations of the four initiatives. In most cases, concentrations of public housing have been demolished, and the subsidies converted to tenant-based Section 8 vouchers. Redevelopment of the sites typically incorporates a mixed-income approach. In some cases, mobility programs have been initiated. In other cities, HUD has agreed to a program of scattered-site public housing to reduce concentrations. Thus, these lawsuits, which HUD was facing as a result of its previous policies, and which had been filed in most cases as discrimination lawsuits independent of deconcentration, were nonetheless used by the agency to accomplish deconcentration-policy objectives. In a few cities, including Minneapolis, the consent decrees incorporated all the elements of the deconcentration strategy.

Redevelopment

The largest single programmatic effort at deconcentrating poverty has been the HOPE VI program. Created in 1992, HOPE VI grew out of a national commission that focused on the worst public housing projects and proposed solutions for improving them. The program funds the redevelopment of large public housing projects across the country, and for the first few years, HOPE VI grants were restricted to the nation's most "distressed" public housing projects. Over time, however, HOPE VI has moved beyond those projects and now applies to any public housing project for which demolition and redevelopment costs are within 10 percent of rehabilitation costs. Typically, HOPE VI involves demolition of some or all of the units in a particular project and redevelopment of the site as a mixed-use, mixed-income development. The number of public housing units is reduced dramatically, owner-occupied housing is combined with rental housing on the site, and an income mix is achieved. Approximately 100,000 public housing units were scheduled for demolition in the first 10 years of program funding, with the net loss of units projected as high as 60,000 (Keating 2000).

What Is at Stake

Close analysis of a single campaign to deconcentrate the poor, such as the one in Minneapolis, provides us an opportunity to carefully consider the entire edifice of this policy approach. The profile of poverty neighborhoods, as it has emerged in both the social scientific literature and the popular press, is one of a devastated social and economic landscape, with pervasive poverty, an almost complete lack of healthy social and economic characteristics, and prevailing norms of lawlessness and antisocial behavior. The concentration-of-poverty discourse was developed and refined during the height of the nation's war on drugs, when fears of inner-city violent crime, drug-induced criminality, and social breakdown were at their greatest. One issue facing this policy approach, however, is whether or not the concentration-of-poverty scenario exaggerates conditions in poor urban neighborhoods. Are the images of lawlessness and social breakdown, if true even in a limited number of extreme cases, nevertheless a distortion of most poor communities? If so, is deconcentration on a national scale an extreme measure, ill suited to the problems of urban poverty?

A second issue is "choice." Is deconcentration about moving people out of particular neighborhoods because the neighborhoods have been declared dysfunctional, or is it about providing housing choices for a class of people who have not had them in the past? This question may be, in many ways, the most difficult issue for policymakers and planners to address. It repeats a long-standing tension in federal housing policy and case law: In our policy efforts, are we trying to reduce incidences of discrimination that rob people of full choice in the housing market, or are we trying in a more proactive (and interventionist way) to desegregate? The desirability of forced racial desegregation is a matter of contention among both blacks and whites.

The desirability of forced *income* segregation in the housing market, however, is equally contentious. The empirical evidence on the effects of concentrated poverty suggests fairly convincingly that such high levels of income segregation negatively impact disadvantaged neighborhoods. Deconcentration, as the term suggests, is about achieving a greater level of income (and—because of the considerable overlap with race—racial) desegregation. However, when this objective is achieved through anything other than voluntary means, it produces significant political conflict. Do all or most of the residents of concentrated subsidized housing want to move to non-concentrated communities? Experience and even common sense might suggest otherwise. Do all or any of the residents of the "receiving communities"—the neighborhoods into which the poor will relocate—welcome the opportunity to increase the diversity of their neighborhoods? Not typically.

Yet, were we to limit our deconcentration efforts to expanding the mobility "choices" of the poor, what might be the result? Mobility choices are the result of a myriad of considerations by households, and depend on a constellation of market and social factors. Neighborhoods, for instance, provide a package of amenities, including employment access, parks, shopping, public transportation, and other public services. In addition, personal support networks and such market factors as the availability of desired rents and certain types of housing units affect location decisions. The poor relate to many of these amenities in ways fundamentally different from more affluent families. For example, buses are less important to the affluent than to poor families without a car. True choice in the housing market means more than providing a poor household with a rent subsidy. A Section 8 voucher may allow a poor family to afford an apartment that costs an additional $300 per month. However, such a voucher does not put a bus line in front of the building, relocate the community college or affordable day care nearby, and bring along the family's network of friends and relatives for emotional and material support. Housing "choice" is a variable term in any market, highly constrained by factors that deconcentration policy as currently formulated does not begin to address. Thus, whether the objective is desegregation or, more fundamentally, greater choice in the housing market, deconcentration efforts face significant constraints.

Third, efforts to deconcentrate the poor lead inevitably to discussions of the proper role of government in shaping neighborhoods and influencing the housing choice and mobility decisions of all households. This question spans the entire range of housing market interventions, from decisions to forcibly move and relocate poor people on the one hand, to using regulatory power to induce or discourage the development of low-cost housing in suburban areas on the other. What principles should guide such intervention—the desire for specific outcomes (i.e., desegregation) or the concern for equitable processes (i.e., antidiscrimination)? Strongly interventionist efforts such as deconcentration (and urban renewal before it) engage us in fundamental questions of community planning. What is the proper use of public authority when it comes to building communities? What are the public purposes involved in such intervention?

Deconcentration efforts require that communities with little or no low-cost housing make room for subsidized families from high-poverty, central-city neighborhoods. No long and rich history of this exists in the United States, however. Suburban communities have traditionally used their local control over land use to limit low-cost and subsidized housing. To succeed at a significant scale, deconcentration would require a modification of that approach. Modifications of local zoning and development prerogatives have been attempted only through regional governance or state growth management, both extremely rare. Instead, deconcentration policy has been about moving the poor, and only about moving the poor.

While deconcentration was designed to help rectify conditions in America's worst neighborhoods, housing markets since the late 1990s have become very heated, even in or near neighborhoods of concentrated poverty. Efforts at deconcentration must walk a fine line between having enough impact to reverse neighborhood decline and establish a viable multi-income community on the one hand, and triggering gentrification on the other. Though gentrification may represent to some the ultimate success, the ultimate turnaround for a high-poverty neighborhood, it will not appreciably deconcentrate poverty as much as simply moving those concentrations to other places.

Beyond these more macro-level concerns, several notable issues arise at the strategy and policy level. The most overriding is the implicit decision within a deconcentration approach that community development approaches are inadequate at best and outright failures at worst. In his widely read account of a half-century of urban community development policy, Nicholas Lemann (1994) pronounced that these policies had failed. Despite the expenditure of millions of dollars and decades of efforts, America's urban neighborhoods continued to decline. To some extent, this analysis complements the 1980s neoconservative attack on the antipoverty programs of the 1960s. According to Murray (1984), for example, these attempts to end poverty in place not only failed, but also actually exacerbated the problem by creating dependency among people and places on government assistance. Other experts, even those who do not quite share Murray's opinion, nevertheless suggest that community development has come up wanting. Orfield (1997), for example, argues that even community development efforts that are considered successful within the field have failed to turn around their central-city communities. Rusk (1999) argues that the "inside game" (community development) is destined to fail without a complementary strong "outside game" (regional efforts). The debate over addressing poverty in place as opposed to facilitating residents' exit from poor neighborhoods is not new. Nor has the question been resolved in any final sense. Forced deconcentration, however, is an emphatic statement. It stakes out a strong position on one side of the question. Deconcentration says that households should leave their central-city neighborhoods for their own good—that they would be better-off in neighborhoods shared with more affluent families.

Finally, disregarding alternative approaches or questions about the premises of deconcentration itself produces more questions. First, is deconcentration of poverty a step back from a fundamental attempt to eliminate poverty to a less-ambitious attempt to merely spread it around? Have we retreated from our effort to attack those processes, whatever they may be, that produce poverty? Proponents of deconcentration would argue that this is not wholly the case. The concentration-of-poverty argument suggests that living in these environments begets even greater social dysfunction than being poor in a predominantly nonpoor community. Thus, there are individual and social benefits to deconcentrating poverty. Troublesome social problems are reduced, and individual families may be better able to work their way out of poverty. They will be closer to jobs, less afraid to venture out to find work. They will benefit from better schools and richer (literally and figuratively) networks of social capital. In addition, their children will be better socialized to succeed. Therefore, according to proponents, deconcentrating poverty will also reduce poverty.

The relative emphasis on forced versus voluntary deconcentration is a central issue. Voluntary mobility avoids many of the more problematic aspects of forced relocation, yet voluntary mobility will probably never achieve the scale necessary to have the impact that proponents desire. The issue of scale is central. The proper and necessary scale for these programs is probably several orders of magnitude higher than what can be achieved purely through voluntary means, and higher, too, than what is politically acceptable to most parties. Political opposition to deconcentration comes from both the right and the left; it comes from both the receiving communities and the communities being deconcentrated. Receiving communities want strict limits to the number of very low income families that are relocated in their midst. The high-poverty communities, too, are quite likely to resist large-scale deconcentration—on several grounds.

A final controversy generated by deconcentration revolves around its impact on the families involved and the communities affected. Proponents point to evidence that deconcentration leads to improvements in employment, education, neighborhood satisfaction, and sense of safety. Opponents point to examples of families in new communities experiencing harassment, higher levels of social isolation, and greater dissatisfaction with public services, such as public transportation, on which the poor rely heavily. Opponents also point to the potential detrimental impacts of subsidized housing units (or families) in receiving communities. Do these families (or units) devalue property, trigger decline in the public schools, or increase incivilities? Proponents suggest that research by and large does not support these claims, and that healthy communities can absorb these families and remain healthy.

The Consent Decree in *Hollman v. Cisneros*

In order to investigate the issues related to deconcentration in a comprehensive manner, this book examines closely one particular case. The city of Minneapolis pursued a deconcentration strategy through most of the 1990s. The initiative's centerpiece, though by no means the only element, was the consent decree in *Hollman v. Cisneros* (originally *Hollman v. Kemp*).

In 1992, attorneys for the Legal Aid Society of Minneapolis filed a lawsuit in U.S. District Court, alleging that the Minneapolis Public Housing Authority (MPHA), HUD, and the city discriminated in siting public housing. The attorneys provided information that they felt showed a clear pattern among Minneapolis and HUD officials of concentrating family public housing projects in the near north neighborhood, the traditional center of the African-American community in the city. The plaintiffs were alleging what had already been demonstrated for Chicago in the *Gautreaux* cases,[2] and what most who were knowledgeable about public housing nationwide knew characterized the program in many cities. When Bill Clinton took office, the lawsuit's name was changed to reflect the new HUD secretary and the change of administration. However, settlement negotiations took a new direction, too.

The "new HUD" in 1993 wanted to take a fresh look at its subsidized (and especially public) housing programs. Part of that fresh look was a willingness to admit past mistakes in concentrating housing units and to attempt to correct those mistakes. HUD officials moved to settle a number of other cases against the agency essentially alleging the same thing: discrimination in the siting and placement of public housing in ways that furthered segregation. This approach was part of HUD's new theory about urban problems, based on the concentration-of-poverty argument.

In Minneapolis, what had been initiated as a discrimination lawsuit on behalf of public housing residents whose housing choices were restricted by the concentration of assisted units on the near north side became, during the process of settlement negotiations, an effort to deconcentrate poverty, facilitate a greater geographic spread of assisted units and assisted families, and reduce the number of public housing units on that site. Referring back to the time when the suit was first filed, the lead attorney for the plaintiffs remarked, "I don't think any of us had heard the term 'concentration of poverty' " (Furst 1996a). However, by the time the settlement was reached, deconcentrating poverty was its main objective.

The *Hollman* settlement-negotiation process fit seamlessly with the objectives of both HUD and the city of Minneapolis at the time. Many of the local officials who were ostensibly defendants in the process, from the city council to MPHA and HUD, shared with the plaintiffs the central goals of the agreement: reducing the concentration of public housing units on-site, and dispersing the very low income residents throughout the local housing market. An element of this consensus was a fundamental agreement that the reuse of the site should include a significantly reduced concentration of public housing units.

In January 1995, the agreement between the parties was announced, and HUD promised to allocate $100 million toward settling the case (Diaz 1995). The agreement, ratified by all parties in April, covered four separate public housing projects—the Sumner Field townhomes, the Olson townhomes, and the Glenwood and Lyndale townhome projects. In all, these projects and the public land on which they stood encompassed 73 acres located just one mile from downtown Minneapolis, directly adjacent to Interstate 94 and bisected by Olson Memorial Highway (State Highway 55) (figure 1.1).

Figure 1.1. The North Side Project Site Relative to
Downtown Minneapolis

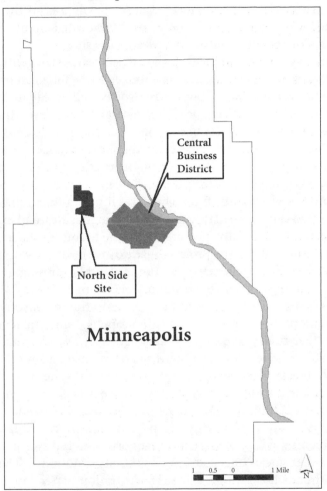

The Near North Side Neighborhood

The near north side site is favorably positioned relative to the city's core and well served by transportation routes. At the same time, however, Interstates 94 and 394 and railroad tracks to the south of the site serve as important physical barriers between the near north side and downtown. In fact, in 1995 the site was virtually surrounded by major transportation routes or industrial properties. Furthermore, several other subsidized housing developments were also adjacent to the site. The Bryant high-rises (for seniors) were located immediately east of the Sumner Field and Olson projects, while several privately owned but publicly subsidized buildings were located northwest of the site.

There was little question that the city's greatest concentration of poverty was located at this site. As mentioned earlier, median household income was one-third that of the city as a whole, and more than 70 percent of all households functioned below the federal poverty level (the typical threshold in identifying areas of concentrated poverty is 40 percent). The percentage of the population receiving public assistance was six times that of the city as a whole. In addition, the residents of the project site were overwhelmingly (94 percent) nonwhite in a city that was 78 percent European-American at the time. There was little argument that the city over time had concentrated its public housing in that area, and in the near north side more generally. The site was home to four of the five family public housing townhome projects that existed in the city. In fact, the project area contained more than 900 units of public housing, 25 percent of the total non–scattered-site inventory owned by MPHA.

Census data for 1990 showed that concentration of poverty among African Americans was greater in the Minneapolis–Saint Paul region than in most other cities in the United States. In fact, as a whole, minorities in the Twin Cities were more likely to live in poverty than in any other major metropolitan area in the country (Draper 1993). The proportion of African Americans living in high-poverty areas of Minneapolis–Saint Paul had increased from 27 to 47 percent between 1980 and 1990 (Jargowsky 1996). The city's siting pattern had concentrated public housing developments not only on the city's near north side, but also along corridors on either side of Interstate 35W on the city's south side. These same neighborhoods housed the highest concentration of Section 8 participants as well. They were home to just 20 percent of the city's total population, but 51 percent of certificate and voucher holders. Furthermore, these neighborhoods were 57 percent nonwhite in a city that was 78 percent white. At the time the lawsuit was filed, 58 percent of all scattered-site units were located in predominantly minority census tracts (Thompson 1996, 244). Thus, the evidence was clear on a number of dimensions that serious problems of residential segregation characterized the public housing program in Minneapolis, and affected minority populations in particular.

Conditions on the North Side

By 1995, the units in the aging north side project site were suffering from physical decline, neglect, and a host of design problems. Few housing officials or advocates were ready to contest such a characterization. The *Star Tribune,* the city's leading daily newspaper, ran stories of mice and cockroaches overwhelming some residents. According to one of the plaintiffs, "[Cockroaches are] inside my washer, they're in my radio, they're in my telephone, and when I turn on my microwave, they come running out. The roaches even used to get up in the smoke detector and set the thing off" (Morrison 1995).

The projects had been built on a floodplain through which Bassett Creek had run. When the projects were built, the creek was diverted through a storm sewer to connect with the nearby Mississippi River. Over the decades, the unstable soil of the former creek bed had led to shifting and cracking in the Sumner Field project buildings until, in some units, one could allegedly see outside through the cracks. The nature of the soils would later play a prominent role in the decision to demolish all the public housing units on the site (the consent decree only explicitly called for the demolition of the Sumner Field project).

Project building and site designs were also criticized. The HUD HOPE VI program officially adopted the view that much public housing built between 1930 and 1980 in the modernist tradition significantly and negatively affected residents' quality of life. The north side projects were offered as examples. Front doors were indistinguishable from back doors, and, as one Minneapolis reporter put it,

> Garbage carts are as likely to stand by the one that looks most like the front door. Doors open directly to the outside, without a vestibule or any way to personalize the entry. Most of the original canopies have rotted away. Yards belong to everybody and, therefore, no one. And the 5.2 miles of sidewalks that crisscross the six square block project make all spaces open to strangers (Mack 1995).

The site included three square blocks (a so-called superblock) that interrupted the street grid and isolated the projects from the residential neighborhood to its west. All these features had, by the 1990s, come to be seen as destructive of good community life, and obstacles to a safe residential experience. The federal government's official public housing revitalization program, HOPE VI, had officially condemned these design features and adopted the principles of "new urbanism," calling for the return of street grids and personalized spaces, and reintegration of public housing with its surrounding communities.

Deconcentration "Unwrapped"

This book analyzes recent efforts to deconcentrate poverty. In particular, the Minneapolis case is presented within the context of the national effort to disperse poor people throughout metropolitan areas. The argument presented here is based both on the *Hollman* consent decree, and, more generally, on the changes in local revitalization efforts triggered by the concentration-of-poverty argument. Chapter 2 lays out the concentration-of-poverty argument. The empirical and theoretical underpinnings of deconcentration are examined, as are the historical contextual conditions that gave rise to it. The strengths and the limits of the neighborhood-effects arguments also are discussed, as are arguments that are corollary to deconcentration, such as the impact of community design on community life.

Chapter 3 looks at the policy history—the evolution of public, mainly federal, efforts to provide poor families with housing choice and reduce concentrations of poverty. This history dates to the Johnson administration, although the first meaningful steps in this direction were taken in Nixon's first term. Though poverty deconcentration is a fairly recent initiative, its heritage is rooted in a range of policies that have evolved since the 1960s. The tour through these initiatives will take us from the efforts to produce scattered-site public housing to the regional initiatives of the 1970s and on to the development of the Section 8 program in 1974. This chapter also surveys the importance of the *Gautreaux* cases in Chicago and more recent policy shifts in tenant-based assistance. We will also briefly look at the development of the HOPE VI program. Finally, the chapter examines the impact of dispersal and deconcentration efforts in cities across the country. Studies of Gautreaux in Chicago, HUD's evaluation of Moving To Opportunity (MTO), collected evidence regarding scattered-site housing, and smaller studies of "vouchering out" and lawsuit settlements across the country provide substantial data on the effectiveness of these approaches. We evaluate deconcentration on its own terms: Does it improve the lives of the families deconcentrated, does it have benign effects on the receiving communities, and does it improve conditions in the target communities? Indeed, does deconcentration clear the way for poor families to improve their lot in life?

Chapter 4 shifts our analysis to Minneapolis. The Twin Cities region is home to one of the nation's leading advocates of deconcentration, Democratic State Senator Myron Orfield. As a state representative from a south side district during the early 1990s, Orfield successfully shepherded regional fair-share housing legislation through the Minnesota legislature three years in a row. In particular, his efforts were notable for their comprehensiveness. He advocated tax-base sharing; reform of the regional governing body, the Metropolitan Council; and efforts to rationalize regional funding for infrastructure as well. All these initiatives were aimed at a better share of costs, responsibilities, and development support between the center of the region and its fast-growing periphery. Orfield's lasting political contribution was the realization that inner-ring suburbs were facing many of the same issues of decline that central cities had been facing for decades. He molded a winning legislative coalition out of central-city representatives and legislators from the inner-ring suburbs. Though Orfield's legislation was vetoed three years running by a governor whose political base was in the developing suburbs, Orfield has had a profound and lasting impact on the politics of the Twin Cities. In fact, in 1995 the legislature passed and the governor signed a compromise fair-share law (written by two other legislators, but dubbed "Orfield Lite" by locals in tribute to its obvious lineage). The implementation of this law and continuing efforts to get suburban communities to accept low-income housing are the subject of chapter 4.

During Orfield's years of tireless advocacy for regional equity, he spread the word among countless community organizations in the suburbs and the two central cities. The spread of this message, coinciding as it did with an unprecedented rise in violent crime in Minneapolis— much of which the public associated with gangs and drugs—was wide and far. By 1995, few community activists and even fewer local politicians were unfamiliar with the dangers of concentrated poverty. This pervasive concentration-of-poverty argument fundamentally shaped local community development politics in the city for the rest of the decade and beyond.

Chapter 5 examines the "new community development" resulting from these changing circumstances and the new awareness of concentrated poverty that shaped local revitalization efforts in the 1990s. Central-city community groups feared more low-cost housing in their neighborhoods, arguing that they had done their fair share already. Minneapolis and Saint Paul council members began to talk about the need for regional approaches to affordable housing, often as a substitute for their own efforts. Officials in the central cities and in some suburban areas began to favor the demolition of some subsidized and low-cost developments in the name of deconcentrating poverty. Affordable-housing advocates found themselves on the defensive, even in communities that had traditionally supported housing rehabilitation efforts.

The main event in deconcentrating the poor in Minneapolis, discussed in chapter 6, was the consent decree in *Hollman v. Cisneros*. Settled in 1995, the *Hollman* decree incorporates every form of deconcentration extant: demolition and forced displacement, mixed-income redevelopment, scattered-site subsidized development, and voluntary mobility. Though not the only site in the country to adopt all these approaches, Minneapolis is the one in which implementation has progressed most rapidly. Thus, the north side of Minneapolis provides a perfect opportunity to analyze the effects of these different approaches and the politics of a comprehensive deconcentration strategy.

In 1995 the north side site was home to more than 900 units of public housing, by far the city's largest concentration of poverty. By 2000, every one of those units had been demolished and the families relocated to other homes and apartments throughout the region. Such massive dislocation did not occur without political conflict—considerable political conflict, as it turned out. Three groups, in particular, opposed demolition and redevelopment. Southeast Asian immigrants, who by 1995 made up the largest single ethnic group in the north side public housing, opposed demolition because, for them, spatial concentration was an asset. African-American activists on the north side opposed redevelopment because they feared gentrification and the loss of a historically black community. Affordable-housing activists also opposed demolition because of the loss of 700 units of low-cost housing at a time when the city was experiencing double-digit appreciation in housing values and the vacancy rate in rental units was less than 2 percent. The public debate on deconcentration was, by most measures, well informed and intelligent. The debate illustrated virtually all the potential controversies inherent in the strategy and is the subject of chapter 6.

Chapter 7 examines the implementation of *Hollman* deconcentration efforts, including relocation of north side families, construction of replacement housing in "non-concentrated" parts of the metropolitan area, and the Special Mobility Program (SMP) that moved families into these non-concentrated neighborhoods. Relocation progressed rapidly to facilitate demolition. Families were not restricted as to where they could move, though relocation counselors tried to facilitate moves to preferred neighborhoods and housing units. Both replacement housing and the SMP, however, involve the placement of housing and families in non-concentrated neighborhoods. In that respect, officials implementing these elements of the decree have faced significant geographical limits. And while replacement housing developments have come about slowly and met with stiff resistance, the Twin Cities' experience does exemplify metrowide cooperation. The progress of this particular element in the decree has been greater in the Twin Cities, in fact, than in most other regions in the country. The Special Mobility Program, however, has fared quite differently. While HUD made more than 900 vouchers and certificates available for SMP candidates, fewer than 100 have been successfully used, even after six years. This chapter examines the difficulties of implementing both replacement housing and the Special Mobility Program.

"*Hollman* families"—those displaced on the north side and those using mobility certificates and living in replacement units—have been scattered throughout the metropolitan area. Some have participated voluntarily; they signed up to participate in the program and used a mobility certificate or moved into one of the replacement units. Others have participated because a bulldozer knocked down their public housing apartment. Chapter 8 discusses what has happened to these families and how they feel about it.

The concluding chapter assesses the deconcentration of poverty, not only on its own terms (how well it serves the families and the neighborhoods involved), but also by other criteria. Critics of deconcentration argue that it constitutes a misguided repetition of previous mistakes from urban renewal, when government power cleared the way for reuse of valuable urban land near the core of American cities. Does deconcentration repeat past mistakes? Can deconcentration efforts, as they are currently conceived, ever achieve the scale necessary to make a measurable dent in the country's race- and class-based settlement patterns? What are the political implications? How does the language of deconcentration change neighborhood planning and politics?

Messy Business

After giving a public talk on deconcentration in 1996, I was asked whether it was not simply overwhelmingly self-evident that the problems of America's central-city neighborhoods of poverty should be solved by deconcentration. The empirical evidence had, by then, shown quite convincingly that such concentrations are bad. Other empirical evidence (at that point, primarily the Gautreaux program) had shown that deconcentration benefits families that participate. I agreed then and still do, for that matter, that the logic is compelling.

What the Minneapolis case provides, however, is an understanding of the difference between that rather clean logic of deconcentration on the one hand, and its messy reality on the other. Deconcentration, as it happens to people and communities, is not a clean process. As it plays out on the streets, deconcentration exposes fundamental questions of urban planning and politics. Those in a position to decide whether deconcentration remains a policy option should, at the very least, regard these questions as seriously as they regard the logic behind the strategy.

NOTES

1. Other housing programs include subsidy programs for low-income people, such as Section 221 (d)(3) and Section 236.

2. In 1969, a U.S. district court ruled in *Gautreaux v. Chicago Housing Authority* that the Chicago Housing Authority had discriminated in the placement and leasing of public housing in Chicago. In a related case, *Gautreaux v. Harris*, the U.S. Supreme Court ordered a regional remedy for the discrimination. See chapter 3.

2

The Case for Deconcentration

In these "deadly neighborhoods," families have to cope not only with their own poverty, but also with the social isolation and economic deprivation of the hundreds, if not thousands, of other families who live near them. This spatial concentration of poor people acts to magnify poverty and exacerbate its effects.
—Paul A. Jargowsky, 1996

Public housing . . . represents a federally funded, physically permanent institution for the isolation of black families by race and class, and must be considered an important structural cause of concentrated poverty in U.S. cities.
—Douglas S. Massey and Shawn M. Kanaiaupuni, 1993

Publication of William Julius Wilson's *The Truly Disadvantaged* in 1987 triggered more than a decade of scholarly and policy discourse about the dynamics of poverty in urban America. Wilson documented the extreme living conditions of the urban underclass and argued that their systematic marginalization from mainstream social, economic, and political life produced an adaptive set of behavior norms. Wilson's work generated three streams of scholarly inquiry: (1) Some argued with him about what factors caused concentrated poverty; (2) others expanded on his research to document the scope of the problem nationwide; and (3) still others examined the consequences associated with extreme and concentrated poverty (Jargowsky 1996).

Figure 2.1 shows the related but distinct foci for discourse about urban poverty. The first stage focuses on the determinants of concentrated poverty. The second (represented by the center oval) is the set of

Figure 2.1.   The Causes and Consequences of Concentrated Poverty

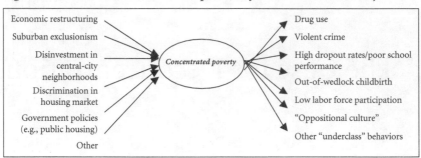

concerns about the extent of concentrated poverty and the empirical efforts to document its scope. The third is the impact of concentrated poverty on the people who live in such neighborhoods and on the communities in which these neighborhoods are located.

Causes of Concentrated Poverty

Explanations for the causes of concentrated poverty have converged on an understanding that stresses the importance of local contextual factors and the variability of causal factors across metropolitan areas. This agreement has transformed the earlier debate that pitted several different explanations against each other. Wilson (1987), for example, argued that macroeconomic changes in the U.S. economy have adversely affected minority central-city residents. Higher concentrations of urban poverty, according to this view, are the result of global economic changes that have restructured local economies and eliminated employment and income sources for many lower- and moderate-income people. Wilson's explanation also connects the exodus of the black middle class from central-city neighborhoods to the Fair Housing Act of 1968 and the limited opening of suburban areas to African-American families.[1]

In a similar argument, the "spatial-mismatch" hypothesis suggests that lower-income populations are trapped in economically obsolete inner cities away from the dynamic growth centers of the economy that are now increasingly located in suburban and non-metropolitan areas (Hughes 1989; Ihlandfeldt and Sjoquist 1998; Kain 1968; Kasarda 1990). In this view, the growth of the urban underclass is tied to the 1970s shift from an industrial economy to a high-skill, technology-oriented economy whose job base is increasingly located in suburban areas. Job requirements with respect to both skill and education increased, and the suburban location of job growth made many of the new jobs physically inaccessible to low-income persons. As a result, residential location explains a large percentage of metropolitan white–black employment rate differences (Stoll 1999).

Yet, as noted earlier, many analyses have shown that people of color disproportionately experience concentrated poverty (Jargowsky 1996; Jargowsky and Bane 1991; Kasarda 1989; Mincy 1988). Thus, explanations of concentrated poverty must take into account the racial character of urban ghettos and the legacy of housing discrimination and segregation that created them.[2] For example, recent studies suggest evidence of continued racial discrimination in employment, particularly in the suburbs.[3] The data simply do not support arguments that suggest a declining significance or occurrence of racial discrimination in housing. Real estate professionals and community "gatekeepers" continue to limit geographic choice among minority groups (Desena 1994; Yinger 1998). Intentional segregation and discrimination in the siting of public and assisted housing also limit minorities' housing choices (Carter, Schill, and Wachter 1998; Holloway et al. 1998; Massey and Kanaiaupuni 1993).

Arguments about the relative roles of structural economic changes, segregation, and public housing complement earlier explanations that emphasize a slightly different set of impediments to economic and racial integration. These arguments also focus on systematic private and public disinvestment from central-city areas in favor of outlying and smaller metropolitan areas, exclusionary housing and zoning policies exercised by suburban communities, and other effectively segregationist government programs, such as the Federal Housing Administration's (FHA's) homeownership assistance programs.[4] Even tax incentives related to the capital gains tax, which defer payments for individuals who sell their homes and purchase others of equal or greater value, have been shown to spread wealthier families outward from the central city (Bier and Maric 1994).

More recently, analysts have explored the relationship between governmental fragmentation and segregation by income and race. David Rusk (1999), for example, suggests that the ability of central cities to annex territory and thus capture the benefits of regional growth is a strong predictor of the level of racial segregation and concentrated poverty across metropolitan areas. Furthermore, the highly fragmented nature of most metropolitan government encourages the kind of development that reinforces economic segregation. Sprawling metropolitan areas, according to Rusk, generally work to keep poverty in central areas and foster a continued and heightened degree of economic polarization. Anthony Downs (1999), on the other hand, reports that quantitative analysis does not link sprawl with concentrated poverty.

The most recent analyses synthesize these different perspectives into an explanation of concentrated poverty that stresses the variability of the phenomenon and the complementary effects of multiple factors. Jargowsky's relatively early observation (1996) of regional variations in the degree and timing of concentrated poverty suggests that causes may vary across regions and cities as well. Holloway and others (1999) and Cooke (1999), for example, argue that concentrated poverty is the result of both distributional forces (forces that spatially redistribute population within a region, such as racial and class-based residential segregation and middle-class out-migration) and rate factors that affect the aggregate amount of wealth and income in a region (such as industrial mix and regional business-cycle characteristics).

In their study of metropolitan Columbus, Ohio, Holloway and others (1999) find that metropolitan-level economic trends increased poor blacks' exposure to neighborhood poverty. At the same time, the spatial redistribution of the nonpoor, and their tendency to further segregate themselves from lower-income households, increased neighborhood poverty rates in the metropolitan area. Cooke's national analysis (1999) of high-poverty census tracts reveals four major clusters that represent different processes producing concentrated poverty. The first cluster, the most common, consists of income-segregated tracts in regions with poorly performing economies. This process is most prevalent in Spokane, Washington; Erie, Pennsylvania; Amarillo, Texas; Denver, Colorado; and Peoria, Illinois, thereby demonstrating no particular regional focus. The second cluster includes neighborhoods in immigrant gateway cities with mixed-race ethnic/immigrant enclaves. These cities include El Paso, San Antonio, Brownsville, and Laredo, Texas, as well as New York, Los Angeles, and Miami. The third cluster occurs in cities with high levels of racial segregation. Cities most characterized by this type of concentrated poverty tend to be mid-sized southern cities, including Atlanta, Georgia; Jackson, Mississippi; Saint Louis, Missouri; Montgomery, Alabama; Shreveport and New Orleans, Louisiana; Memphis, Tennessee; and Baltimore, Maryland. The fourth cluster occurs in cities hit the hardest by economic restructuring and deindustrialization. These communities, which include Chicago, Philadelphia, Milwaukee, and Cleveland, are also beset by high levels of racial segregation.

The Scope of Concentrated Poverty

Empirical investigations into the extent of the problem and its implications have been characterized by greater consensus. Danziger and Gottschalk (1987) operationalized concentrated poverty as neighborhoods (or census tracts) in which more than 40 percent of the population lives below the federal poverty level. Jargowsky and Bane (1991) validated that threshold with field observations in several cities. Alternatively, the scope of concentrated poverty has been determined by measuring behavioral patterns associated with the underclass.[5]

Studies show that while concentrated-poverty census tracts were rare in American cities in 1970, such tracts were much more prevalent by 1980 and widespread by 1990 (Danziger and Gottschalk 1987; Jargowsky 1996).[6] From 1970 to 1990, the number of high-poverty pockets more than doubled and the number of persons living in these neighborhoods increased from 4.1 to 8.0 million. Concentrated poverty is most severe in the Midwest and Northeast, and members of minority groups are far more likely to live in high-poverty neighborhoods than whites.

There is, however, some debate as to whether the focus on concentrated poverty distorts the picture of poverty in America, as well as the picture of urban poverty. Jargowsky (1996), using the 40-percent-below-poverty threshold for defining "high-poverty areas," suggests that about eight million people live in these neighborhoods. Yet, despite these high numbers, most poor people do not live in neighborhoods of concentrated poverty (Ellwood 1988). In the 1980s, less than 10 percent of the nation's poor lived in such neighborhoods within urban areas. Furthermore, the common perception of these communities underestimates the diversity in areas of concentrated poverty.[7]

The Effects of Concentrated Poverty

What happens when poverty becomes so heavily concentrated? There are typically two levels of concern. The first is about poverty's impact on individuals and their life opportunities. Do the poor (and nonpoor) living in these communities face problems greater than others with similar income, living in more diverse communities? The second is at the scale of the community. What does it mean for a neighborhood to have concentrated poverty? What are the implications for the larger city and the region? How do communities of concentrated poverty affect regional development patterns?

Neighborhood Effects on Individuals

How is it that neighborhoods affect the social and economic outcomes of their residents? How are neighborhood effects transmitted to individuals? According to Ellen and Turner (1997), previous studies highlight six different ways neighborhoods impact residents.[8] The first is through the differential quality of services available to people in different neighborhoods, the most important being public schools, after-school programs, child care and day care centers, and medical care. When the quality and quantity of these programs are reduced in some neighborhoods, residents' ability to work and compete in the labor market can be seriously impaired.

The second way is through the socialization of young people by adults. Wilson (1996) argues, for example, that growing up around few working adults means that children may end up underestimating or undervaluing the human-capital return on education, and learn less about developing personal habits necessary to succeed in the workforce.

Third, neighborhood effects can be transmitted through peer influence. This is, essentially, the "contagion theory" of neighborhood effects, or the importance of "the company you keep."[9] These influences are generally greatest in adolescent years, and can be positive or negative. Neighborhoods where school dropout, teen pregnancy, and illegal drug use rates are high, for example, produce a different set of peer influences than do neighborhoods in which these rates are lower.

The fourth way neighborhoods affect individuals is through social networks. The composition and density of social networks determine the degree of social capital to which one has access. An individual whose network contains few people with decent employment will be less likely to hear of good job opportunities and less likely to gain a personal job recommendation from an employed person. Similarly, if one's network is extremely dense, then information about outside opportunities can be redundant and less extensive than that received from looser networks (Wacquant and Wilson 1989). On the other hand, evidence shows that greater levels of social cohesion can reduce rates of violent and property crime within a neighborhood.[10]

The fifth dynamic is exposure to crime and violence. People living in areas of high crime have a higher risk of victimization and can become more isolated through fear, thus reducing the size of their social networks. In addition, the desensitizing nature of exposure to violent crime can alter a person's perspective on the world, and lead to greater acceptance of norms of violence and criminality.

Sixth, and last, according to Ellen and Turner (1997), is the sheer physical distance from employment and educational opportunities for people living in neighborhoods undergoing economic disinvestment. This is an adaptation of the spatial-mismatch hypothesis, which suggests that distance from social and economic opportunities constrains an individual from taking advantage of those opportunities.

All six of these perspectives assume that greater economic diversity in a neighborhood will benefit all residents, including the poor. Research evidence shows substantial support for this proposition. High school graduation rates, child cognitive development, and rates of teenage childbearing can be sensitive to neighborhood effects (Brooks-Gunn et al. 1993; Crane 1991). Some evidence indicates that African Americans who attend desegregated schools have more white friends, work in jobs with more white coworkers, and have higher wages than blacks educated in segregated schools (Wells and Crain 1994). Living in areas of concentrated poverty has been shown to have an adverse effect on a range of life experiences, from isolating youth from employment opportunities to consigning them to inferior education, dangerous neighborhood conditions, and harmful environmental conditions. Studies have shown that neighborhood affects employment prospects, exposure to toxic wastes, and criminal behavior.[11] These neighborhood effects are produced through the creation of a "ghetto culture" that stresses short-term goals (Anderson 1990, 1991); through a lack of role models and stabilizing institutions (Wilson 1987, 1996); or through underfunded schools and reduced access to new jobs in suburban areas (Kain 1968). While some analysts object to the concept of the underclass, and others argue that the association of underclass behaviors with minority groups is an empirical exaggeration, there is general consensus regarding the set of behavioral pathologies associated with concentrated poverty.[12]

The form of these effects has also been the subject of research. Galster, Quercia, and Cortes (2000), for example, suggest that the relationship between neighborhood conditions and individual effects might be non-linear; that is, that conditions might need to reach some threshold before effects are felt at the individual level. In addition, they argue that although direct family effects are stronger than neighborhood effects, neighborhood effects are greatest in families with the fewest resources.

Neighborhood effects also vary across the life cycle. Such effects on infants and toddlers are manifest indirectly through parents. Several studies suggest that the degree of social and institutional supports available to parents can have a significant impact on the development of young children (Coulton 1996; Ellen and Turner 1997; Furstenberg 1993). Other studies show that neighborhood effects are strong for low-birth-weight infants in their first year (Brooks-Gunn et al. 1993; Duncan, Brooks-Gunn, and Klebanov 1994; Ellen and Turner 1997).

The effects of neighborhood on school-age children and adolescents, however, are more direct, the strongest being on school achievement.[13] Young people experience effects far beyond education, however. Evidence on the impact of neighborhood on employment for youth is mixed (Ellen and Turner 1997), but evidence on sexual activity, crime, drug use, and church attendance is well documented.[14]

Studies of neighborhood effects on adults tend to focus on employment. The growth of low-skill jobs on the fringe of urban areas disadvantages inner-city residents, not only because of spatial mismatch, but also because of continuing racial discrimination in employment in suburban areas (Bendick, Jackson, and Reinoso 1994; Ihlandfeldt and Sjoquist 1998; Schill 1991; Stoll 1999; Turner 1998).

Some research shows benefits to lower-income households through proximity to higher-income neighbors. For example, studies indicate that the presence of neighbors with incomes more than $30,000 has a significant positive impact on low-income youth.[15] Contagion, socialization, and social-capital theories suggest that benefits are produced when low-income people interact or share space with higher-income people or people who are well tied into the economy and labor force (Briggs 1997). Briggs distinguishes between two types of social capital: social support and social leverage. Social support is what people rely upon to get by on a daily basis, such as short-term babysitting or transportation to the grocery store, and so on. Social leverage (or what is sometimes termed social "bridging") is the kind of assistance that could result in improving one's situation, such as information on job opportunities or a reference to a potential employer (Briggs 1998).

Advocates for dispersal identify numerous potential benefits, including access to better jobs and schools, reduced fear of crime, greater housing satisfaction, and the benefits of diversity in neighborhoods (Burby and Rohe 1989; Downs 1973; Kain 1968; Rosenbaum 1991, 1995). Dispersal is also a response to spatial mismatch because it places lower-income families closer to areas of job growth on the urban fringe. According to this argument, proximity to employment opportunities would improve information about potential job prospects, as well as make commuting more possible (Schill 1991). On the other hand, this viewpoint assumes that spatial mismatch is the only employment obstacle for low-income persons. In fact, it is possible that dispersal could be ineffective in situations where discrimination is prevalent. Indeed, as Stoll (1999, 94) argues, many fear that even if young, lower-income minority men "overcome the problem of place, they are likely to encounter the problem of race in suburban labor markets."

Community-Scale Impacts of Concentrated Poverty

Neighborhoods of highly concentrated poverty produce negative community-level effects for cities. Obviously, high-poverty neighborhoods suffer from lack of private capital investment. At the same time, they create high service burdens for core governments. These two effects mutually reinforce each other, since disinvestment reduces property values, in turn reducing revenues for city government. Pack (cited in Cisneros 1995) suggests that the increased social problems brought on by concentrated poverty in central-city neighborhoods lead to increased public costs. Her study of large American cities shows that those with high poverty levels have higher per capita expenditures for most municipal functions.

The negative social effects of highly concentrated poverty accentuate trends of middle-class flight, reinforce negative images of the central city and the poor, and reinforce the exclusionary impulses of suburban officials and residents. This progression in turn creates greater spatial disparities in regional development and ultimately threatens the fiscal viability of the central city. It also produces further inequities, as residents of poor neighborhoods subsidize growing areas on the periphery of metropolitan areas (Orfield 1997).[16]

The Politics of Deconcentrating Poverty

The concern about concentrated poverty has never been solely an academic one. It has pervaded popular discourse on urban America. Although the debate over the causes and scope of concentrated poverty has become more academic over time, the discussion of outcomes has always been a matter for more popular concern. In fact, over time, popular attention to the entire issue has moved away from causes and scope and focused solidly on the behavior of the poor in response to concentrated poverty. The shift was facilitated by several factors, two of which stand out—the drift to the Right in the policy environment of the 1980s and 1990s, and the recent "moral panic" in response to drugs and drug-related violent crime.[17]

Wilson (1987) argues that the Left generally ceded the analytical ground on the poverty question to neoconservatives during the 1970s and 1980s. The result was a discourse that focused on the poor's deviant and self-destructive behaviors. Indeed, the research represented by the third stage in figure 2.1 identifies the social pathologies associated with extreme and concentrated poverty. Though much of the research in this third stage was produced by academics who do not share a neoconservative political ideology, their work has carried on the tradition of linking poverty to the behaviors of the poor. Within this realm, the discussion of concentrated poverty intersects with prevailing images of the poor and public debate over dealing with this group. The popular view suggests that ghettos are the product of the personal failings of the people who live in them (Goetz 1996; Jargowsky 1996). Reeves and Campbell (1994), for example, identify the central role of the news media, which "not only facilitated the ascendancy of a punitive strategy in national drug control policy, but . . . generated a 'new consensus' that attributes the many human troubles attending economic distress to 'individual deviance, immorality, or weakness' " (250).

The moral panic about drugs complemented concerns regarding concentrated poverty, because it, too, focused on the behaviors of poor, minority, central-city inhabitants, and it blossomed at the same time (mid-1980s through mid-1990s) that concentrated poverty was entering the national consciousness.[18] During these years, the nation's drug war targeted the minority population of poorer central cities and led to severely disproportionate sentencing and arrest rates for young African-American males (Chambliss 1994; Maurer 1992; Tonrys 1995).

From the nation's almost 15-year preoccupation with concentrated urban poverty, a policy approach has gradually emerged. It is, quite simply, to break up concentrations of poverty wherever possible. This is done sometimes by facilitating greater economic diversity in place; often by moving poor families to other, less-poor communities; and frequently by both methods. What can be referred to as the deconcentration paradigm is not without its contradictions and significant limits. It is, nonetheless, a fairly coherent response to the issue of concentrated poverty. Before understanding its specific characteristics, however, it is necessary to understand one more element of concentrated poverty in the United States—the role of subsidized housing programs.

The Location and Impact of Subsidized Housing

Several analyses across a number of decades have made the connection between the location of public housing and high levels of racial segregation and concentrated poverty.[19] Public housing has been referred to as "vertical ghettos" and implicated in the growth of the urban underclass.[20] Schill (1991), Schill and Wachter (1995), and Turner (1998) claim that the overconcentration of public and subsidized housing has had measurably negative impacts on urban neighborhoods and has hastened neighborhood decline and disinvestment.[21]

Two features of the federal public housing program led to housing unit concentration in central-city neighborhoods. The first was the marriage of public housing with slum clearance in the Housing Act of 1949; the second is the program's high degree of local autonomy.

Slum Clearance

One of the chief justifications for public housing has been its role in clearing previous slums. From the time Congress began considering public housing in the 1930s, and even more so before enactment of the 1949 Housing Act, public housing was tied to slum clearance (Weiss 1985). In its original form, the public housing program incorporated a clause calling for the "equivalent elimination" of dilapidated housing. That is, for every unit of public housing created, one unit of dilapidated housing was to be demolished. Hirsch (1996) argues that this coupling of public housing and slum clearance ensured that the new housing would be built in areas already characterized by high poverty and minority concentrations— leading to the creation of what he calls a "federally sponsored second ghetto."

Slum clearance meant that public housing was located primarily in central cities, not outlying areas. It also meant that, within cities, public housing was built in the most troubled neighborhoods and on relatively expensive land near the urban core, rather than in less expensive, outlying, and undeveloped areas. Because land was expensive, cities tended to economize by building at high densities.

Local Authority and Site Selection

The 1935 federal district court decision in *U.S. v. Certain Lands in the City of Louisville* ruled that the federal government could not use the powers of eminent domain to clear slums for public housing. State courts, on the other hand, were not so limiting; local authorities were allowed to combine eminent domain with public housing construction. The 1935 decision eliminated the possibility of a federally run public housing program, a constraint the federal government accepted when it chose not to appeal. Congress simply incorporated the idea of local authority into the public housing program. As a result, public housing is not owned and operated by the federal government, but rather by local public housing authorities created by states and localities.

The public housing program incorporated a strict policy of local control based on two mechanisms. First, there were various controls over participation in the program. Jurisdictions that wanted to participate had to take highly public and positive steps before any units could be built. Localities had to create a local public housing authority (PHA) to receive the federal funds to construct, manage, and operate public housing. In some places, state law required special referenda before a PHA could be established. In addition, a "cooperating agreement" between the PHA and the local government was necessary before units could be built. Second, once a locality had moved to participate, local governments had absolute control over siting. This ensured that low-rent public housing would be located only in neighborhoods approved for such housing. Since public housing was the federal government's only housing assistance program for low-income families between 1939 and 1959, local officials regarded this policy of local veto power as their right—one that could naturally be extended (and often was) to other forms of subsidized and low-cost housing.

Local autonomy also provided communities the opportunity to opt out of subsidized housing programs altogether, an option adopted by many suburban areas. Most suburbs avoided public housing by simply never creating local housing authorities (McDonnell 1997). In states where enabling legislation allowed housing authorities to cross jurisdictional boundaries and operate in neighboring communities, some communities created PHAs for no other purpose than to avoid unwanted public housing. For example, DuPage County, Illinois, established a PHA in 1942 that existed more than 30 years before building a single unit, and the Housing Authority of Fulton County (Georgia) was created to prevent the Atlanta Housing Authority from developing public housing units in unincorporated parts of the county (Danielson 1976). There is even some evidence that local officials in charge of the program contributed to its spatial bias. In Cuyahoga County, Ohio, the PHA built all of its units in Cleveland, and for 25 years did not build a single unit of public housing in any of the 66 suburban municipalities (Rabin 1987). A 1967 survey of local PHA board members in cities across the nation discovered considerable reluctance to use public housing to promote racial integration (Hartman and Carr 1969).

That local politicians from the 1940s through the 1970s were responsible for decisions related to the placement of public housing virtually ensured its construction in high-poverty and high-minority neighborhoods. Decisions over the placement of public housing in many cities were made "to keep the Negroes where they were and so prevented the deterioration of property values and the other undesirable effects which were said to come from the movement of Negroes into outlying white areas" (Meyerson and Banfield 1955, 210).

Most public housing units nationwide (nearly 700,000) were built before the civil rights laws of the 1960s. Thus, antidiscrimination as a principle of public policy, and desegregation as an objective, did not exist when the original public housing projects were built. These units conformed to local patterns of segregated residential living. In this respect, local authority and slum clearance were complementary. For example, to avoid having to relocate displaced blacks to other neighborhoods, the Chicago city council decided to build public housing on slum sites even before tearing down the slums (Meyerson and Banfield 1955).

Thus, projects housing blacks were built in or near existing black neighborhoods, reinforcing existing segregation (Goldstein and Yancey 1986).[22] During this time, almost 100 percent of potential project sites located in white Chicago neighborhoods were vetoed, compared with 10 percent of potential sites in nonwhite neighborhoods (Tein 1992).

From the mid-1950s until the mid-1960s, the mayor, city council, and the Chicago Housing Authority (CHA) pursued a public housing siting protocol that guaranteed locating all new CHA developments in exclusively black or racially changing areas. During the early years of the program, public housing nationally was run according to the "neighborhood-composition" rule, requiring that public housing residents must mirror the ethnic distribution of their surrounding neighborhood. This was another way of ensuring that public housing, far from discouraging segregation, simply continued it.

This model of local veto over low-cost housing was not abandoned until the Fair Housing Act of 1968. The Section 235 and 236 programs created in 1968 required only a nonprofit or limited-dividend partnership to secure construction funds from the federal government. These programs ended 30 years of discrimination, during which the principle of local autonomy established by the public housing program provided "the most widely employed and effective suburban defense against subsidized housing" (Danielson 1976, 93).

Tenant Selection

Income qualifications for public housing have also worked to concentrate poverty. Over time, Congress has enacted selection criteria that have targeted the most disadvantaged among the poor. This has led to lower-income residents, with more social problems and economic obstacles, and, in turn, generated selective migration into the projects themselves and the neighborhoods that contain them (Massey and Kanaiaupuni 1993).[23] For example, income limitations grew more stringent with the 1949 Housing Act requiring that PHAs establish income ceilings and force out those whose incomes exceeded them. This legislation also mandated that PHAs give preference in admissions to those displaced by slum clearance. In 1979, Congress established preferences for families displaced or living in substandard housing. Two years later, Congress mandated an income limit of 50 percent of the area median for most units. Homeless families were given preferences to public housing during the 1980s, as were households paying more than 50 percent of their income on housing. In 1974, 1 percent of all households living in nonelderly developments earned less than 10 percent of the area's median income; by 1991, however, this proportion had grown to 19 percent (Schill and Wachter 1995).

The Spatial Concentration of Public and Assisted Housing

Concentration of Units in Central Cities

All these factors, then, have served to concentrate public housing and, to a lesser extent, other forms of subsidized housing in the central cities of America. By the 1990s, more than 61 percent of all public housing units were located in central cities. Suburban areas accounted for only 19 percent of all such housing units, and non-metropolitan areas another 19 percent.

One study shows that public housing units exceeded the central city's share of income-eligible residents by 20 or more percentage points in 7 of the 10 metropolitan areas studied (Gray and Tursky 1986). In Yonkers, New York, most of the city's 13,000 units of public housing were located in the southwest quadrant of the city. In addition, more than 95 percent of the city's other subsidized units were located in or adjacent to the southwest quadrant (Briggs 1997). A study of Philadelphia's public housing shows that its projects were located near the core, in areas of low housing value, and were not accessible to industrial job opportunities (Goldstein and Yancey 1986). Other forms of subsidized housing, such as Section 236, Section 221(d)(3), and project-based Section 8, are less spatially concentrated than public housing; nevertheless, they provide evidence of concentration (Gray and Tursky 1986; Newman and Schnare 1997; Warren 1986, 1987).

Though more units of subsidized housing have been built outside central cities in recent decades, the patterns of concentration have not changed dramatically. Close to one-third of federally subsidized units (1.1 of 3.5 million) for low- to very low income families were built in the suburbs (Schill and Wachter 1995). However, most of those have been built in close-in suburbs, in low-income areas. Burchell, Listokin, and Pashman (1994) estimate that only 250,000 low-income housing units were built in middle- or upper-income suburbs between 1973 and 1993. Such units are typically reserved for existing suburban residents or the elderly (Polikoff 1995).

The tenant-based Section 8 program is the least concentrated of all federal housing assistance programs. As this program has grown over time and become a larger share of all subsidized housing, the overall picture of subsidized housing concentration has diminished. Nevertheless, even with the Section 8 program, clearly the most mobile form of housing assistance, the percentage of subsidies used in central cities is disproportionate to the number of eligible households (Gray and Tursky 1986; Pendall 2000).

Concentration by Racial Makeup of Neighborhoods

As described above, local siting decisions allowed public housing to be erected in areas that reinforced local patterns of racial segregation. In Chicago, more than 99 percent of its public housing units were situated in areas that were more than 50 percent black (Massey and Kanaiaupuni 1993). Studies in other cities confirm the same basic pattern.[24] Nationally, 37 percent of public housing is located in neighborhoods that are more than 80 percent minority, compared with only 21 percent in low-minority (i.e., less than 10 percent minority using 1990 census data) neighborhoods (table 2.1). Privately owned subsidized housing and tenant-based subsidies are significantly less likely than public housing to be located in high-minority communities (only 10 percent of tenant-based subsidies and 15 percent of private, subsidized housing can be found in neighborhoods with more than 80 percent minority, while 42 percent of private developments and 44 percent of tenant-based subsidies are located in neighborhoods with a minority population of less than 10 percent).[25]

Concentration by Neighborhood Income

Despite the strong patterns of concentration by race, the evidence also indicates that subsidized housing is even more highly concentrated by income. Nationally, 53.6 percent of public housing is located in census tracts in which more than 30 percent of the population is below the federal poverty level, while only 7.5 percent is located in low-poverty (less

Table 2.1. *Distribution of Federally Subsidized Housing in the United States, by Neighborhood Minority Status*

	Public (%)	Privately owned (%)	Tenant-based subsidy (%)
Low-minority neighborhood (<10% minority residents)	21	42	44
High-minority neighborhood (>80% minority residents)	37	15	10

Source: Adapted from Newman and Schnare (1997).

than 10 percent) neighborhoods (table 2.2). In contrast, only 21.9 percent of privately owned, publicly subsidized units and 14.8 percent of tenant-based subsidies are found in high-poverty neighborhoods (Newman and Schnare 1997; Turner 1998).

Similarly, very low income neighborhoods (census tracts with a 1990 median income of less than $10,000) account for 26 percent of public housing, compared with only 2.3 percent of certificates and vouchers. At the other end of the scale, just 9 percent of public housing is located in neighborhoods with a median income of more than $30,000, while these neighborhoods represent 27 percent of privately owned subsidized housing and 26 percent of certificates and vouchers (Newman and Schnare 1997).

Concentration by Neighborhood Housing Stock Characteristics

Public housing is also more likely to be located in neighborhoods with other assisted units. Nationally, neighborhoods in which fewer than 10 percent of the units are assisted contain only 24 percent of public housing units, but are home to 41 percent of privately owned subsidized units and 80 percent of tenant-based subsidies. At the other end of the spectrum, 29 percent of public housing is located in neighborhoods where more than 50 percent of all units are subsidized, yet only 12 percent of privately owned subsidized units and just 1 percent of tenant-based subsidies are represented in these neighborhoods (Newman and Schnare 1997).

Segregation within Public and Subsidized Housing

Finally, a high level of segregation according to race exists in public housing projects. A 1990 study indicates that African Americans generally pre-

Table 2.2. Distribution of Federally Subsidized Housing in the United States, by Neighborhood Poverty Level

Poverty rate	Public (%)	Privately owned (%)	Tenant-based subsidy (%)
Low (<10%)	7.5	27.4	27.5
Medium (10–29%)	38.9	50.7	57.8
High (30–39%)	17.1	11.5	9.5
Very high (>40%)	36.5	10.4	5.3

Source: Adapted from Newman and Schnare (1997).

dominate in family projects, comprising 58 percent of all units in this category, and segregation within subsidized housing is greatest among authority-owned family projects, compared with elderly projects or privately owned projects. The authors of this study judged that the housing stock of more than one-fifth of all local public housing authorities is "highly segregated," and another 45 percent is moderately segregated (Bickford and Massey 1991).[26] More recent analysis of public housing data shows a decline in segregation since the 1970s and considerable variation across metropolitan areas (Goering, Kamely, and Richardson 1997).[27] Segregation within public housing is generally greater in larger metropolitan areas, and seems to be greater in areas where black population growth is coupled with declining white population.

Table 2.3 describes the degree of segregation in public housing. The left-hand column represents the project and neighborhood characteristics of the typical African-American family in public housing; the right-hand column describes those same conditions for the typical white family in public housing. The typical African-American public housing resident lives in a project in which 85 percent of residents are also African American. The typical white public housing resident, on the other hand, lives in a project in which only 27 percent of the residents are black and 60 percent are white. Furthermore, these differences carry over to the neighborhoods

Table 2.3. Project and Neighborhood Characteristics for Average African-American and White Public Housing Residents in the United States, 1990

	African American (%)	White (%)
Characteristics of the public housing project		
African American	85	27
White	8	60
Residents employed	25	27
Single female-headed household	53	47
Below poverty	80	74
Characteristics of the neighborhood in which project is located		
African American	68	15
White	25	78
Residents employed	81	89
Below poverty	47	26

Source: Adapted from Goering, Kamely, and Richardson (1997).

in which the projects are located. As the table shows, the average African-American resident lives in a neighborhood that is 68 percent black; the average white resident lives in a 78 percent white neighborhood.

The Effects of Concentrated Public Housing

Six published studies directly measure the impact of concentrated public housing on the racial and poverty characteristics of communities. Most evidence suggests that concentrated public housing does result in socioeconomic changes in neighborhoods. The effects occur in two ways—one direct, the other indirect. First, as we have described, the families that reside in public housing are among the poorest in society. To the extent that many public housing units are concentrated in a single neighborhood, the very fact of the overwhelming poverty of these residents will result in a concentration of poverty. One such example is the four-block area of Chicago's south side that includes the Robert Taylor Homes. In 1980, this community was the poorest in the country because of the high number of units in the project and its residents' low income. Second, the indirect effect of public housing concentration results from the stigma associated with public housing and the subsequent out-migration of the nonpoor (Holloway et al. 1998; Massey and Kanaiaupuni 1993).

These studies have, in fact, found substantial evidence for both the direct and indirect effects of concentrated public housing. In a study of Chicago, researchers found that public housing was built in predominantly black neighborhoods, and that the existence of public housing was related to the subsequent growth of poverty in those neighborhoods. The concentration of poverty was higher even in census tracts with public housing nearby. The 1980 poverty rate increased an average of 11 percentage points in tracts with at least one public housing project. The study also found that public housing led to out-migration of higher-income households from poor neighborhoods (Massey and Kanaiaupuni 1993).

A similar analysis of Columbus, Ohio, also supports both the direct and indirect effects of public housing on neighborhood status. Interestingly, these authors find that a concentration of public housing resulted in a steeper increase in poverty rates for blacks than whites. For blacks, public housing has the effect of concentrating the groups most vulnerable to economic dislocation. For both races, housing market changes also contribute to concentrated poverty in public housing neighborhoods.

More recent efforts to disperse public housing in Columbus have avoided concentration effects. Dispersed public housing built since 1980 in tracts that did not previously contain any such housing was not associated with an increase in poverty levels among blacks (Holloway et al. 1998).

Evidence presented in another study of Philadelphia confirms that the existence of public housing in a neighborhood contributes substantially to concentrated poverty (Schill and Wachter 1995). Increased levels of public housing in that city's neighborhoods had a dramatic effect on neighborhood poverty. The average neighborhood with no public housing units demonstrated a 13 percent poverty rate. However, neighborhoods containing just the average proportion of public housing had poverty rates that averaged 31.8 percent. Another study of Yonkers, New York, shows only a slight direct impact of public housing on subsequent changes in racial composition of census tracts (Galster and Keeney 1993).

Two analyses, however, do not support the causal link between the siting of public housing and subsequent concentration of poverty. Goldstein and Yancey (1986) indicate that public housing in Philadelphia was built in neighborhoods that were already becoming black and lower income, and introducing such housing did not alter the neighborhoods' trajectory significantly. Furthermore, a national study indicates that the presence of subsidized housing reduces the likelihood of the nonpoor entering a neighborhood, but is not associated with the nonpoor moving out of a community (Freeman 2001).

Toward a Policy Response

This legacy of the spatial concentration of public and subsidized housing and its demonstrated effects in neighborhoods have been influential in shaping the American policy response to concentrated poverty. Though concentrated poverty is clearly a larger phenomenon than concentrated public housing, and has been related to a range of factors beyond public housing (including the mobility patterns of the nonpoor), U.S. deconcentration policy, nevertheless, has been focused primarily on the dispersal of subsidized families.

In practice, this policy has meant scattering subsidized units over a greater geographic area within regions, providing families with a different form of subsidy that allows them to choose a unit on the open market, and not constraining them to units financed by the public sector. Deconcentration has also meant, to a very significant extent, demolishing or converting existing subsidized housing and forcing assisted families to relocate to other neighborhoods. Chapter 3 reviews the history of these policy approaches.

NOTES

1. See also Jargowsky (1996) and Schill (1991).

2. See, for example, Bullard and Lee (1994); Massey and Denton (1993); and Massey and Eggers (1990).

3. See Cohn and Fossett (1998) and Stoll (1999).

4. See Jackson (1985) and Judd (1999).

5. Errol Ricketts and Isabel Sawhill developed an alternative method of measuring the "underclass" in Ricketts and Sawhill (1988).

6. See also Schill (1991).

7. See Jargowsky (1996).

8. See also Jencks and Mayer (1990).

9. This phrase is taken from Case and Katz (1991).

10. Information on the relationship between social cohesion and violent crime is presented in Sampson (1999). The relationship between social cohesion and property crime is one of the central hypotheses of urban crime research. See also Sampson and Raudenbusch (1999) and Donnelly and Kimble (1997).

11. See, for example, Anderson (1991); Bullard (1990); Case and Katz (1991); Ellen and Turner (1997); and Massey, Gross, and Eggers (1991).

12. See Hughes (1989) for criticism of the term "underclass." See Alex-Assensoh (1995, 1997) for patterns of "underclass" behavior among lower-income whites.

13. See, for example, Aaronson (1997); Corcoran et al. (1989); Crane (1991); Datcher (1982); Duncan (1994); Haveman and Wolfe (1994); Jencks and Mayer (1990); Rosenbaum (1991); and Wells and Crain (1994).

14. See, for example, Case and Katz (1991) and Crane (1991).

15. See, for example, Aaronson (1997); Brooks-Gunn et al. (1993); and Duncan (1994).

16. Rusk (1999) argues that concentrated poverty contributes to patterns of sprawled development. See Downs (1999) for a contrary argument.

17. See Goode and Ben-Yehuda (1994) for more on the concept of "moral panic."

18. See Gordon (1994) and Tonrys (1995) on the social, racial, and geographic targeting of the war on drugs.

19. See, for example, Bauman (1987); Carter et al. (1998); Goering, Kamely, and Richardson (1997); Hirsch (1996); Holloway et al. (1998); Massey and Kanaiaupuni (1993); and Taeuber and Taeuber (1965).

20. The term is Hirsch's. See Hirsch (1996).

21. For a dissenting view, see Freeman (2001).

22. See also Bickford and Massey (1991); Meyerson and Banfield (1955); and Rossi and Dentler (1961).

23. See also Schill and Wachter (1995) and Spence (1993).

24. See Goldstein and Yancey (1986) and Hartung and Henig (1997).

25. See Gray and Tursky (1986); Newman and Schnare (1997); and Warren (1987).

26. See also Bauman (1987) and Hirsch (1996).

27. See also Bickford and Massey (1991).

3

Programs to Deconcentrate the Poor

Achieving the American Dream for everyone requires opening up all of a metropolitan area's resources and opportunities to all of its residents.

—Henry Cisneros, 1995

If . . . the planned subsidized housing goes up, I think you can get out an eraser and cross out the line between the Bronx and Yonkers, because that's what it's going to look like in a few years after it's built.

—Yonkers City Council Member Nicholas Longo, 1988

Henry Cisneros, former mayor of San Antonio and secretary of the U.S. Department of Housing and Urban Development (HUD) under President Clinton, called "highly concentrated minority poverty urban America's toughest challenge" (HUD 1996, 1). In 1995, Cisneros toured the country, talking about HUD's previous and mistaken policy of "warehousing poor people in high-rise buildings" (Hartung and Henig 1997, 404). While acknowledging that "many Americans are dismayed by the seeming magnitude of urban poverty," Cisneros (1995, 10) argued that "the problem's size is an illusion created by its concentration." During Cisneros's term as HUD secretary, the objective of deconcentrating poverty drove a range of new HUD initiatives to disperse subsidized housing and families into communities with less poverty. These initiatives, in fact, constituted a "second generation" of federal efforts to deconcentrate subsidized housing and disperse assisted households. The first generation had emerged at the end of the 1960s as a result of the "open housing" movement.

43

The course of first-generation dispersal policy was very closely tied to the evolution of federal policy on housing discrimination. As we discussed in chapter 2, the first few decades of federal housing policy contributed directly to concentrating the poor. Similarly, federal policy also fostered discriminatory practices against racial minorities. Public housing's neighborhood-composition rule, for example (requiring a project's racial makeup to match the surrounding neighborhood), and the routine practice of segregation within public housing were both blatantly discriminatory. The government's advocacy of racially restrictive covenants in its FHA homeownership assistance program, and its refusal to provide such subsidies in diverse neighborhoods, were also overt acts of racial discrimination. Because of the large overlap in American society between race and income, those discriminatory actions also contributed to the concentration of poverty between 1930 and 1970.

Dispersal of subsidized housing was a way of both reversing past discrimination and promoting integration. Thus, the first generation of dispersal marked a turnaround for the federal government and its housing policy. After decades of contributing to residential segregation and discrimination, the federal government in the 1960s moved toward acknowledging the problems and taking some initial, hesitant steps to reverse direction. These steps included President Kennedy's Executive Order 11063 (1962), which ended discrimination in federally assisted housing programs; enactment of the Fair Housing Act of 1968; creation of scattered-site public housing; the end of high-rise public housing developments; and first steps toward support for regional housing initiatives to disperse subsidized units.

These first steps toward antidiscrimination and dispersal were halting and, for the most part, ineffective. The Fair Housing Act was limited in important ways and proved very cumbersome in the fight to end racial discrimination in housing.[1] Implementation was undermined by the lack of interest in enforcement demonstrated by successive presidential administrations and by cuts in enforcement staffing. Dispersal policy and scattered-site efforts have been similarly limited. In fact, scattered-site public housing has never amounted to more than a very small percentage of units in most cities (Hogan 1996). HUD's first regionalism initiatives of 1970 to 1972, including support for regional councils of government and regional "fair-share" housing approaches, quickly evaporated in the face of suburban resistance. Dispersal, as a policy objective, was put on the back burner. HUD did not consciously return to old practices of concentrating assisted housing, yet visible attempts to significantly disperse subsidized housing disappeared from its agenda.

Scattered-Site Programs

For three decades, from 1937 to the mid-1960s, the dominant model of public housing was the high-density high-rise or townhouse "project." Though efforts to disperse public housing began as early as the 1950s, the Section 23 program, enacted in 1965, was the first significant program to facilitate a more scattered approach (Chandler 1990; Hogan and Lengyel 1985). Section 23 allowed PHAs to lease private homes on a scattered-site basis to public housing tenants. The shift to a scattered-site approach was gradual, however. Fewer than one-fourth of the housing authorities in a national survey had initiated such programs by the end of the 1960s (Hartman and Carr 1969). The acceptance and spread of scattered-site public housing increased during the late 1960s and early 1970s, however, a time when the fair housing movement gained momentum and the first generation of HUD-sponsored regional approaches to housing emerged.

In the 1960s, many officials running local housing authorities were simply not prepared to use their programs for achieving desegregation. One survey in 1967 found that close to half of all PHA officials did not think public housing should promote integration (Hartman and Carr 1969). Almost two decades later, many of these attitudes still were unchanged. In 1985, the *Dallas Morning News* published a series showing racist attitudes among housing officials across the country, as well as open criticism by PHA officials of judicial efforts to desegregate public housing (Goering 1986, 200).

Thus, despite the fact that most public housing authorities began their scattered-site programs in the early 1970s, these units constituted only 9 percent of all assisted housing by the early 1980s. After another decade, scattered-site housing still represented less than 10 percent of all assisted units in urban areas, although local officials generally regarded it as successful (Hogan 1996). Ultimately, the growth of the scattered-site program has been limited by high land and property costs outside of core neighborhoods, the opposition of residents in receiving neighborhoods, and lukewarm commitment from local housing officials. Political opposition to public housing has especially restricted the widespread application of scattered-site principles. Resistance is generally the norm, and dispersal has rarely proceeded without opposition—typically from middle-class communities fearing property value decline and increased social problems (Hogan 1996; Polikoff 1995). Finally, because public housing authorities are restricted from buying or leasing properties outside their jurisdictions, most scattered-site programs involve dispersal within a jurisdiction.

In addition to embarking upon dispersal in a limited way through scattered-site development, HUD also moved away from building public housing in high-rises during the 1960s. The President's Commission on Urban Disorders in 1968 called for an end to constructing public housing in high-rise buildings.

HUD experienced further pressure for dispersal from the courts. In *Gautreaux v. Chicago Housing Authority* (1969), the courts ruled that the CHA had to end its policy of concentrating public housing in minority and poor neighborhoods. The courts mandated that the city disperse future public housing throughout the city and, more specifically, build it in low-minority neighborhoods. Several years later, the U.S. Supreme Court would rule in *Gautreaux v. Harris* that housing for Chicago public housing families should be made available on a regional basis (Rubinowitz and Rosenbaum 2001). In *Shannon v. United States Department of Housing and Urban Development* (1970), the courts ruled that HUD and local PHAs could no longer locate subsidized housing only in nonwhite areas. HUD responded with regulations adopted in 1972 that restricted new construction of subsidized housing in nonwhite areas except where there were comparable opportunities for nonwhite families in white neighborhoods.

Fair-Share Housing Programs

Concurrent with these efforts, HUD and Congress also began to feel their way into supporting regional initiatives in subsidized housing dispersal. During this period, several special presidential commissions focused on the exclusionary practices of predominantly white suburban areas and the lack of subsidized, affordable housing outside central cities. The National Advisory Commission on Civil Disorders, created in 1967 after the Detroit and Newark riots; the National Commission on Urban Problems (the Douglas Commission); the President's Committee on Urban Housing (the Kaiser Committee); and the President's Task Force on Suburban Problems each called for greater dispersion of federally subsidized housing and, more specifically, for greater development of such housing in suburban areas. The Kaiser Committee went so far as to suggest that HUD be given the authority to override local zoning regulations that were exclusionary in intent and effect. Even the Task Force on Urban Renewal, reporting two years into the Nixon administration, recommended withholding federal aid from communities that did not make an effort to expand low-income housing (Danielson 1976).

In the years following the Fair Housing Act of 1968, the federal government supported and funded the development of areawide councils of government and briefly supported metropolitan dispersal of assisted housing (Keating 1994). HUD's Open Communities Program, for example, provided water, sewer, and infrastructure funds based on local governments' compliance with fair-share housing concerns. In addition, Congress authorized metro-wide councils of governments (COGs) to review local applications for federal aid to ensure that proposed projects were consistent with regional development plans. The number of COGs nationwide grew dramatically in response to this new procedural requirement. Some COGs, notable among them the Metropolitan Council of the Twin Cities, used this authority to downgrade applications from communities that had not made progress in meeting affordable housing goals. This mechanism led to the creation of fair-share housing programs in several metropolitan areas.

Fair-share programs, according to one expert, are designed to "improve the status quo by allocating units in a rational and equitable fashion . . . [A] primary impetus for and emphasis of fair share is expanding housing opportunity usually, but not exclusively, for low- and moderate-income families" (Listokin 1976, 1). Because they require the cooperation of municipalities throughout a metropolitan area, fair-share programs typically are operated by regional governments. The cities of Dayton, Chicago, San Francisco, Washington, D.C., and others conducted brief experiments with fair-share programs (Craig 1972; Keating 1994; Listokin 1976). As the federal government withdrew support, however, fair share became strictly a local initiative. It survived where local interest was sufficient in assuring that subsidized housing opportunities existed equitably throughout the central city and developing suburban areas. It survived, that is to say, almost nowhere. Instead, as with the dispersal of HUD-subsidized housing, fair share continued only where the courts demanded it.

The *Mount Laurel* (New Jersey) case, decided by the New Jersey Supreme Court in 1975, held that communities could not zone to exclude low-income housing. Two subsequent lawsuits were required to fully implement the court's mandate of regional fair-share strategies throughout the state. In 1985, the New Jersey legislature created the Council on Affordable Housing (COAH) to oversee statewide implementation of fair-share requirements. Communities in New Jersey are assigned low-income housing obligations based on existing housing mix, present and projected employment, and amount of open land (Anglin 1994). COAH was also responsible for setting time limits for compliance and was given the power to enforce its regulations. In the first six years, COAH facilitated development of 16,000 new affordable housing units in New Jersey suburbs, and 6,500 rehabilitated units between 1985 and 1997 (Wish and Eisdorfer 1997). New Jersey continues to conduct the country's largest fair-share housing program.

Methods of achieving fair share are quite varied. They include inclusionary zoning programs (e.g., Montgomery County, Maryland, and New Jersey) that require a percentage of units in new developments to be set aside for low- and moderate-income occupancy, "builders' remedies" (as in Connecticut, Rhode Island, and Massachusetts) that provide opportunities for developers to appeal permit and zoning decisions by local governments, and state programs (as in California, New Hampshire, and Oregon) that require local communities to provide reasonable opportunities for the development of affordable housing. These objectives typically are achieved through incentives or direct regulation of the development process, and shift the costs of supplying subsidized housing to developers and market-based homebuyers. If the housing market is strong, the potential for significant production of affordable units—in areas that traditionally, or otherwise, would not have them—is considerable. For example, in Montgomery County, Maryland—one of the wealthiest suburban counties in the nation—more than 12,000 units of low- and moderate-income housing have been built since 1974.

These "first-generation" programs, born of the urban unrest of the 1960s and closely associated with efforts to eliminate racial discrimination in housing, had taken on the issue of suburban exclusionism. Various means were considered for overriding local prerogatives in land use and assisted housing. Even HUD attempted, very briefly, to withhold grants from exclusionary communities. The siting of HUD housing developments came under new guidelines aimed at greater dispersal.

These programs produced a brief flurry of activity that, in the end, was soundly beaten back by the substantial and growing political clout of suburban areas. Whenever a proposal or existing program came close to "forcing" low-cost housing on suburban municipalities, the federal government retreated in the face of fierce suburban resistance. Nixon quickly reined in his secretary of HUD after the agency became too enthusiastic in its efforts to open the suburbs. In this, Nixon was moving to protect his own sizable suburban constituency, and also responding to the dominance of suburban interests in Congress (Danielson 1976). In the end, the Nixon administration decoupled the issues of antidiscrimination and dispersal. Though compelled by a strong civil rights lobby to continue antidiscrimination efforts, Nixon backpedaled on efforts to promote subsidized housing in the suburbs.

By 1973, it had become clear that Congress would initiate no regional housing legislation unacceptable to suburban interests. Metropolitan-wide efforts were dead at the federal level. What emerged in their place were renewed emphasis on local discretion, as seen in the 1974 Housing and Community Development Act, and a new way of delivering subsidized housing that relied on individual tenants and the market to achieve dispersal.

Tenant-Based Programs

In 1968, the President's Committee on Urban Housing, known as the Kaiser Committee, recommended a tenant-based form of housing allowance for lower-income families. The committee's argument for this type of assistance focused on three matters. First, tenant-based assistance was less expensive, the committee's answer to growing criticism that unit-based programs were too costly and not serving enough families. Second, tenant-based assistance allowed families greater choice in units and neighborhoods, and represented a lesser degree of interference in the private market. Finally, tenant-based assistance could reduce the levels of segregation by race and poverty that characterize unit-based programs.

In reality, tenant-based housing assistance dates back to the formation of the public housing program (Friedman and Weinberg 1983). Congress considered tenant-based assistance when creating the Housing Act of 1937, and again in 1944. A housing shortage had emerged during the Great Depression and grown during the Second World War, and Congress decided in both instances that slum clearance and the construction of more and newer housing were national priorities. Furthermore, it was felt that tenant-based assistance might merely maintain the profitability of slum areas (Friedman and Weinberg 1983; Semer et al. 1976). The idea did not go away, however. Congress considered and rejected it again in 1949 and 1953. The riots of the 1960s, however, highlighted the extent of residential segregation and substandard housing for the poor in central cities, and brought the issue of dispersal to center stage.

Though no immediate action was taken on the Kaiser Committee's recommendation, Congress in 1971 authorized a national experiment in tenant-based assistance—the Experimental Housing Allowance Program (EHAP). This initiative was meant to run for the better part of a decade, and the results were to be used to determine if a national program would be created. However, in 1974, Congress and the Nixon administration decided not to wait for the results, and proceeded to create the Section 8 program. Section 8 was then expanded in the 1980s to include vouchers as well as certificates. Vouchers worked in a slightly different way than certificates and were meant to increase the choices available to participating families.

The Section 8 Programs

Section 8 Existing

Section 8 of the 1974 Housing and Community Development Act consisted of three separate housing assistance programs. The Section 8 New Construction and Section 8 Substantial Rehabilitation programs worked very much like the old project-based programs, in which the subsidy was tied to the units built (or rehabilitated). The Section 8 Existing program, however, was a truly tenant-based subsidy in which the household could use the certificate in the marketplace. The tenant-based Section 8 program caught on quickly and in just five years became the nation's second largest low-income housing program, behind public housing (Rasmussen 1980).

The program worked by allowing certificate holders to rent any unit in the market that met certain quality standards and rented at or below a HUD-established fair market rent (FMR) for the region. The certificate paid for the difference between the unit's market rent and 25 percent of the household's income. In 1982, the certificate formula was changed so households were responsible for paying 30 percent of their income. HUD adjusts FMRs annually, and by law they were set at the median rent for units of similar size in each regional market. In 1984, FMRs were reduced to the 45th percentile, and in 1995, they were reduced again, to the 40th percentile.

Vouchers

At the urging of the Reagan administration, Congress in 1983 created a demonstration program of housing vouchers. Vouchers were similar to Section 8 certificates, except that they had fewer geographic restrictions, and families could rent units above the FMR if they absorbed the extra cost (and thus paid more than 30 percent of their income on housing). Section 8 certificates were limited to the jurisdiction of the local administering agency, while vouchers were valid throughout the United States. The voucher program became permanent in 1987, and in 1998 Congress merged the certificate and voucher programs, retaining most of the voucher features.

Over time, federal housing policy has shifted emphasis and expenditures from building units to providing housing allowances (Hartung and Henig 1997; McClure 1998; Struyk 1991). Between the 1970s and early 1990s, the ratio of tenant-based to project-based subsidies increased from 0.6 vouchers and certificates to 4.75 vouchers and certificates for every unit of project-based public or subsidized housing (Hartung and Henig 1997). By 1997, 72 percent of new federal rental assistance funds went to tenant-based assistance and only 28 percent to project-based programs (McClure 1998). By the end of the 1990s, roughly one-third of all households assisted by the federal government received allowances (McClure 1998; Newman and Schnare 1997). Indeed, the record of Section 8 showed a much greater dispersion of assisted households than project-based programs. The introduction of vouchers accentuated this effect, allowing families to venture into neighborhoods where prevailing rents were above FMR limits. Because households receiving allowances are more evenly distributed across metropolitan regions than residents in project-based subsidized housing, the overall geographic dispersion of HUD-assisted households has increased over time (Gray and Tursky 1986).

Portability

During the 1970s, HUD took some preliminary steps to encourage the use of Section 8 housing allowances across jurisdictional boundaries.

HUD's voluntary Areawide Housing Opportunity Plan and Regional Housing Mobility Program encouraged municipalities within metropolitan areas to collaborate in planning for low-income housing and facilitate cross-jurisdictional mobility by certificate holders. The Regional Housing Mobility Program, which was designed to assist areawide planning organizations in facilitating the interjurisdictional mobility of low-income and minority households, was abandoned by HUD, however, at the beginning of the Reagan administration.

In 1987, Congress amended Section 8 to allow certificate holders to use their subsidies throughout the metropolitan area in which the subsidy was issued, or in a contiguous area. Congress then expanded the so-called portability provision in 1990, allowing statewide mobility by certificate holders. Despite these changes, most local housing authorities did not implement portability guidelines quickly. A national survey in 1991 found that only 3 percent of Section 8 certificates and vouchers had been transferred across jurisdictional boundaries (Polikoff 1995). Local housing authorities did not vigorously adopt portability for several reasons. First, many local authorities established residency preferences for admission to the Section 8 programs. An internal HUD survey of the 51 field offices found that 42 percent of 2,541 local public housing authorities had such residency preferences (Tegeler, Hanley, and Liben 1995). Second, the program often resulted in a loss of administrative revenue to local authorities each time a family exercised portability. In 1992, Congress pulled back on portability, requiring recipients who did not already live in the jurisdiction of an issuing housing authority to remain within that jurisdiction for at least 12 months before moving. Portability was made permanent in the new, combined voucher program in 1998.

The Gautreaux Program

The most notable lawsuit dealing with desegregation and deconcentration is the *Gautreaux* case, named after the lead plaintiff in this class action suit, Dorothy Gautreaux, a long-time resident of Chicago public housing. There were, in fact, two *Gautreaux* cases. In the first, *Gautreaux v. Chicago Housing Authority* (1969), the federal district court found that the Chicago Housing Authority had discriminated in the placement and leasing of public housing, and ordered it to provide additional units on a scattered-site basis in predominantly white areas. Over the next two decades, there were several court-ordered modifications to this remedy. The second *Gautreaux* case, *Gautreaux v. Harris,* was decided by the U.S. Supreme Court in 1976. The Court's ruling produced a metropolitan-wide "mobility program" that came to be known as the Gautreaux program. This program provided Section 8 subsidies for public housing residents, enabling them to move to predominantly white neighborhoods in Chicago and its suburbs. During the 20 years in which the program operated, 6,000 participants were moved out of racially segregated Chicago neighborhoods. The majority moved into about 115 predominantly white suburbs (Rubinowitz 1992).

The Gautreaux program provided an orientation workshop, an initial credit check, and a home visit for interested families. Each participating family was then assigned a mobility counselor, who helped participants find an appropriate apartment within the required six-month period. Counselors also provided information tenants would need after their move, such as referrals to local service agencies. Rubinowitz (1992) argues that many families would not have participated except for the counseling element.

To encourage landlord participation, the Gautreaux program also provided applicant screening. Program officials obtained credit checks, made home visits, and also required reference letters from each applicant. Participating landlords were assured both of confidentiality and that the program would avoid reconcentrating participants.

The experience of the Gautreaux program convinced many that mobility programs that integrate landlord recruitment, tenant counseling, and placement services could begin to overcome patterns of residential segregation and improve the lives of poor families (Goering, Stebbins, and Siewart 1995).

Second-Generation Dispersal

In the early 1990s, as the concentration-of-poverty argument was reaching ascendancy, the framework for federal housing policy shifted. Congress began not only to recognize the "failures" of public housing, but also to associate them with an emerging understanding of concentrated poverty as the driving problem in American urban areas. In 1988, along with encouraging portability in Section 8, Congress also created the National Commission on Severely Distressed Public Housing. Legislators were searching for a way to change the face of existing public housing by looking at options for the worst examples in the stock and increasing the income diversity of public housing residents, an orientation shared by the Clinton appointees who ran HUD from 1993 to 2001. From the late 1980s through most of the 1990s, HUD policy moved toward and finally adopted a paradigm that emphasized dispersion. Unlike the first generation of dispersion efforts, which was tied to racial segregation, this generation was firmly tied to concentrated poverty. Work demonstrating the connection between federal housing policy and concentrated poverty provided a greater rationale for dispersion. HUD was not simply correcting old mistakes; it was addressing what it regarded as the most significant problem facing American cities at the end of the century.

Political considerations also helped foster HUD's interest in deconcentrating public and subsidized housing recipients. After midterm elections in 1994 gave control of both houses of Congress to the Republicans, HUD found itself in a precarious situation. With House Republicans publicly advocating the agency's demise, HUD Secretary Henry Cisneros privately acknowledged his agency's need "to quickly reposition itself rightward to survive" (Weisman 1996, 2517). His plan called for "reinventing" the agency, disavowing old supply-based housing strategies and embracing policy options that had always been more favored by conservatives. This meant reducing support for subsidized housing development, and shifting to demand-based subsidies that work through the market and block grants that give local governments more discretion in using federal housing subsidies. The resulting document was the 1995 HUD Reinvention Blueprint, which called for the collapse of dozens of HUD programs into just three—most notably a conversion of public housing into an essentially privatized system relying entirely on tenant-based subsidies. One national observer called the blueprint "a sheer act of desperation" by an agency attempting to stave off its own elimination by a hostile Congress (Weisman 1996).

The second generation of dispersal has been a two-pronged approach. On the one hand, a growing number of cities have created "mobility programs" that use tenant-based Section 8 subsidies to move families out of neighborhoods of concentrated poverty. These programs are part of a larger shift in federal housing subsidies, from project-based to tenant-based assistance, that has been unfolding for more than 20 years. On the other hand, housing authorities are making a concerted effort to redefine and redevelop existing public and assisted housing projects by introducing a greater mix of incomes and uses at the project sites, and improving site design to encourage community-building within the projects.

Mobility Programs

Programs that combine Section 8 tenant-based assistance with mobility counseling and other special efforts, or require the deconcentration of subsidized households, are referred to as "mobility programs." Mobility programs go beyond the regular Section 8 program in any of three different ways: They (1) require participants to move to non-concentrated neighborhoods, (2) incorporate mobility counseling to assist households in choosing neighborhoods they would not necessarily have chosen without greater information, and (3) include an active recruitment of landlords in neighborhoods not traditionally receptive to Section 8 families.

As described earlier, the barriers to interjurisdictional mobility using Section 8 are significant. Suburban communities often establish residency preferences for Section 8 and other assisted-housing programs that work to reduce opportunities for central-city residents to take advantage of suburban subsidized housing. Public housing authorities cannot own or operate facilities outside their jurisdictions unless they enter into agreements with housing authorities in those jurisdictions, which have been rare (Polikoff 1995). Mobility programs attempt to overcome the limited amount of dispersal typical of the regular Section 8 program.

Five major categories of mobility programs operate in the United States. The first is the result of recent federal efforts to shift project-based subsidies to tenant-based assistance. In HUD-subsidized buildings that are no longer financially viable, have high vacancy rates, or where project-based subsidies have expired or are prepaid, families are given Section 8 vouchers in a process called "vouchering out." These families are then instructed and assisted in using their vouchers on the open market, relocating to neighborhoods and housing units of their choice. We include this as a mobility program because of the mobility counseling provided to households and because one of the major policy objectives in vouchering out is to disperse subsidized households.

The second category stems from a set of litigation settlements across the country. These lawsuits were typically filed as housing discrimination cases in which it was alleged that the local housing authority and HUD willfully and negligently segregated subsidized housing projects in predominantly minority neighborhoods. The most famous case, *Gautreaux v.*

Harris, resulted in a mobility program that became a national model. More recently, HUD has settled these cases out of court where possible (Hartman 1995). Many of the resulting consent decrees, including the settlement in *Hollman v. Cisneros,* incorporate Gautreaux-like mobility efforts.

Third is the federal Moving To Opportunity (MTO) program. This demonstration, enacted by Congress in 1992, was influenced by the documented outcomes of the Gautreaux program and incorporated many of its features. Fourth, HUD has created several Regional Opportunity Counseling programs around the country to promote collaboration in Section 8. They combine landlord recruitment and mobility counseling to enhance mobility. Finally, a variety of local programs combine elements of counseling and placement to facilitate the mobility of low-income households. In all, more than 50 programs of all types operate in more than 35 metropolitan areas across the country (Williams 1998).

MOVING TO OPPORTUNITY

Moving To Opportunity (MTO) was authorized by Section 152 of the 1992 Housing and Community Development Act. Congress appropriated $20 million in 1992 and another $50 million in 1993 for this program. The program is designed to provide Section 8 tenant-based assistance to families living in public housing located in high-poverty areas and those living in Section 8 project-based developments in neighborhoods with high poverty concentrations (greater than 40 percent of residents below the federal poverty level). Though modeled after Gautreaux, MTO differs from it in one important way: The receiving neighborhoods are defined by their degree of poverty, not minority concentration. Similar to Gautreaux, however, MTO uses nonprofit agencies to recruit participating landlords, screen program participants, and provide mobility counseling and support in the search and resettlement process.

Authorized as a demonstration, MTO operates in five cities—New York, Los Angeles, Chicago, Boston, and Baltimore—and was operational in all five by February 1995. Each local housing authority established a waiting list of eligibles and then proceeded with recruitment and random assignment of volunteers to one of three groups—the MTO experimental group, the Section 8 comparison group, and the stay-in-place control group. Experimental-group members were referred to the nonprofit counseling agency to begin their counseling and search for housing. Participants were given Section 8 tenant-based subsidies and required to relocate into census tracts where less than 10 percent of the population was below the federal poverty level. Section 8 comparison group members were also given Section 8 certificates, but thereafter treated no differently from other regular program participants. Thus, their housing search was not restricted to low-poverty areas, and they received no special mobility counseling. Finally, the in-place, control group members remained in their public housing or project-based Section 8 units. Program participants were randomly assigned to a group to determine more precisely whether differences in outcome across the groups were attributable to the counseling and assistance. HUD plans to monitor the families over 10 years to document their educational, employment, and social experiences (HUD 1996, 1999).

In Baltimore, program implementation was delayed because of strong reaction from politicians in some inner suburbs. Ironically, those suburbs' poverty rates already exceeded 10 percent and therefore they were not eligible to receive MTO families; nevertheless, several political candidates in the area picked up the issue. The trouble was such that Maryland's two senators, including the nominally liberal Barbara Mikulski, moved to cut future funding for the program. In the end, the Baltimore program recovered and operated as the others, but MTO as a whole was restricted by Congress to the $70 million that had already been appropriated. According to one observer,

> The experience of Baltimore suggests that public authorities should lay careful political groundwork for housing mobility programs to minimize the ability of demagogues to distort plans and inflame passions. Ultimately, white suburbs in most cases are willing, if they do not seem overwhelmed with their own economic and social problems, to accept some inner-city black poor in their midst (Moberg 1995, 13).

VOUCHERING OUT

"Vouchering out" occurs when HUD project-based assistance is terminated, either through conversion of a building to market-rate rents, or demolition of an older project, and the displaced households are provided with tenant-based subsidies for new apartments. Typically, families that are vouchered out are given some form of mobility or relocation counseling and assistance. As Polikoff argues, programs that demolish housing units and replace them with Section 8 certificates have the largest impact on "eliminating localized poverty clusters" (1995, 20). Vouchering out, however, is significantly different from other mobility programs in that the families are involuntarily displaced, and this situation can have important implications for what the families experience. The success of such "involuntary" dispersal efforts depends upon tenants' desire to move, availability of affordable units, landlords' acceptance of housing certificates, and housing discrimination (U.S. General Accounting Office 1995). Chicago, for example, lost 40,000 housing units in the 1980s and most were lost by low-income families. Even at some of the most notorious projects in the city, resident associations opposed public housing demolition because they feared not enough suitable, affordable housing units were available in the private market to absorb all the public housing families being displaced (Wright 1998).

Mixed-Income Developments

Mixed-income developments (referred to as mixed-income new communities, or MINCs) are attempts to create a greater range of incomes within a single subsidized project (Schill 1997). The 1990 Cranston-Gonzalez National Affordable Housing Act authorized four public housing authorities to experiment with a demonstration program. The program consisted merely of relaxing HUD preference guidelines and allowing PHAs to lease up to half the units in selected developments to families with low but not very low incomes. The Public Housing Reform Act of 1998 (The Quality Housing and Work Reform Act) institutionalized the mixed-income approach. This act directs local housing authorities to reserve as little as 40 percent of public housing units for the very poor, opening the rest to families with higher incomes. At the same time, this legislation also tries to facilitate the deconcentration of the very poor by setting aside 75 percent of all new vouchers for very low income households.

What separates mixed-income from scattered-site housing is that it reverses the dispersal model. Instead of mixing low-income people into wealthier neighborhoods, mixed-income development attempts to attract higher-income groups into more disadvantaged communities by offering attractive housing options in previously concentrated project areas. This formula requires several elements to be successful. The developments must offer amenities attractive to market-rate residents, and the projects must be considered safe, thus necessitating strict enforcement of management rules and tenant screening (Schill 1997).

Mixed-income developments, and recent reforms in the resident preferences for public housing, signal a shift, or return, to the original premise of public housing. Public housing originally was meant as a way station for the working poor. Over time, resident-preference policies targeted the program to the neediest families, while changes in the program's fiscal structure and in the larger, urban political economy ensured that the experience would be long-term, even multigenerational for some families.[2]

The rationales for a mixed-income approach are similar to those for dispersal. Communities simply are not viable without a cadre of employed residents to sustain businesses, provide role models, and increase social capital. A greater mix of incomes allows public housing to fit more completely into a surrounding community; that is, it reduces the chances that public housing will be seen as a pocket of disadvantage in the larger community. Finally, proponents of the neighborhood-effects argument expect that very low income households will benefit from the inclusion of higher-income families.

HOPE VI

The federal HOPE VI program incorporates elements of both project-based and tenant-based assistance. The program works primarily to demolish or rehabilitate large and troubled public housing projects, and redevelop the sites into lower-density, mixed-use, mixed-income developments. The redevelopment usually includes some units of public housing on site, but also results in converting many public housing families into Section 8 voucher holders. Thus, the program results in a net loss of public housing units, reduces concentrations of subsidized families, and contributes to the general federal conversion to household-based forms of housing assistance.

The National Commission on Severely Distressed Public Housing reported in 1992 that approximately 86,000 units, or 6 percent of public housing, could be considered severely distressed. Congress reacted to the commission's report by introducing the HOPE VI program. First authorized in 1992, HOPE VI aimed to eliminate the worst public housing developments. For this to happen, however, HUD and Congress had to revise several important policies. First, the one-for-one replacement law, originally part of the 1987 Housing and Community Development Act, which required housing authorities to produce a new unit of affordable housing for every one they demolished, was abolished. Second, HUD eliminated the federal preferences that reserved public housing for the lowest-income households, and, finally, HUD authorized the use of public housing development funds and operating subsidies for projects owned by a private entity. Thus, HOPE VI results in a triple deconcentration when combined with the guidelines of the new public housing law. HOPE VI redevelopment sites are characterized by fewer public housing units, more non–public housing units, and a greater income mix. In most HOPE VI programs, the physical design of the redevelopment site incorporates many of the precepts of new urbanism, which are intended to increase the informal socializing that takes place in a community and build social capital.[3]

DEMOLITION

The one-for-one replacement law was the largest obstacle to implementing HOPE VI. Combined with the lack of federal funding for developing new units, the one-for-one replacement rule made demolition of even dysfunctional public housing developments virtually impossible. HOPE VI could not result in any large-scale activity until the replacement requirement was repealed. HUD Secretary Henry Cisneros was instrumental, during the first two years of his administration, in convincing fellow Democrats to waive the rule for public housing. One senate Republican aide said the secretary was "doing what no Republican housing secretary could have gotten away with" (Weisman 1996, 2517). Cisneros advocated repeal of the rule even before the 1994 election gave Republicans the majority and threatened HUD's very future. After the election, according to one national housing advocate, "every word out of Cisneros' mouth . . . [was] about the need for demolition". One-for-one replacement was eliminated in 1995 and permanently repealed in the 1998 public housing bill.

In the first three years, only PHAs from the 40 largest U.S. cities or PHAs on HUD's list of troubled housing authorities were eligible for HOPE VI funds. From the beginning, there was little doubt that HOPE VI's biggest impact would be the demolition of thousands of public housing units. HUD initially targeted 100,000 units for demolition by the end of the century and accomplished almost one-quarter of that goal by the end of 1996 (Weisman 1996). HOPE VI projects in the first five years planned to demolish 37,449 units and replace 27,526 (U.S. General Accounting Office 1997). The difference was to be made up with vouchers. By the end of the 1990s, HUD had planned to replace roughly 60,000 of the 100,000 units targeted for demolition.

Though replacement housing is a program goal, HOPE VI does not provide such funding. PHAs are required to channel other sources of public housing funds into replacement housing. In Atlanta, for example, housing officials made plans to build replacement housing off site, using the cash flow from the profitable, on-site HOPE VI housing (Salama 1999).

In some cities, the HOPE VI guidelines have virtually remade the face of public housing. In Chicago, which had a high percentage of distressed projects, HUD guidelines called for demolition of 18,000 of the city's 41,000 public housing units. Many of the city's most notorious projects are being demolished under HUD plans. The Robert Taylor Homes, for example, have seen close to 4,000 units demolished, with plans to rebuild only 1,276 units. On the city's north side, Cabrini-Green is slated to lose 1,200 units, with fewer than 600 being rebuilt (Bennett and Reed 1999; Rogal 1999; Wright 1998).

Involuntary Deconcentration
An important feature of HOPE VI is that residents displaced by the demolition of their public housing units are, like vouchered-out households, involuntarily dispersed. This has implications for the enthusiasm program participants may have for it, and, because displaced households are not required to relocate to non-concentrated neighborhoods, implications also for the degree to which families are dispersed and the experiences they encounter in their new communities. Another group of HOPE VI participants stays in whatever public housing units are rehabilitated and maintained on site, so they experience deconcentration in place, similar to existing residents in mixed-income developments, as discussed earlier.

Desegregation Lawsuits
Though the *Gautreaux* cases are the oldest and perhaps best-known cases alleging discrimination and segregation in public housing, a number of other lawsuits also have been filed across the country. During the Clinton administration, HUD decided to settle these cases whenever possible. HUD has entered into consent decrees in more than 12 cases nationwide, the *Hollman* case in Minneapolis being one. Although the settlements differ in detail, they share several common themes. Typically, the settlements call for demolition of some public housing, construction of scattered-site replacement housing, and development of mobility programs (with counseling) in which those in the plaintiff class are provided with tenant-based assistance to make desegregative moves (Popkin,

Buron, et al. 2000). Elements not included in the *Hollman* settlement are the merging of Section 8 and public housing waiting lists and community development in areas surrounding the public housing.

The combination of demolition, redevelopment, and mobility programs makes these settlements hybrids of the HOPE VI and MTO programs. The settlements deal with older public housing, much as HOPE VI does, by emphasizing demolition and redevelopment into lower-density, mixed-use developments. Many of the consent-decree sites have, in fact, used HOPE VI funds to accomplish just those objectives. In addition, however, the lawsuits also incorporate the MTO model of geographically restricted Section 8 vouchers and mobility counseling to facilitate deconcentration.

A recent Urban Institute baseline evaluation offers some early findings on how the decrees are being implemented (Popkin, Buron, et al. 2000). Typically, demolition has proceeded without much delay. This is not surprising, given the local housing authorities' almost total control over the process, and the priority HUD has given to demolition in recent years. Dallas, for example, has demolished more than 2,500 units, and in Omaha, more than 700 units were taken down in two years. "In Omaha, tenants were relocated so quickly that some ended up in substandard housing and [had] to be relocated a second time" (Popkin, Galster, et al. 2000, 42). Changes in tenant-selection procedures and the merging of waiting lists also have occurred quickly at most sites. Even modernization and rehabilitation have taken place without problems where they are called for by decrees.

Other elements of the decrees, which require greater cooperation between agencies, have been more difficult to implement. Development of replacement housing, for instance, has not occurred on a large scale at any of the sites studied by Popkin, Galster, et al. (2000). In some cases, the delays have been due to community resistance to scattered-site housing, and in other cases, because of a lack of interest from private developers.

Popkin, Galster, et al. (2000) identify a number of factors that have impeded progress in implementing the decrees. The first, as suggested above, is conflict among agencies implementing the decrees, and difficulties in coordinating multiple agency activities. In most cities, multiple defendants are responsible for implementing portions of the decrees. In some cases, contractor selection has been a source of conflict; in others, simply coordinating the agendas and resources of multiple agencies has slowed implementation. Additional impediments include community opposition to deconcentration, resident opposition to demolition, and tight rental markets that make implementing mobility programs difficult.

The National Experience with Deconcentration

The preceding pages have described two generations of deconcentration policy. The first began in the mid- to late 1960s and lasted for only a few years, essentially fading away by 1974. It was closely aligned with efforts to reduce racial discrimination in housing and open the suburbs to families of color. When opponents were able to uncouple these issues, and the dispersal of subsidized housing had to be justified on its own account, the entire effort came to a grinding halt.

Less than two decades later, however, a second generation emerged and, from the beginning, was based on creating income diversity in neighborhoods of both concentrated poverty in central cities and concentrated affluence in suburban areas. It is therefore understandable and indeed predictable that the two generations share, if anything, a legacy of stiff opposition from residents and officials in receiving communities.

Resistance to Deconcentration

The ugly American history of residential intolerance predates, of course, the advent of subsidized housing programs. Efforts to maintain the racial purity of neighborhoods throughout the 20th century often included brutal and mob violence, official acts of government, and rulings from the nation's highest courts.[4] When publicly assisted housing programs finally were created, they were easily assimilated into prevailing real estate practices that reinforced, if not increased, patterns of race and class segregation. The siting of public housing became so concentrated precisely because of the opposition of white and middle-class communities.[5] When the federal government moved to reverse 30 years of its own actions, and decades more of officially sanctioned private market activity, it ran into the same resistance.

Scattered-site programs generated resistance in virtually every city that tried them (Hogan 1996). Residents of middle-class neighborhoods objected to "low-income minorities," who would ruin their communities and depress property values. Congressional fears that white suburban communities would suffer from "incursions by housing projects to be occupied predominantly by low-income Negro families" (Keith 1973, 178) limited funding for some of the original initiatives aimed at scattering assisted households. The political fate of scattered-site housing depends upon local housing market conditions and the program's scale and visibility. Neighborhood reaction may also be triggered by media coverage. One key factor in neighborhood reaction is whether the units being introduced are scattered, single-family homes or small complexes, which are more identifiable.[6]

Yonkers

The most notorious case of scattered-site housing is undoubtedly Yonkers, New York. Yonkers is a first-ring suburb of New York City, just north of The Bronx. Subsidized housing in Yonkers followed the classic pattern of concentration. Virtually all (97 percent) subsidized housing in the city was located in its southwest quadrant; "all of the city's high-rise buildings [were] visible from a single street corner" (Briggs 1998, 190), and none of its 27 family projects was located in the predominantly white eastern and northwestern sections of the city.[7] In 1980, the U.S. Department of Justice and the NAACP filed suit against Yonkers, charging deliberate segregation of public housing and schools. On November 11, 1985, a federal district judge ruled for the plaintiffs in finding that the pattern of siting subsidized housing in Yonkers reinforced segregation.

The remedial order, issued six months after the ruling, required desegregation of public schools and provision of subsidized housing in areas other than the southwest quadrant. Desegregating schools was achieved through busing and magnet schools. Desegregating public housing was to be achieved through 200 townhouse units to be built in white, eastern neighborhoods. The city council, however, resisted the order to disperse public housing. City council chambers were filled with white-led homeowner groups complaining about the potential negative effects of such desegregation on property values, crime rates, and "the social fabric" of their neighborhoods (Briggs 1998).[8] One city councilman suggested that the court order would, in essence, erase the line between Yonkers and The Bronx. The mayor, whose support of the desegregation plan ended his political career, received bullets in the mail because he refused to oppose the plan completely (Abramsky 1998; Belkin 1999).

The city spent more to stop the new housing units (more than $20 million) than was spent to build them. The judge who issued the order in the first place responded by imposing ever-increasing fines upon the city until it complied. City officials finally relented in September 1988, when it became clear that accumulating fines would soon bankrupt the city. Between 1990 and 1993, 200 public housing units, consisting of two- and three-bedroom townhouses, were developed on seven different sites that each contained 14 to 48 units. According to Briggs (1998), the city council preferred fewer and larger sites so fewer areas would be "contaminated." The opposition was centered among male homeowners who lived near the sites, held fairly conservative ideological views, and apparently subscribed to racial stereotypes, though NIMBY ("not in my backyard") attitudes against in-movers were based not only on race but also on class (Briggs, Darden, and Aidala 1999).

Regional Efforts

Even certain programs not explicitly or implicitly designed to disperse subsidized housing ran into stiff suburban opposition. For example, Operation Breakthrough, a program aimed at facilitating manufactured housing in response to a housing shortage during President Nixon's first term, was fiercely resisted by suburbs because it might have resulted in racial and class diversity (Danielson 1976). Programs consciously designed to induce diversity fared even worse. HUD's brief efforts to open the suburbs during the Nixon administration were buried in an avalanche of suburban opposition. A proposal for HUD review of local zoning was immediately killed in Congress. The wrath of suburban congressmen against HUD's practice of making water and sewer grants contingent on affordable-housing progress brought an end to that practice. A 1972 plan to distribute housing subsidies through metropolitan agencies was also killed by suburban opposition.

Resistance to scattered-site and fair-share approaches has endured over the decades. The intransigence of New Jersey suburbs to a court mandate to reduce exclusionary barriers led to a second and then third lawsuit in the *Mount Laurel* case. Even HUD's timid attempt in 1979 to facilitate Section 8 portability through a $2 million funding for housing counseling suffered intense criticism, both from those who feared what would happen to the receiving communities and those who felt it was an attempt to facilitate gentrification in core neighborhoods (Goering 1986). In Hartford, Connecticut, a regional mediation process centering on affordable housing resulted in the transformation of a fair-share effort to build affordable housing units into a regional agreement to increase "housing opportunities." Housing opportunities, as defined in the Hartford case, can be provided primarily through Section 8 tenant-based subsidies. Even this watered-down version of "fair share" was further compromised when suburban jurisdictions imposed preferences for their own residents (Polikoff 1995).

Second-generation dispersal policy also has met with fierce resistance. Hysteria over Baltimore's MTO program in 1994, for example, brought swift congressional action. A Republican gubernatorial candidate called the program "social engineering," while another statewide candidate made the program a main campaign issue, denouncing the prospect of public housing families moving out of Baltimore and into the suburbs. Intense opposition also arose in a number of inner-ring suburbs (ironically, their poverty levels were too high even to qualify for any MTO families). The reaction, according to one observer, "bordered on mass hysteria" (Moberg 1995). One political candidate, perpetuating negative images of public housing families, suggested that residents of "the projects had to be taught to bathe and how not to steal" (American Friends Service Committee 1994; Moberg 1995). Anti-MTO buttons and T-shirts were produced and distributed to people fearing an "onslaught of inner-city blacks." In the end, Maryland Senator Barbara Mikulski, chair of the relevant appropriations subcommittee, killed further funding for the program. As one HUD source was quoted as saying, "The congressional message was clear: 'We don't want to hear anything more about HUD programs to move poor blacks into white neighborhoods' " (Rusk 1999, 274).

Lawsuit settlements have generated significant reaction in many receiving communities, as evidenced by arson attacks in New Haven and countersuits in Dallas that ended that city's scattered-site effort. In Allegheny County, Pennsylvania, local government officials in receiving communities vocally opposed the scattered-site program, and a crowd of 250 protested the housing authority's purchase of three townhouses. "In November 1998, local councilmen organized a petition to secede from Allegheny County rather than accept these three units of subsidized housing" (Popkin, Galster, et al. 2000, 75). In New Haven, several homes purchased by the housing authority for the scattered-site program were the targets of arson. Public hearings in New Haven and Omaha have been extremely contentious on the issue of developing affordable units in non-impacted neighborhoods.

The Dallas countersuits were brought by homeowners associations to stop the development of scattered-site units in suburban areas. A district court dismissed the first, but the second, *Highlands of McKamy et al. v. the Dallas Housing Authority*, was favorably decided for the plaintiffs by the Fifth Circuit Court of Appeals.[9] The ruling in favor of the homeowners association essentially holds that, under the 14th Amendment's Equal Protection Clause, the development of close to 500 units of scattered-site public housing in predominantly white areas violates the constitutional rights of the homeowners by subjecting them to the potential of reduced property values, crime, and disorder (Popkin, Galster, et al. 2000, 3–66). This extraordinary decision, in effect, ends the scattered-site program in Dallas. The court of appeals preferred a more race-neutral, tenant-based remedy over scattered-site development.

Impacts of Deconcentration

Deconcentrating the poor brings about two main benefits, yet still faces a significant barrier. First, social problems decrease in previously concentrated neighborhoods. Second, dispersed low-income families experience improved living conditions and life opportunities. Any assessment of deconcentration needs to address whether either effect actually occurs. Yet, as has been demonstrated virtually everywhere dispersal is attempted, perceived risk to receiving communities substantially limits deconcentration. Thus, three main research questions relate to dispersal programs. First, how are the communities from which the poor are dispersed affected? Second, how are the dispersed families affected? Third, how are the receiving communities affected? We now examine the record of deconcentration nationwide in search of answers.

Impact on Concentrated Poverty

Determining the impact of dispersal on concentrated poverty involves a two-stage analysis. First is the question of how dispersal programs impact communities of concentrated poverty. Do they result in a greater distribution of incomes within previously concentrated areas? Do they facilitate new investment and gentrification in previously distressed neighborhoods? Or, is there little spillover impact, outside of the changes made within assisted projects? Second is the issue of how well the programs actually disperse the families involved. Do dispersal programs achieve significant deconcentration?

Very little research, in fact, has been done on the first question, especially for programs not targeted to concentrated neighborhoods. For example, though mobility programs such as Gautreaux and MTO are inspired by concentration of poverty, they do not seem to be regarded as solutions to the problems facing communities characterized by concentrated poverty. Nowhere in the Gautreaux studies, for example, is the issue of the condition of participants' "old" neighborhoods ever raised, except to compare them unfavorably with the new ones. Mobility programs are seen as individual-level or "people" programs, not place based. Thus, the impact that the Gautreaux or MTO programs have had on poverty concentration in the cities in which they operate has not been investigated. Despite the generally positive impact of mobility programs on the individuals involved, there is little evidence they have had any impact on poverty neighborhoods. The scale at which the programs operate reinforces the presumption that little if any neighborhood effect has occurred. Even supporters, such as Polikoff (1995, 19), argue that such programs "so far have been too modest to show a definite impact on poverty concentrations in central cities."

Though there is no evidence mobility programs have had a positive impact on concentrations of poverty, there is some reason to suspect they might have had a negative effect. Voluntary mobility programs "cream" from the households living in highly concentrated public housing. The Gautreaux program screened families very carefully, for example, and families using mobility certificates were able to achieve a relatively low "lease-up" rate (the percentage of families that are able to successfully lease up an apartment using their Section 8 subsidy). These two factors, combined with the self-selection involved in voluntary programs, suggest that those who move out of neighborhoods of high poverty are different from those who remain.

For programs targeted to neighborhoods of concentrated poverty, the impacts are easier to determine. HOPE VI, vouchering out, and the conversion of existing projects to mixed-income developments all result in the immediate deconcentration of poverty on site. The Public Housing Reform Act of 1998 may work on a more gradual basis by reducing concentrations of very low income families over time, as housing authorities use vacancies to introduce higher-income families into public housing projects. What has yet to be determined through research, however, is whether these changes in the micro-community of a subsidized housing project have any wider impact in the very poor neighborhoods where they are located.

Only HOPE VI research extends to the question of impacts on communities of concentrated poverty. Virtually all of it, however, is in its early stages and, thus, is unavailable for review. Work that has been done suggests that redevelopment efforts must walk a fine line between triggering large-scale gentrification and being forced to heavily subsidize redevelopment in communities where the market is not so anxious to reinvest. The transformation of public housing sites at many HOPE VI projects has been remarkable. The worst projects have been demolished, with more demolition still to come. In their place are new, mixed-income, mixed-use communities developed along neotraditional design principles aimed at maximizing a sense of community and the development of social capital. The new developments are undeniably more attractive than the typically modernist structures they replaced.

One study of HOPE VI in three cities, however, indicates that redevelopment has not leveraged much private-sector investment. For example, public subsidies were required in San Antonio for all phases of the project—from relocation to demolition to infrastructure development—and even for the development of market-rate housing on site. Furthermore, total development costs per unit for several HOPE VI projects were well above those for the low-income housing tax credit program (62 percent over in Atlanta, 81 percent over in Chicago, and 113 percent over in San Antonio) (Salama 1999).

On the other hand, the transformation of public housing can lead to quick gentrification in some cities. More recent HOPE VI projects have involved smaller, less-distressed public housing sites "with greater potential to attract private investment" (National Housing Law Project 2002, 14). Bennett's (1999) analysis of Chicago, for example, notes that the heated real estate market there has responded swiftly to the redevelopment (and, in some cases, even the planned redevelopment) of several of the city's public housing projects. Cabrini-Green was in the middle of a north side neighborhood undergoing aggressive real estate investment and upgrading as early as the late 1970s. By the mid-1980s, one political analyst actually predicted that the project, perhaps the most notorious public housing site in the country, would face strong pressures for redevelopment and gentrification.[10] Ten years later, redevelopment occurred, families were relocated, and the area experienced rapid gentrification.

Median sales prices of single-unit homes increased from $138,000 to $700,000 during the 1980s. Nearly three times as many building permits were issued in 1990 as in 1977. During the 1980s, the area lost 7,000 African Americans and gained 4,000 whites (Bennett and Reed 1999).

The same process also occurred two miles from the Loop, in an area next to the University of Illinois at Chicago campus. Gentrification began, followed closely by plans to demolish three-quarters of the ABLA (Addams, Brooks, Loomis, and Abbott) projects and replace them with 1,000 public housing units, 1,000 market-rate units, and 450 affordable units. Elsewhere, the city has invested millions of dollars in neighborhood infrastructure improvements that have generated private market improvements in neighborhoods with large public housing projects. In fact, dramatic real estate appreciation in neighborhoods near the Henry Horner Homes has slowed development of off-site replacement housing for demolished units. Furthermore, the Horner replacement units have met with neighborhood opposition from homeowners groups worried about an influx of public housing families (Bennett 1999).

The same scenario has played out in the city's south side public housing as well. The downsizing of public housing is becoming such an accepted occurrence that private investors are now bidding up property values in the vicinity of public housing projects in anticipation of redevelopment (Bennett 1999). As a result, the redevelopment of public housing in Chicago has become a central element in very significant neighborhood transformations. This situation makes the nature of the redevelopment (and the percentage of new units for public housing) an important consideration in examining its impact. Bennett (1998) argues that because the Cabrini-Green redevelopment plan limits public housing to 30 percent of new construction, it facilitates the economic and racial transformation of the neighborhood.

The Extent of Deconcentration

The other aspect of dispersal's impact is how well families actually are dispersed throughout a metropolitan region. That is, where have they gone? Have they moved to neighborhoods with lower poverty rates? Have they dispersed into suburban areas?

According to census indicators, most families that either voluntarily deconcentrate or are forcibly relocated experience improved neighborhood conditions. Voluntary participants are better-off because they relocate to neighborhoods that are below defined thresholds for poverty or minority status. Involuntarily displaced households experience improvements because the neighborhoods from which they were displaced are often the very worst in a community. The actual degree of dispersion, however, is greater under voluntary mobility programs because they mandate that participants move to non-concentrated neighborhoods. What the studies have not detailed, however, is the extent to which families remain in those neighborhoods or subsequently move back into neighborhoods of concentrated poverty. Rubinowitz and Rosenbaum (2001) report, for instance, that 20 percent of the Gautreaux participants who had originally moved to the suburbs and been resurveyed had moved back to the city. Involuntarily displaced households, on the other hand, tend not to move very far from their old neighborhoods, and many move into other poverty or minority concentrations.

Tenant-based subsidies produce greater dispersion than project-based subsidies.[11] But the passive administration of tenant-based assistance does not, on the whole, lead to deconcentration of poverty, compared with the settlement patterns of the nonsubsidized poor. Participants in the Experimental Housing Assistance Program (EHAP) experienced virtually no change in the income profile of their neighborhoods and only a slight reduction in the percentage of minority residents in the communities to which they moved (Cronin and Rasmussen 1981; Frieden 1985; Leger and Kennedy 1990; Lowry 1983; Weicher 1990). The overall experience of the Section 8 program has reinforced this pattern (Cronin and Rasmussen 1981; Pendall 2000). Studies show that many participating families remain in their current neighborhoods. For those who do move, the increase in neighborhood income is quite modest (Leger and Kennedy 1990; Schill and Wachter 1995). Clearly, families may weigh the expected benefits of a move against the costs, including the out-of-pocket costs of searching and moving, loss of length-of-tenure discounts, loss of information capital, and psychological costs. The net effect of Section 8 allowances on mobility might therefore best be interpreted as accelerating moves that would have been made otherwise.[12] Certificate and voucher holders remain concentrated in tracts with lower incomes and more affordable housing because of the distribution of available low-cost apartments (Hartung and Henig 1997; Pendall 2000).

Studies of the portability features of Section 8 have generated mixed outcomes. Hartford (Connecticut) voucher holders who exercise portability enjoy improvements in neighborhood quality. In fact, a regular voucher holder in Hartford lives in a census tract with a poverty rate four times that of the average participant who transfers out of the city. In addition, the minority population for a regular voucher holder in a census tract within the city is just under four times greater than for the average mobility-program participant. In fact, 90 percent of these participants live in census tracts with less than 40 percent minority population (Donovan 1994).

Polikoff (1995) argues that portability is a way of "reaching scale" in mobility programs. For example, in a survey of Section 8 participants in Hartford, 68 percent indicated they were interested in living elsewhere, if possible. This high interest resulted from the participants' desire to move away from crime (32 percent) and to better schools (19 percent). Portability is limited, however, by the difficulty low-income families face in leaving neighborhoods and support networks. In a New Haven survey, 52 percent thought they would have obstacles to moving, such as a lack of transportation (cited by 33 percent) and difficulty separating from relatives and friends (11 percent).[13]

Despite the success of the Hartford program, other evidence reveals little sign of large-scale deconcentration of subsidized households. Researchers found evidence of only 41 households that transferred from Washington, D.C., to Maryland in the early 1990s, and only 7 that moved from Washington, D.C., to Virginia, while 99 moved (changing jurisdictions) within Maryland and 657 moved within Virginia (Pope 1995). Most Section 8 participants exercising portability out of Berkeley, California, went to Oakland, a lower-income city with a greater supply of low-cost housing (Barton 1998). Portability in the Minneapolis–Saint Paul region actually facilitated a greater concentration of Section 8 families in the two central cities; Minneapolis and Saint Paul were the two largest recipients of Section 8 households (Malaby and Lukermann 1996).

Voluntary mobility programs that require a move to neighborhoods with less poverty or fewer minority residents achieve the greatest level of deconcentration. Those who volunteer are typically less tied to their current neighborhoods. Results from the Baltimore MTO program, for example, show that 5 percent of the participants wanted to relocate elsewhere in their neighborhood, 60 percent wanted to move to different neighborhoods within Baltimore, one-quarter (26 percent) expressed a preference for the suburbs, and 7 percent wished to leave the Baltimore area entirely (Norris and Bembry 1998). In actuality, 38 percent of the experimental group moved outside the city compared with only 3 percent of the comparison group (Ladd and Ludwig 1997). Most indicated they wanted to move into integrated neighborhoods, while, at the same time, indicating that race was not an important factor in their ultimate choice. The Baltimore MTO group was one-third less likely to move to a neighborhood that was mostly African American, compared with the control group (Norris and Bembry 1998).

A summary examination of mobility programs that allow a move to suburban areas indicates that roughly 15 to 20 percent of the participants choose to move. That figure is higher for programs (such as MTO) that require a move to a low-poverty area. Mobility programs typically result in significant changes in neighborhood characteristics for participant families (Polikoff 1995). For example, in the Cincinnati HOME program, the average destination census tract is 86 percent non-Hispanic white (Rosenbaum and Miller 1997). Furthermore, scattered-site participants in Cleveland moved from neighborhoods that were less well-off to neighborhoods with higher median incomes, median housing values, median rents, and ownership rates (Chandler 1990).

The record is quite different for those who are involuntarily deconcentrated. Former public housing residents in Chicago displaced through demolition typically moved into segregated areas where the residents were equally as poor. Of the first 1,044 families relocated out of public housing, 79 percent moved into census tracts that were 90 percent or more black, and 94 percent live in tracts that average $15,000 or less in household income, a record worse than the Section 8 program as a whole (Rumbler 1998).

Many of the displaced residents wanted to remain in the community where they had been living. For example, most families vouchered out of HUD projects in four study sites made short moves. In Baltimore, 40 percent remained in the West Baltimore neighborhood from which they came. Most of the rest moved elsewhere in the city. In San Francisco, though only 10 percent remained in their original neighborhood (Visitacion Valley), the rest moved into Bayview Hunters Point and the Western Addition, the two nearest high-poverty, high-minority neighborhoods. In Newport News, Virginia, about 50 percent remained in the east end of town, 27 percent moved to other parts of town, and the rest went to the neighboring city of Hampton. In Kansas City, Missouri, 99 percent stayed in the city (HUD 1998).

Vouchered-out families in the HUD study cited their own lack of transportation, a desire to remain close to their support systems (including family, friends, and church), a tendency to search in familiar areas, and a fear of discrimination in searching as reasons for restricting their searches. Many were directed to nearby units through referral lists of landlords from the relocation process. About one in four vouchered-out families reported being the victim of discrimination in its housing search, most frequently because of the family's status as a Section 8 certificate/voucher holder. HUD estimates the rate was not higher because many families restricted their searches to areas in which they felt welcome and more comfortable (HUD 1998).

The new neighborhoods of the vouchered-out families had, on average, higher median incomes than the old ones. In three of the cities, a slight majority of households moved to neighborhoods with fewer African Americans as a percentage of all residents. In Baltimore, however, only 10 percent of the families made such moves. The housing values in the new neighborhoods were lower than in the original ones at all sites except San Francisco.

Evidence going back as far as the Experimental Housing Allowance Program indicates that mobility counseling can significantly influence locational choices (Cronin and Rasmussen 1981). This has been confirmed by more recent studies showing that mobility counseling and housing-search assistance are very important to families that want to move to non-concentrated areas (HUD 1995). The experience of programs in Hartford, Dallas, and Alameda County indicates that even simple information about regional housing opportunities can be helpful in facilitating moves to lower-poverty areas. However, counseling can also just as easily result in reconcentrating blacks (Cronin and Rasmussen 1981; Polikoff 1995). Data from the HUD study of vouchered-out projects in four cities showed that those who used the relocation services were no more likely to learn about opportunities in distant places than were nonparticipating families.

Project-based dispersal programs, such as fair-share and scattered-site programs, also tend to achieve very modest dispersal outcomes. Scattered-site programs, for example, involve only dispersal within a particular jurisdiction because public housing authorities are restricted from buying or leasing properties outside their municipal boundaries. Thus, scattered-site public housing is not typically a metropolitan-wide approach. However, even when such a metropolitan-wide approach is taken, either as the result of a fair-share program or a court mandate, it still results in only a modest dispersal of low-income, central-city families.

The country's largest fair-share program (New Jersey) allows communities to fulfill up to half their low-cost housing obligation by paying other localities to build such housing within their boundaries. In practice, this has meant that whiter, more affluent communities have paid poorer communities with greater percentages of people of color to take a portion of their obligation. Among the 54 regional contribution agreements (RCAs) reached in New Jersey between 1987 and 1996, all but one involved the transfer of affordable housing obligations from wealthier to poorer communities. The average sending community had a 2 percent African-American population, while the average receiving community was 27 percent African American (Field, Gilbert, and Wheeler 1997). Suburban areas can fulfill the rest of their obligation by providing low-cost housing for the elderly and by imposing residency preferences for families already residing in the community.

Among those units that are built in suburban areas, most are occupied by white families that had previously lived in the suburbs. In fact, the amount of city-to-suburb dispersal of lower-income and minority households through the Mount Laurel program has been minuscule. Only 6.8 percent of more than 2,600 households were families that moved from the cities to the suburbs, and less than 2 percent were African Americans. When the movement of African Americans from the suburbs back into the cities is taken into account, the net rate of African-American dispersal is less than 1 percent (Wish and Eisdorfer 1997).

Participant Experience

Methodological Approaches

A significant amount of research has been completed on how mobility programs impact lower-income households. Typically, families are interviewed after they have moved and asked a series of questions about their experiences in their new homes as compared with their retrospective assessment of their previous residences. In the case of the Gautreaux program, which has been in operation for a long time, follow-up interviews were also conducted several years later to determine long-term impacts. However, Briggs (1998) argues that methodological problems with these studies hinder our ability to apply their findings across the entire population of low-income households. The most notable limitation is selection

bias. Since most mobility programs are voluntary and incorporate participant screening, participating households are systematically different from
the entire population of subsidized (or low-income) households. That is,
it is impossible to determine whether the improvements that occur in
their lives stem from their new environment or occur because these households may have, on average, more resources or initiative to improve their
situations than nonparticipating families have. In the Gautreaux studies,
where a comparison group is used, participants volunteered for either
group, indicating the high potential for selection bias. In some studies, no
comparison group is used, making causal inferences impossible. Most
studies have failed to distinguish between direct and indirect effects, and
have poorly specified how effects may have occurred. For example, many
studies do not attempt to establish whether mobility families have,
indeed, experienced the level of contact and exposure to the environments
thought to influence behavior.

The Moving To Opportunity program was designed to rectify the
selection-bias problem as much as possible. Participants still volunteer
for it, however; therefore generalizing the findings to the entire population of public housing residents is not possible. However, assignment to
the mobility program, the regular Section 8 program, and to the group
receiving no further assistance (the stay-in-place control group) is done
randomly. Therefore, outcome differences across these groups should be
related only to program treatment and not to systematic differences
between those who move and those who do not.

Satisfaction

In a study of single-parent African-American families in Durham, North
Carolina, residents of scattered-site units reported more residential satisfaction and less fear of crime than a comparison group (Burby and Rohe
1989). In a separate study of 340 households participating in Cincinnati's
scattered-site program, residents did not report any greater levels of social
isolation than a comparison group, though there was some evidence of
isolation from employment opportunities (Varady and Preiser 1998). This
latter finding, of course, is the opposite of what would be expected by the
spatial-mismatch theory. It suggests that low-income groups are more isolated from employment opportunities in disadvantaged central-city
neighborhoods than in more dispersed locations.

Two other studies show that residents of scattered-site public housing report high satisfaction with their housing, although neither had a comparison group (Hogan and Lengyel 1985). In Cincinnati, 75 percent reported they were satisfied or very satisfied with their housing, but there was no difference between the scattered-site households and those living in traditional public housing in the city. Scattered-site residents did report significantly greater levels of neighborhood satisfaction and reduced fear of crime compared with traditional public housing residents (Varady and Preiser 1998).

In Cleveland, 79 percent of the residents of scattered-site units rated their housing better than their former, traditional public housing. This study did not incorporate a comparison group. Rather, the author examined reported changes in behaviors and satisfaction that took place after residents moved into scattered-site public housing. In addition, 74 percent of former private-housing residents also considered the scattered-site public housing an improvement over their former residences. The Cleveland movers felt services—with the notable exception of transportation—were better in their new communities (Chandler 1990).

A study of the Yonkers families compares the experiences of those residents who moved into the scattered-site units with a comparable group of public housing residents who stayed in their old units. The comparison group's neighborhoods exhibited higher poverty rates, lower labor force participation, lower educational attainment, and higher rates of female-headed households. The movers, who moved anywhere from two to seven miles away, perceived their neighborhoods as safer than did those who stayed (Briggs 1997).

In the only published research on families vouchered out of HUD-assisted buildings, more than half surveyed at three of four sites stated they were unhappy about moving or would have preferred to stay. Long-term and older residents were the least happy to move. Despite this, approximately two-thirds were more satisfied with their new homes than their original developments. The other one-third said their current housing conditions were worse, or the same as, their previous conditions. Similarly, households were more satisfied with their new neighborhoods than their previous ones. Respondents reported a greater sense of safety at their new homes, as well as improvements in shopping and proximity to friends. Interestingly, the HUD study indicated that housing satisfaction was greatest among those who confined their searches to their immediate neighborhood and relocated nearby. Similarly, those who began to look for a new apartment relatively soon after learning they had to move were more likely to be satisfied with their new homes than were those who waited. Housing expenses for vouchered-out families rose in two of the sites (considerably so in San Francisco) and fell at the other two (HUD 1998; Varady and Walker 2000).

Both city and suburban movers in the Gautreaux program reported higher levels of satisfaction after moving out of their public housing units. Suburban movers reported significantly greater satisfaction with police and schools, but significantly less satisfaction with medical and transportation services. City movers reported more satisfaction in all four areas. There were no differences, however, between city and suburban movers on respondents' reporting they had "more money" or "better housing" (Rosenbaum and Popkin 1990).

Early MTO findings report higher satisfaction with neighborhood, much lower fear of neighborhood crime, low exposure to violence, and higher-quality schools. In Baltimore, for example, 61 percent of the comparison group reported problems with drugs and violence in their new neighborhoods, compared with 28 percent of the treatment group. The comparison group was, however, more satisfied with the public transportation in their neighborhoods (Norris and Bembry 1998).

Education

Among the suburban movers in the Gautreaux program, youth age 17 or younger were less likely to drop out of high school compared with city movers (5 versus 20 percent), more likely to be in a college track (40 versus 24 percent), and more likely to attend college (54 versus 21 percent). Among those attending college, half of suburban movers went to four-year institutions, and two-thirds were working toward an associate's degree, compared with only half of city movers (Kaufman and Rosenbaum 1992).

The research also showed that, compared with reports by city movers, suburban teachers offered more educational assistance to children. Compared with city-mover parents, suburban parents felt that teachers responded better to the educational needs of their children, treated them better, helped more often, and went out of their way to help their children more frequently (Rosenbaum, Kulieke, and Rubinowitz 1987). Grade school children had difficulty adjusting to higher expectations of suburban schools, but their grades (relative to the city movers) did not suffer, indicating "an impressive ability of these children to respond to the higher demands in the suburbs" (24). Parents also noted that their children's attitudes toward school improved after moving to suburban areas.

Despite these positive outcomes for suburban movers, significant problems were noted in the suburban schools that received these African-American inner-city children. First, participants reported a racial bias in the suburban schools that made their children's adjustment difficult. Second, and perhaps most troubling, was the tendency for suburban schools to place these children in special education programs (for learning disabled and educable mentally retarded children) at a significantly higher rate than city schools. Pre-move, 7 percent of families reported children in special education tracks, compared with 19 percent post-move in the suburbs and 5 percent post-move in the city. Most parents attributed this to the racism of suburban school officials. Despite these reservations, suburban participants reported significantly greater overall satisfaction with their schools than did city movers (Rosenbaum ct al. 1987, 1988). Suburban movers also reported that their new environment increased their children's motivation. The environmental effects mentioned included higher school expectations along with positive role models and peer pressure (Kaufman and Rosenbaum 1992; Rosenbaum and Popkin 1991).

In the Baltimore MTO program, however, there was no difference between the movers and control groups on satisfaction with schools (Norris and Bembry 1998). The Cleveland study of scattered-site housing found that program residents reported improved school performance and interest in school among their children. As for the adults themselves, one-third became enrolled in training or education programs after moving, a small increase over the 28 percent who had enrolled in such programs prior to moving (Chandler 1990). Ludwig, Ladd, and Duncan (2001) document higher achievement scores for children in the Baltimore MTO program than in the stay-in-place control group, but no difference between MTO participants and the Section 8 comparison group. Whether such improvements occur for children of involuntarily displaced families is less clear (Johnson, Ladd, and Ludwig 2002).

Employment

Dispersal is thought to facilitate employment gains through a number of means. First, movement out of poorer central-city neighborhoods and into more economically vibrant suburban communities may solve the spatial mismatch for some families, putting them in closer proximity to areas of job growth. Second, feelings of greater personal safety that accompany a move out of the poorest neighborhoods may allow some previously unemployed individuals to participate in the labor market. Third, living among more middle-class people may provide potential workers with different role models and/or access to better job prospects through word of mouth than were available in their old neighborhoods.

The record of dispersal programs on employment, however, is somewhat mixed. The studies of Gautreaux families do indicate some employment benefits associated with a move to the suburbs. Significantly more suburban youth than city youth were working (75 versus 41 percent) (Kaufman and Rosenbaum 1992). Among adults, the work experience prior to moving was identical for city and suburban movers; after relocating, however, suburban movers were 13 percent more likely to have a job than city movers were. Even controlling for human-capital factors, suburban movers were more likely than city movers to become employed. Among those unemployed prior to moving, 46 percent of the suburban movers found jobs, compared with only 30 percent of the city movers; however, there was little difference between city and suburban movers in hourly wages and hours worked (Rosenbaum and Popkin 1991). Suburban youth reported higher pay than city movers, though there was no difference in job prestige across the groups. Suburban youth were also more likely to have benefits—such as vacation, sick leave, and health and education benefits—than city movers were (Kaufman and Rosenbaum 1992; Rosenbaum and Popkin 1990).

Suburban movers in the Gautreaux program indicated that the greater number of jobs in the suburbs was a factor in their employment success. They also mentioned that their increased sense of personal safety and the safety of their children allowed them to leave their homes and go to work. Participants did report, however, that a lack of transportation, difficulties in securing child care, and discrimination were significant obstacles to employment in the suburbs (Rosenbaum and Popkin 1990). Among MTO families, participation in welfare programs is lower for those families that move than for those that remain in concentrated public housing (Ludwig, Duncan, and Pinkston 2000).

On the other hand, several studies show little or no employment effect. Vouchering out did not lead to any increase in employment among the families studied by HUD (1998). Apparently, most of the moves were very short, and, as a result, most families did not improve their chances of accessing more employment opportunities. The early MTO results showed some gains in employment and earnings in Los Angeles, but not Boston.[14] In Cincinnati, employment rates among movers were significantly higher than rates among public housing residents, though there were differences between the groups even before the move. In Cleveland, less than one-third of scattered households reported feeling their employment opportunities had improved, compared with more than half who felt no change. The group also experienced no changes in actual employment rates, hours of work, or wages, compared with their pre-move status.[15]

Social Interaction

Levels of social interaction among poor families dispersed into predominantly white, middle-class areas are of interest for several reasons. First, the neighborhood-effects literature suggests that different behavioral expectations in the new neighborhoods may positively impact relocating families. More economically and socially diverse neighborhoods may increase the diversity of social networks for poor families and increase access to better job prospects. These effects, however, presume some level of contact between the relocating families and their new neighbors. If, instead of social integration in their new environments, the relocating families experience isolation and hostility, then the move can be damaging instead of beneficial. The empirical studies have found evidence of both, sometimes among the same families.

Among children in the Gautreaux program, there were no differences between the city and suburban movers in "feeling a part of the school," in receiving respect from other students, or in overall social integration. Moving to the suburbs did not seem to affect the size of the social circle reported by youth in the Gautreaux program. Suburban movers did report, however, having fewer black friends and more white friends than did city movers.[16] Suburban movers reported a higher degree of interaction with white children on a number of dimensions, including contact outside of school, sharing homework, and visiting homes. Suburban movers agreed more than city movers with the statement that "whites are friendly" (Rosenbaum and Meaden 1992).

At the same time, however, 52 percent of young people in the suburbs reported at least one incident of name-calling, compared with only 13 percent of city movers. The percentage of suburban movers who reported harassment reduced over time to 25 percent, a percentage not statistically different from that reported by city movers. Both city and suburban movers reported less interaction with neighbors after moving. Suburban movers were, however, twice as likely as city movers to complain of isolation and loneliness.

In Yonkers, where the scattered-site program consisted of several clustered developments of between 14 and 48 units, movers were not well integrated into the social environment of their new neighborhoods. Social interactions tended to be with others living in the same subsidized development (Briggs 1998). Kleit (2001a, b) found that families that moved into scattered-site housing in Montgomery County, Maryland, had more diverse social networks than a comparison group that had moved into more clustered developments. However, compared with the clustered families, the scattered residents were significantly less likely to use their more diverse neighbors in a job search, and reported looser ties to their neighbors. Mixed-income developments have typically not generated significant levels of social interactions across income groups.[17]

Other Effects

Early findings from several MTO studies across the five demonstration sites indicate some program effects in criminal behavior, health, and parenting. The findings on criminal behavior are mixed. In Boston, male children in MTO families engaged in less criminal activity than did their counterparts in the public housing control group (Katz, Kling, and Liebman 2001). In New York, however, treatment and comparison groups exhibited no differences in delinquency rates (Johnson et al. 2002). In Baltimore, the male children of MTO families showed lower rates of violent criminal offenses (though the rate was even lower among the non-MTO Section 8 comparison group), but higher rates of property crime, than did the male children in the public housing control group (Ludwig, Duncan, and Hirschfield 2001).

Compared with the stay-in-place group, MTO families in New York reported better physical and mental health (the Section 8 group also showed many of these benefits) and a lower likelihood of punitive or restrictive parenting. Among the three groups, however, MTO parents were the least involved in their children's school activities (Johnson et al. 2002).

Impact on Receiving Communities

One limitation on dispersal programs is the perceived risk to "receiving" communities. That is, suburban and outlying communities are not generally anxious to receive very low income households, based on the argument that concentrating such households negatively affects communities. Receiving communities anticipate an increase in neighborhood stressors similar to those associated with concentrated poverty, including crime, delinquency, declining schools, and depreciating property values.

The potential negative effects of dispersal programs on receiving communities have been inadequately theorized and researched, however. Galster and Zobel (1998), for example, argue that there are several potential forms to the relationship between the introduction of poor households to a community and the social and economic well-being of that community.[18] If the relationship is linear, then one neighborhood's gain (in losing a poor household) is another's loss. This, however, is unlikely to be the case; the addition of each new poor household is unlikely to add an equal increment of strain to the receiving community. In one type of nonlinear relationship, a gentle slope gives way to an ever-steeper one. In this scenario, the first few poor people entering a receiving neighborhood have very little impact. At some point, however, a threshold is attained and additional poor people create ever-larger detrimental effects. An opposite, nonlinear pattern would posit a very large effect from the first poor families in a neighborhood, with diminishing effects thereafter. Finally, an S-shaped curve suggests that the first and last poor households make little neighborhood impact, while greater impacts occur somewhere in the middle. Nonlinearity, however, is rarely, if ever, considered. Furthermore, neighborhood-impact studies fail to stratify by neighborhoods in order to determine the differential impacts of subsidized housing across community types, and fail to account for the possibility that subsidized housing is located in neighborhoods already experiencing declines in quality of the sort the housing itself is presumed to produce (Freeman and Botein 2002).

Opponents of scattered-site public housing suggest a range of negative outcomes in receiving neighborhoods. Analysis of the actual impact has been pursued in two ways—by surveying residents' attitudes in the receiving communities and by measuring objective indicators (typically property values) to examine patterns of change that could be attributed to the introduction of the scattered-site units. Even though decisions by realtors, mortgage lenders, and others who typically do not reside in a target neighborhood are critical in determining the effects of subsidized housing on that neighborhood, studies of scattered-site public housing have not incorporated analyses of these reactions (Briggs, Darden, and Aidala 1999).

Resident Perceptions

If scattered-site public housing indeed produces negative neighborhood outcomes, one would expect residents to notice such outcomes and alter their feelings toward the neighborhood. By this standard, the impact of scattered-site development on nearby residents seems minimal in most cases. A survey of 56 residents of market-rate units in Montgomery County, Maryland, found that 93 percent were either very satisfied or satisfied with their neighborhoods, which included scattered-site public housing. Though there was no control group, the absolute percentage of those expressing satisfaction was very high (Innovative Housing Institute 1998). Furthermore, introducing scattered-site units in Yonkers has had no substantial negative effects on the psychological sense of community in receiving neighborhoods (Briggs, Darden, and Aidala 1999). In many of these locations, residents are probably unaware that scattered-site subsidized units exist in their neighborhoods (Chandler 1990). Neighbors' perceptions about subsidized housing are often incorrect. An Urban Institute study reports that members of focus groups identify subsidized housing with the most rundown buildings in a neighborhood, whether or not those buildings turn out, in fact, to be subsidized (Galster et al. 1999).

Property Values

Research is mixed on the impact of subsidized housing on nearby property values. Early studies indicated that subsidized housing positively or imperceptibly influenced the receiving neighborhoods (Babb, Pol, and Guy 1984; Baird 1980; DeSalvo 1974; Nourse 1963; Rabiega, Lin, and Robinson 1984; Saunders and Woodford 1979; Schafer 1972; Sedway and Associates 1983; Warren, Aduddell, and Tatalovich 1983). More recently, some studies have shown slight negative effects from public housing and other forms of subsidized housing, while others have found no effect or even slight positive impacts.[19] The evidence suggests that whatever effects there are, they depend highly on the local context and type of neighborhood (Briggs et al. 1999; Freeman and Botein 2002; Galster et al. 1999).

In Yonkers, where 200 units of scattered-site public housing were developed in projects of anywhere from 14 to 48 units each, overall proximity was shown to have no detectable price effect. White homeowners living near the scattered-site housing were not particularly concerned about racial tipping, nor were they more likely to move than were their counterparts citywide (Briggs et al. 1999). The public housing units themselves tended to be sited in lower-value areas within the new neighborhoods, a pattern seen in other studies (Innovative Housing Institute 1998).

A Denver study found that dispersed public housing positively influenced housing prices. House prices for properties within 500 feet of a public housing site were higher relative to similar homes outside the radius. The effect was not universal, however. Dispersed public housing in predominantly low-income black neighborhoods actually had a negative effect on nearby housing values, suggesting that negative effects are most likely in more vulnerable neighborhoods (Santiago, Galster, and Tatian 2001). A similar finding is reported in a study of how the concentration of Section 8 certificate and voucher units in Baltimore County impacted nearby property values. Within a 500-foot ring of sales, lower concentrations of Section 8 units were associated with positive effects on property values, except in lower-income neighborhoods where the effects were small but negative (Galster et al. 1999).

Ambiguous Objectives, Equivocal Policy

Dispersal policy is an arena in which the objectives have not always been clear. Emerging first in the late 1960s after decades of explicitly discriminatory and segregationist practices in siting subsidized housing, dispersal policy marked a significant redirection for federal housing policy. Housing officials, long accustomed to old ways, were sometimes reluctant to embrace dispersal or integration. Even after the federal policy shift, differences occasionally remained between official Washington policy and the practices of local housing authorities.[20]

Even when dispersal was agreed upon, the real objective remained ambiguous. Were dispersal efforts aimed at merely eliminating discriminatory barriers, or attempting to achieve actual integrative outcomes?[21]

The first generation of dispersal witnessed a clear merging of antidiscrimination efforts and integrationist objectives. When this combination proved politically insupportable, however, the Nixon administration separated the two objectives. Stripped of legitimacy stemming from its antidiscriminatory foundation, dispersal quickly died, as political support for integration also came up insufficient. Echoing the first wave of dispersal, many of the lawsuits that served as the foundation for current dispersal programs, including *Hollman* in Minneapolis, originated as antidiscrimination suits. Current remedies, however, focus on dispersal, or integrating low-income families into more affluent neighborhoods. This time, antidiscrimination impulses combine uneasily with a desire to deconcentrate poverty. The elimination of discriminatory, subsidized housing–siting practices, which enjoys significant political consensus, will not, by itself, lead to deconcentration of poverty. The more direct steps needed to facilitate deconcentration, through integrating the poor into more affluent communities, simply do not possess that same level of consensus.

Congressional support for deconcentration and dispersal has been uneven and inconsistent. In the early 1970s, Congress would not support a direct effort to integrate suburban areas. In 1974, however, it supported creation of the Section 8 program in an effort to offer greater choice for subsidized households. Congress approved the MTO program in the 1990s, but halted program expansion at the first sign of suburban resistance. All this has left the court system, in both the first and second generation of dispersal, as the most important initiator of dispersal and integration efforts.

Equivocal policy has limited the impact of dispersal over both generations. Gautreaux operated in Chicago for more than two decades, but the program had to carefully screen tenants (limiting its scope) and limit the number of families it introduced to any one receiving community. These practices not only avoided reconcentration, but also kept the program under the political radar in receiving communities. Furthermore, fair-share efforts at the national level have been aborted early, and scattered-site efforts to build affordable housing in nontraditional neighborhoods have also been greatly limited. More passive attempts to disperse show virtually no effect.

Dispersal efforts, even voluntary mobility programs, face significant barriers to achieving the scale necessary to make a dent in patterns of concentrated poverty. Mobility programs launched as a result of the desegregation lawsuits, for example, have faced several challenges. First, many people are reluctant to make desegregative moves. Many participants fear discrimination in their housing search and harassment in their new communities. Others shy away from such programs because of perceived financial barriers to the relocation process, while still others hesitate to move away from familiar areas and necessary support networks. In Omaha, for example, "many residents were so unwilling to make desegregative moves that they waited until the 120-day restricted period was lifted and they could use their Section 8 certificate or voucher in an impacted area" (Popkin, Buron, et al. 2000, 76). In New Haven, members of the plaintiff class did not want to move to the suburbs, away from friends and support networks (Popkin, Galster, et al. 2000). The authors suggest that relocated families need long-term support to keep them from moving back into impacted areas.

Mobility programs have also been hindered by a lack of units available at or below fair market rents. Very tight rental housing markets in New York City, Dallas, and Omaha have resulted in very intense competition for units, making it difficult for housing authorities to recruit landlords to participate. Many mobility participants have suggested that a lack of transportation in non-impacted communities is a barrier to mobility. Even where bus routes exist, significant distances make getting to and from work and stores very difficult. Finally, landlord behavior and management practices may also limit the scope of dispersal efforts. In Chicago, for example, tenant-screening criteria in suburban areas have made it impossible for many of the plaintiff class to move into the suburbs (Wilen and Stasell 2000).

> Even a HUD-commissioned assessment of the Regional Housing Mobility Program concluded that "enabling a household to move to a greater number of jurisdictions without increasing the available supply of affordable, decent housing there merely increases the number of areas where a household may look for yet unavailable housing" (Metropolitan Action Institute of New York [December 1982], quoted in Goering 1986, 201).

Massive and consistent suburban opposition to deconcentration, backed in Congress and state houses by the growing political clout of America's suburbs, leaves deconcentration in a precarious place. What can be agreed upon without much political contention, and therefore what has occurred in greatest quantity, is the demolition of "dysfunctional" or "pathological" central neighborhoods dominated by the poor and people of color. The questions of where the poor should go and what low-income, central-city neighborhoods should look like, however, are still a matter of debate.

NOTES

1. See, for example, Massey and Denton (1993); Meyer (2000); and Schill and Friedman (1999).

2. See the argument in Spence (1993).

3. See Epp (1996) and Lang and Hornburg (1998).

4. See the detailed history provided by Meyer (2000).

5. Goldstein and Yancey (1986); Hirsch (1996); and Meyerson and Banfield (1955) all provide accounts of this type of process.

6. See Briggs (1997); Chandler (1990); and Hogan (1996) for the various elements that condition the political reception of scattered-site programs.

7. See also Tein (1992).

8. See also Belkin (1999) for an extensive description of the events surrounding the Yonkers controversy.

9. *Highlands of McKamy IV and V Community Improvement Association; Ginger Lee; Preston Highlands Homeowners' Association, Incorporated; David Beer v. The Dallas Housing Authority*, United States Court of Appeals for the Fifth Circuit, no. 97-11083, March 16, 1999.

10. Bennett and Reed (1999, 177–78) use a quote from a book written by a former aide to Mayor Richard J. Daley, who wrote in 1986, "In the near future . . . the Cabrini-Green high-rises will be at the center of a classic confrontation between political constituencies with clashing interests; between onrushing affluence and defensive poverty. . . . Hence, the Cabrini-Green public housing project faces an unsure future. Inevitably, Cabrini-Green's high rises will be recycled or torn down, their residents relocated."

11. See Goering, Stebbins, and Siewart (1995); Hartung and Henig (1997); and Newman and Schnare (1997).

12. This is the argument of Cronin and Rasmussen (1981).

13. The information on the Hartford program is from Donovan (1994).

14. See Hanratty, McLanahan, and Pettit (1997) for the Los Angeles results, and Katz, Kling, and Liebman (2001) for Boston.

15. Both of these studies are summarized in Polikoff (1995).

16. The Gautreaux education results are reported in Rosenbaum and Meaden (1992) and Rosenbaum and Popkin (1990).

17. See Brophy and Smith (1997); Nyden (1998); Popkin, Buron, et al. (2000); Rosenbaum, Stroh, and Flynn (1998); and Schill (1997).

18. See also Freeman and Botein (2002).

19. See Briggs, Darden, and Aidala (1999); Cummings and Landis (1993); Goetz, Lam, and Heitlinger (1996); Innovative Housing Institute (1998); Lee, Culhane, and Wachter (1999); and Lyons and Loveridge (1993).

20. See Goering (1986).

21. See Galster (1990).

4

Concentrated Poverty and Regional Politics in Minneapolis–Saint Paul

The need for low- and moderate-income housing within Apple Valley must be identified on a regional basis because Apple Valley is a suburb within the Minneapolis/ Saint Paul Metropolitan area and there is nothing of particular significance within the community that would cause it to stand apart from regional considerations.
—Apple Valley, Minnesota, Comprehensive Plan, 1979

The City is in the best position to determine the most responsible option for meeting the future needs of Apple Valley rather than the Metropolitan Council, especially as it relates to residential densities.
—Apple Valley, Minnesota, Comprehensive Plan, 1999

The Minnesota Land Use Planning Act of 1976 requires regional fair-share assessments of housing needs in the Minneapolis–Saint Paul metropolitan area. In addition, the Twin Cities area is one of the few regions in the entire nation with a regional governance body—the Metropolitan Council—to implement and enforce such a program. In the 1970s, this combination produced one of the most effective regional, affordable-housing strategies in the country. Twenty-five years later, both the law and the "Met" Council still exist. However, despite a second state law in 1995, which provided incentives for the development of affordable housing throughout the region, individual communities and the Met Council now routinely ignore the fair-share housing provisions of the 1976 law. The council no longer calculates affordable-housing-need allocations, and resistance to affordable housing characterizes the stance of most suburban governments.

What happened? Things changed. The social profile of the region changed, the distribution of economic resources changed, and the political environment of the Twin Cities changed. One major element that represents both cause and effect in each of those trends is the increasing concentration of poverty and minority groups in the region's central cities. This chapter charts the path of regional fortunes over the past quarter-century and examines how concentrated poverty impacts local and regional housing policies.

The Region

The 13-county Minneapolis–Saint Paul metropolitan area is the 15th largest in the United States, with a population of close to three million. Though the city of Minneapolis lost population during the 1960s and 1970s, the central city stabilized during the 1980s and grew by 3.9 percent during the 1990s. The city remained predominantly white, non-Hispanic (66 percent) in 2000, but significantly less so than in 1980. The city's population is more highly educated and wealthier than the population of most other cities of its size (Schwartz and Glickman 1992).

The regional economy grew by 225,000 new jobs in the 1980s, with the overwhelming majority in the suburbs. In fact, between 1980 and 1990, 164,000 new jobs were created in developing suburbs, 52,000 in developed suburbs, but only 5,400 in central cities. Furthermore, the rate of job creation increased during the 1990s. Early in the decade, the region led the country's 33 largest metro areas in new job creation (Economic Research Corporation 1994; Metropolitan Council 1992). In fact, the region's per capita income ranked seventh among the 25 largest metro areas in the country. The Twin Cities metropolitan area is currently home to 31 "Fortune 500" industrial and service companies, 20 of which are in Hennepin County, with Minneapolis the county seat.

Downtown Development

As in most U.S. metropolitan regions, the area's economy shifted during the 1980s from a base of manufacturing, agricultural processing, and trade to domination by corporate headquarters and producer services (including financial, business, professional, and communication services). In

Minneapolis, the rapid redevelopment of the downtown area accelerated this shift.

Minneapolis, in fact, pursued an extremely aggressive downtown-development strategy during the 1980s.[1] The city's development agency, the Minneapolis Community Development Agency (MCDA), made extensive use of tax-increment financing to leverage private commercial/retail investment. In the 1980s alone, 70 new development projects occurred in the downtown area, along with 80 major rehab projects (Schwartz and Glickman 1992). As a result, downtown multi-tenant office space grew from 8 million to more than 21 million square feet between 1980 and 1994. An additional 6 million square feet in government offices, medical office buildings, and single-tenant buildings were also constructed during this time. Employment downtown increased by more than half during the 1980s alone, and the city currently hosts headquarters for 82 major public and private companies. Moreover, downtown development went beyond simple office space to include a new convention center, thousands of hotel rooms to service it, a multipurpose sports stadium, and new and renovated theaters. Minneapolis is the leading corporate and financial center in the upper Midwest and has a strong commercial-industrial tax base. In fact, the growth in downtown commercial property values during the 1980s and 1990s put the city's commercial-industrial tax base well above the regional average (Wascoe 1998). Moreover, from 1980 to 1990, the property tax base per household in Minneapolis rose from $1,299 to $2,462, a 90 percent increase (Metropolitan Council 1992).

Poverty and Unemployment

The recent economic history of the city and the region reveals the regional economy's strength and the downtown's redevelopment success. However, it hides the unevenness of growth. Non-downtown neighborhoods, primarily those surrounding the core and those with larger minority populations, have not always shared in the economic boom.

Though overall unemployment for the metro area has remained consistently low, with a rate 50 percent lower than the national rate over the past 15 to 20 years, core areas of Minneapolis experienced 18 percent unemployment in 1990—a rate two and one-half times the rest of the region. Lack of transportation and low wages in newly created jobs continue to prevent central-city residents from taking advantage of the growing labor shortage regionally (United Way of Minneapolis Area 1995).

As the 1990s began, the Twin Cities region had the sixth highest level of wealth disparity between central cities and wealthy suburbs when compared with the 25 largest metropolitan areas in the country. During the 1980s, the poverty rate in Minneapolis had increased from 13.5 to 18.5 percent. In Saint Paul, it had risen even faster. For the region as a whole, however, the overall poverty rate stayed essentially the same, increasing only from 4.1 to 4.5 percent (Berg 1993; Metropolitan Council 1992; United Way 1995).

As in most American cities, poverty in Minneapolis is highly concentrated in minority communities, and minority communities are concentrated in the central city. The city's minority population is much more likely to be poor than other city residents. For example, though the overall poverty rate was 13.5 percent in 1980, it was 30 percent for African Americans and 40 percent for Asians and Native Americans (Metropolitan Council 1992) (figures 4.1 and 4.2). Furthermore, the percentage of blacks living in high-poverty areas increased from 27 to 47 percent between 1980 and 1990. The spatial location of black communities and poverty communities shows significant overlap, with both types ringing the southern downtown and near northwestern areas. As the 1990s began, minorities in Minneapolis and Saint Paul were more likely to live in poverty than were minorities in any other major metropolitan area in the country (Draper 1993).

These neighborhoods of concentrated poverty are also areas of high social service needs. In the mid-1990s, four of the core neighborhoods of Minneapolis (Phillips, Near North, Powderhorn, and Central) were the top four communities in the region in number of residents receiving public assistance, number of Hennepin County social service clients, and percentage of residents receiving social services (United Way 1995).

White and minority neighborhoods in Minneapolis are also differentiated by housing stock. Single-family detached homes account for, on average, more than 66 percent of the housing stock in homogeneously white census tracts (defined as having a white population of more than 94 percent), but only 46 percent of homes in the city as a whole. Additionally, white tracts contain significantly fewer housing units in large apartment complexes (more than 10 units) when compared with minority tracts (Urban Coalition 1994).

Minneapolis displays some evidence of the pattern that William Julius Wilson describes for minority neighborhoods, in which the concentration of poverty in central-city neighborhoods is substantially the result of an

Figure 4.1. Non-White Population in the Twin Cities Seven-County Metropolitan Region, 2000

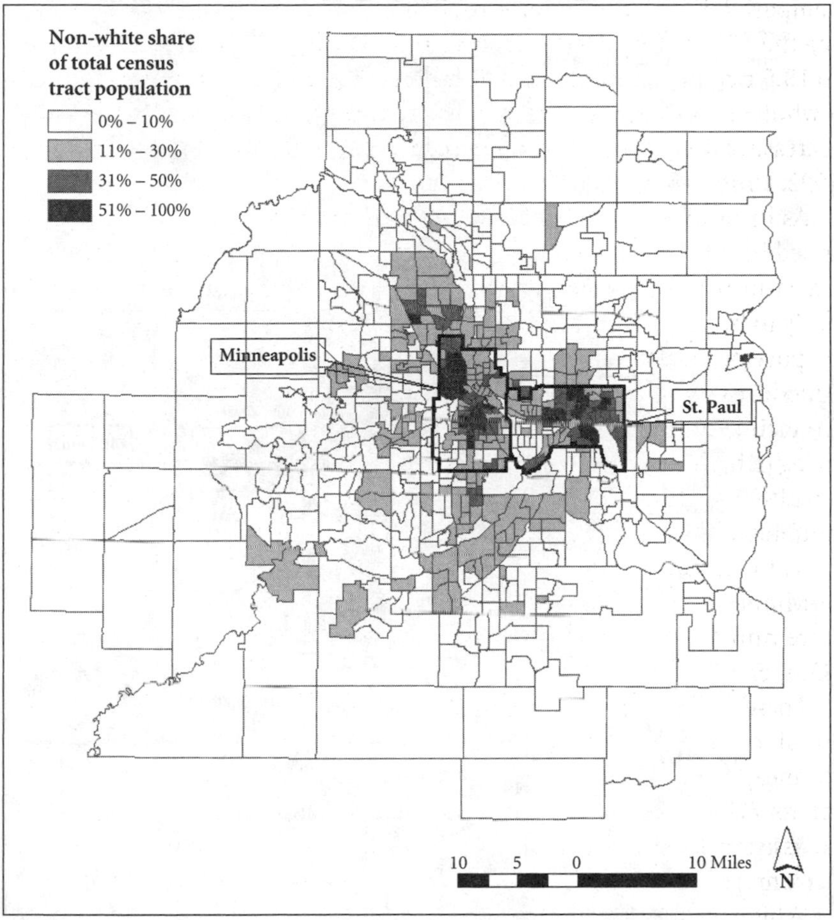

Non-white share of total census tract population
- 0% – 10%
- 11% – 30%
- 31% – 50%
- 51% – 100%

Minneapolis

St. Paul

10   5   0   10 Miles

N

Source: 2000 U.S. Census.

exodus by the black middle class. Blacks who moved from Minneapolis and Saint Paul between 1985 and 1990 had a far lower poverty rate (24 percent) than either those who stayed in the central cities (34 percent) or those who moved into them (49 percent) (Gillaspy 1993). In fact, Minneapolis in the 1980s experienced the emergence of the "Detroit Scenario" (suggesting a city overcome with neighborhoods of high poverty, in which the middle class has fled to relatively safe and secure havens of racial and class exclusivity).

Figure 4.2. Population below the Poverty Level in the Twin Cities Seven-County Metropolitan Region, 2000

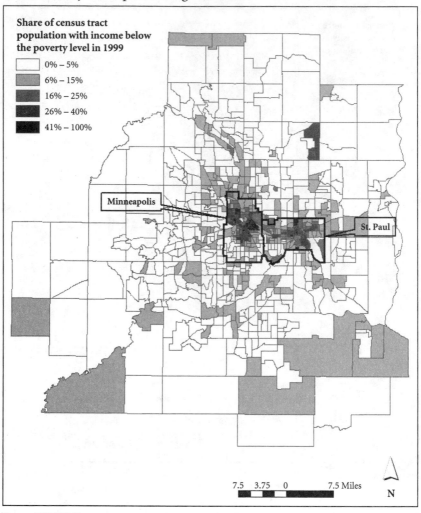

Source: 2000 U.S. Census.

The 1990s

Minneapolis in the early 1990s was a city in fear—in fear of losing its status as one of the most livable urban communities in the nation. It had long had a reputation, for the most part deserved, of being well governed and managed. The area was a leader in regional governmental cooperation, with local governments successfully combining efforts to head off nascent ecological problems and agreeing to share a portion of their tax base to achieve greater regional equity. The city was clean, by American standards for large central cities, and boasted of a world-renowned park system focusing on its many lakes, the Mississippi River, and Minnehaha Creek. For its size, Minneapolis enjoyed a remarkably active cultural life of theater, music, and art. Because of its diverse economy, it had essentially escaped the severe economic crisis experienced by most Midwestern cities during the late 1970s and 1980s. The region's active philanthropic sector and history of activist, progressive government had resulted in a low incidence of urban decay and the type of social problems evident in most American cities. By the 1990s, however, this tidy sense of well-being was eroding fast.

The mid-1980s brought to Minneapolis, as it did to virtually every American city, the plague of crack cocaine. Crack's impact was multifaceted and significant: increased joblessness among the poor, higher incidence of family breakup, increased juvenile delinquency stemming from parental incapacity, increased gang activity and competition for control of the lucrative drug market, and the inevitable increase in violent crime associated with illegal drug commerce.

Violent crime in the cities increased dramatically during this time, peaking during the mid-1990s. Fear of crime escalated even more rapidly. In 1993, 61 percent of the respondents to a public opinion poll of metropolitan residents identified crime as the single most important issue in the region, the peak in a rise that had begun in 1986. The issue mentioned second, in contrast, was listed by only 11 percent of respondents. The local media became obsessed with crime. In 1992, a white policeman was executed while sitting at a table in a south side restaurant, allegedly murdered in response to police abuses. The resultant manhunt, capture, and trial of the suspects (all of whom were young African-American males) dominated the local news scene. (In fact, one local television station actually aided in one suspect's surrender to the police.) In the first six months of 1995, a record year for homicides in Minneapolis, a crime story led local evening newscasts approximately 40 percent of the time, and the percentage increased as the summer progressed ("Body Count" 1995). By 1995, Minneapolis's homicide rate far exceeded New York City's.

In addition, the city experienced other social changes. Close to 70 percent of the students in the public school system were people of color, evidence of white, middle-class withdrawal from both the city and the public institutions upon which it had prided itself for so long. These trends toward greater income and racial disparities within the region continued to increase during the 1990s.

Regional Cooperation in Housing

Historically, the Minneapolis–Saint Paul region has been a leader among American urban areas in regional cooperation. In 1967, the state legislature created the Metropolitan Council of the Twin Cities (mentioned earlier) to guide regional development. The council's early activities focused on transportation planning and regional growth direction through the phased extension of the area's Metropolitan Urban Service Area (MUSA) line. In 1971, the Minnesota legislature created a regional tax-base sharing program through the Fiscal Disparities Act, in which growth in the commercial-industrial tax base is shared among all municipal governments in the region. The legislature then added the Land Use Planning Act (LUPA) in 1976, which required communities to create comprehensive plans for growth. In these plans, communities had to match their own growth scenarios with the Metropolitan Council's regional approach to highways, transit, airports, sewers, and regional parks. A supportive governor and legislature and a substantially homogenous regionwide population gave the Metropolitan Council, by the mid-1970s, a significant mandate and substantial leverage to accomplish a regional growth agenda. The council's efforts in housing, for example, were representative of that influence.

In 1971, the council formally adopted a policy of dispersing "modest-cost" housing throughout the region. To implement this policy, the council weighed communities' records in producing modest-cost housing as it reviewed their applications for federal infrastructure grants. (This "A-95 Review" process was named for the federal Office of Management and Budget [OMB] statement providing regional councils of government the power to review communities' grant applications.) The council began reviewing applications for federal housing assistance in 1973 and, the following year, became a regional housing authority, empowered to implement federal housing programs in suburban areas not served by their own agencies. This step effectively circumvented the suburban tactic of avoiding subsidized housing by simply not creating local implementing agencies, an existing problem in many regions. During these years, the council also created a fair-share formula for determining a community's share of the regional need for low-income and modest-cost housing. This formula took into account a community's share of existing population and projected population growth, its share of the existing job base and projected job growth, and its subsidized units relative to its low-income population (Listokin 1976).

In addition to directing localities to produce plans in conformance with regional infrastructure systems, LUPA also mandated that communities incorporate into their comprehensive plans a "housing element" that provided a strategy for meeting the community's "share of the metro-area need for low- and moderate-income housing." This language ostensibly institutionalized the regional fair-share program, and required that each community have an affordable-housing strategy approved by the Metropolitan Council to meet fair-share requirements.

Through the end of the 1970s, this was, indeed, the case. The original round of comprehensive plans submitted by communities and approved by the council typically met both the letter and spirit of the law. The council provided each community its fair-share target range. These targets were directly referenced in the housing elements, and specific implementation plans were developed. Most plans included statements demonstrating community willingness to address low- and moderate-income housing needs. The council even provided localities with guidelines on zoning standards (including densities and minimum square footage) that would reduce the costs of residential construction.

Overall, significant progress toward a more even distribution of low- and moderate-income housing took place during these years. In 1975, "82 percent of all subsidized dwellings were located in the two central cities. At the end of 1983, by contrast, those cities had only 59 percent of such homes" (Metropolitan Council 1985). By the end of the 1970s, a well-functioning, fair-share program accepted by suburban communities was in place in the Twin Cities. The Met Council provided the necessary data and planning guidelines to implement the program effectively. Subsidized units were dispersed, and the overall regional concentration of low-cost units was noticeably reduced. It was, in short, one of the most, if not the most, effective program of its kind in the nation.

Then in the 1980s, things changed.

Whither Fair Share?

Three components of the political and administrative environment that had framed fair-share housing in the Twin Cities changed in the 1980s—

the governor, the level of HUD funding for subsidized housing, and the demographics of the region. Rudy Perpich, a Democrat, became governor and "had less interest in metropolitan planning than . . . his predecessor" (Johnson 1998, 42).[2] Perpich tended to ignore the council on important decisions in which it might have been involved, and appointed council members who shared his disinterest in regional planning. As a result, the council became disinclined to insert itself directly in local development issues. This trend accelerated with the election of Perpich's successor, Republican Arne Carlson.

In the early 1980s, low- and moderate-income housing was synonymous with federal subsidies. In fact, the Metropolitan Council adjusted the fair-share formula in 1980 so that the "share" determined for each community was not a share of housing units, but a share of the regional total of federal housing subsidies. Most low- and moderate-income housing in the region (and the nation, for that matter) depended on direct and sizable federal subsidies. In most cases, federal programs provided the sole source of financing. However, HUD's dramatic budget cuts early in the decade, totaling 80 percent in budgetary authority over six years, reduced the availability of subsidies local governments could use to build low- and moderate-income housing. As the 1980s wore on, affordable-housing producers and local governments were instead forced to generate alternative sources and begin piecing together various subsidies from state, local, federal, and private sources. The HUD budget reductions, therefore, devastated the fair-share approach in the region.

In addition, the Met Council ended its practice of reviewing grant proposals in the light of communities' affordable-housing records. So while this procedure, Policy 39, remained official agency policy, the council simply stopped following it. This decision, while undoubtedly connected to the realization that local communities had fewer resources for addressing affordable housing needs, was also consistent with the council's general withdrawal from intervention in local development patterns.

Finally, demographic changes in the region's central cities during the 1980s clinched the retreat from fair share housing. More people of color moved to the area. Greater concentrations of poverty, and their attendant social problems, emerged in core neighborhoods. The social and economic homogeneity, which had been the foundation of almost two decades of regional problem solving, began to disappear. With it disappeared the language of regional commitment to low-cost housing needs. When the Metropolitan Council discontinued the practice of determining fair-share requirements, local communities stopped referring to "fair share" as a concept. In most cases, they even stopped referring to low- and moderate-income housing goals at all. Housing elements of community plans in the 1980s and 1990s utterly ignored low- and moderate-income regional housing needs.

The contrasting quotes from Apple Valley's comprehensive plans (see chapter opening) typify the shift in planning priorities among suburban communities throughout the region. Apple Valley's 1979 plan, and those of several other communities throughout the region, specifically acknowledged the superiority of a regional approach to defining housing needs. The most recent round of comprehensive plans, on the other hand, asserts the locality's primacy in determining housing needs and strategies.[3] In fact, official plans of suburban communities after the mid-1980s include no evidence of regional cooperation in defining and meeting low-cost housing needs.

Suburban planning for low-cost housing after the 1980s also became less aggressive in identifying ways to reduce local regulatory barriers. A study of 25 suburban communities found that regulatory techniques to promote low- and moderate-income housing were twice as prevalent in the early plans as they were in the more recent ones (Goetz, Chapple, and Lukermann 2002a). In some cases, the best a community could offer was a vow not to "unduly increase the cost of raw land" within its jurisdiction. Other plans stated there was no need to increase affordable units, given their current supply.[4]

The lack of a regional framework allowed suburban communities to withdraw from a cooperative effort to address low-cost housing needs regionally. What followed shortly were high-profile cases of developing suburbs resisting subsidized housing and ugly scenes of suburbanites packing hearing rooms to denounce efforts to bring "those people" into their communities. The fall from the heady days of the late 1970s had been far and fast.

Growing Awareness of Concentrated Poverty

As the 1980s ended, many residents may have begun sensing the growing concentration of poverty and the greater divisions within the region stemming from uneven economic growth. The first few years of the 1990s, however, brought a spate of official reports documenting the changes and elevating the issue to the top of the regional agenda. The Metropolitan Council (1992, 1994) issued two such reports. The first, "Trouble at the Core," provided data showing that the central cities of Minneapolis and Saint Paul were lagging far behind the rest of the region on most indicators of economic health and social well-being. The second report, "Keeping the Twin Cities Vital," warned of increasing regional inequities and the central cities' growing social and economic woes.

In 1991, the Saint Paul daily newspaper ran a series of articles by Neal Peirce, the syndicated urban affairs columnist, on how to revive the city's neighborhoods. In the summer of 1993, the Minneapolis daily ran a series called "Strengthening the Core," which focused on the city's decline relative to the rest of the region and attempted to set out a policy response. The newspaper also ran a series that examined the 1990 census, particularly concentrating on growing regional inequities and the movement of people and wealth out of the central cities.[5] The Citizen's League, a private good-government group of concerned (and typically influential) citizens, also took up the subject of regional inequities and issued its report in 1994. Other public interest groups—the League of Women Voters and the local Urban Coalition—published their findings on housing segregation and regional disparities in housing, income, and job opportunities. In addition, a private-public finance consulting firm sponsored "Reviving the Core," a 1994 conference examining regional housing disparities and their solutions. Then in 1996, the University of Minnesota's Institute on Race and Poverty hosted a two-day conference at which a number of national experts addressed regional and local approaches to concentrated poverty.[6] Meanwhile, local media contributed to the greater awareness of central-city problems by recounting in detail the daily violence in the war to control the cities' illicit drug market.

The growing differentiation between the housing markets in the core and the developing portions of the region negatively affected, as might be imagined, the area's few nascent efforts to deconcentrate poverty. For instance, landlord participation in the Section 8 program in suburban Hennepin County declined steadily during the 1990s. Fewer units in the suburbs had rents that qualified them for the program (i.e., at or below the HUD-established fair market rent for the area). Even among units that qualified, fewer landlords accepted households with Section 8 subsidies. In 1995, for example, only 27 percent of more than 49,000 rental units surveyed in the suburban areas of the county met Section 8 rent guidelines and accepted Section 8 subsidies. In each of the next five years, that percentage declined further, bottoming out at just 7 percent in 2000 (Community Action for Suburban Hennepin 1995; HOME Line 2000).

During this same period, the "porting" of Section 8 subsidies across municipal lines in the region actually reinforced concentrated poverty rather than alleviating it. The two central cities gained more than 450 Section 8 households from the suburbs between 1990 and 1995, a larger gain than any jurisdiction in the region. A regional study concluded, "rather than instigating an exodus of lower-income households to less economically depressed areas, portability appears to be having the opposite effect. It is opening the central cities to greater concentrations of poverty" (Malaby and Lukermann 1996, 14). Households that transferred into the central cities cited the lack of housing options and public transportation in the suburbs as factors in their moving.

The Twin Cities in the early 1990s seemed caught in a spiral of increasing social and economic disparities between cities and suburbs. Emerging understanding of the region's growth trajectory produced contradictory political effects. On the one hand, political resistance to subsidized housing increased in suburban areas, whose residents fervently desired to keep "those problems" in the central city. At the same time, the Detroit Scenario generated a political movement to reestablish the area's tradition of regional cooperation.

Suburban Resistance

In the face of the Detroit Scenario's growing influence, suburban opposition to low-cost housing peaked in the mid-1990s. Opponents, in fact, were concerned with rental housing, high-density development, and subsidized housing. According to one suburban official in 1993, the economic plight of Minneapolis—which he labeled "not a pretty picture"—resulted from a concentration of rental units and the negative effects of the more transient nature of renters (Elam 1993). Developers in the region bemoaned the lack of high-density land on which to develop affordable housing. Despite the requirements of the Land Use Planning Act, suburban communities simply did not zone enough land for higher-density development, which is the most likely to be affordable.[7] Even when rental housing and high densities were not the issue, however, affordability alone produced opposition. In southwest suburban Chanhassen, for example, residents organized against townhomes in 1996. One existing resident said, "I'm a little sick and tired of government's imposition on the housing market. I don't understand the socialist mentality that can . . . say, 'This goes here, this here [and] this goes here' " (Kaszuba 1996). The city council voted unanimously to reject the development, which would have produced townhomes valued from $85,000 to $150,000. Similar townhome projects faced resistance and ultimate rejection in several suburban areas during the mid-1990s (Lynch 2001).

From Maple Grove to Eagan

In the "pantheon" of suburban resistance to affordable housing in the Twin Cities, special places must be reserved for the communities of Maple Grove and Eagan. Maple Grove, a developing suburb northwest of Minneapolis, is an affluent community. Eagan, southeast of Minneapolis, is less affluent, but still enjoyed significant growth throughout the 1980s and 1990s. In the early 1990s, Maple Grove gained a national name for its virulent opposition to affordable-housing efforts. In 1993, the Maple Grove City Council rejected an affordable-housing project after an angry group of residents protested its construction. Though the housing would have rented for $550 month (in 1993), residents perceived it as a low-income project that would attract "undesirable elements."

Maple Grove residents also objected to a proposed Habitat for Humanity project. Usually, Habitat for Humanity is able to capitalize on its very positive image and gain a foothold, even where other affordable-housing proposals fail. Its projects are typically small in scale and, therefore, nonthreatening. In addition, Habitat projects involve volunteer work (often from local organizations and congregations) and contributions from the families that ultimately will inhabit them. Furthermore, Habitat typically builds or rehabs single-family homes for owner-occupants. For all those reasons, Habitat is a "feel-good" version of assisted housing. Yet even Habitat was run out of Maple Grove, told to "get the hell out of our neighborhood" by Maple Grove residents in 1997.[8] Habitat's original proposal for 16 to 20 homes was rejected. Instead, the organization ended up constructing four single-family homes on city-owned land behind a fire station in 1999.

Soon after the Maple Grove city manager tried to initiate modest efforts to introduce affordable housing, he was relieved of his duties by the council. "In his place was put a recalcitrant local official who confidently told the Maple Grove City Council that it 'is doubtful that affordable housing will ever happen in Maple Grove' " (Orfield 1997, quoting from a Maple Grove City Council transcript, October 21, 1996). Maple Grove became the region's symbol of suburban opposition to low-cost housing. The city's name was even used disparagingly in other cases in the area; for example, proposed projects were described as being "Maple Groved." In 1997, ABC-TV's *Nightline* featured Maple Grove as an example of the growing social, economic, and political distance between central cities and their developing suburbs.

In the midst of all this, Maple Grove requested a 1,800-acre extension of its metropolitan growth boundary and a $43 million sewer extension to facilitate more development. In the past, the Metropolitan Council would have exercised its leverage over development policy in this type of situation. Met Council policies clearly state that, when making regional infrastructure decisions, it should take into account a community's record of providing low- and moderate-income housing. Despite Maple Grove's clear resistance to affordable housing, despite Met Council staff's own judgment that nothing in the city's comprehensive plan "would seem to encourage construction of moderate cost housing," and despite the Met Council's encouragement to the city on two previous occasions to promote more affordable housing, the council granted the sewer extension.

Even though permitting the extension directly contradicted stated policy, the council did extract Maple Grove's agreement to take steps toward improving its housing record. The city pledged to increase the share of new rental housing built to 25 percent of all new housing construction, to make at least 35 percent of the additional rental housing affordable (which, at that time, meant rents of $638 or less per month), to convene a review group of builders, citizens, and city staff to examine land use controls and their impact on housing costs, and to increase overall density in its single-family development.

Though Maple Grove residents still offer considerable resistance to low-cost housing, the city has begun to approve affordable projects in mixed-income developments. A mixed-income senior development, for example, was built in 1997; 48 units of affordable townhomes were completed in 1998; and another 19-unit townhome development was approved that year, though not without strong community opposition. A mixed-income development went up in 2000, and the city has agreed to allow 20 units of

Hollman replacement housing to be acquired on a scattered-site basis throughout the city (see chapter 7).

Even at the height of Maple Grove's intransigence, Eagan was emerging as a new leader in opposition to subsidized housing in the suburbs. In December 1994, Eagan residents and its city council opposed a low- and moderate-income townhouse development. As one resident told the council, "What I'm looking at is [*sic*] the people. I hate to say that because that sounds like I'm being prejudicial here, but I'm looking at the caliber of the neighborhood. Not only the aesthetic looks of it, but the people that are coming in" (Cassano 1994). The townhomes would have required buyers with an average income of $20,000, and households with income up to $30,000 would have qualified. Ironically, the Dakota County housing authority was actually asking the city to downzone the land from high-density to medium-density residential to accommodate the project. The city rejected the project, an action the then mayor (who supported it) called "arbitrary, capricious, and very discriminatory" (Gardner 1994). In response to the rejection, the county housing authority sued the city, and a judge ordered the zoning change to permit the development to move forward. The city councilwoman who led the opposition, however, was subsequently elected mayor. Eagan was on its way to becoming a poster child for suburban resistance to low-cost housing.

In 1999, Eagan turned its back on state development funds because they were attached to affordable-housing requirements. The Met Council rejected the city's comprehensive plan in 2000 because it did not set aside enough land for high-density development.[9] Since then, the city has refused to budge. The Met Council, calling the city irresponsible for developing at such low densities, indicated that Eagan would not receive regional infrastructural grants and other financial aid from the council if it did not produce more affordable housing. Eagan's mayor responded that the city had not benefited from Met Council funding in the past and did not need it in the future. According to the mayor, people "move here from the inner city because they want to live on a safe cul-de-sac." Furthermore, she claimed that Eagan has enough low-cost rental housing. Naming one development, she stated, "This is where all our crime is. It's mostly African Americans fighting with African immigrants. It's everything—drugs, assaults, knife fights. We had to have a police presence there. This is what you get," she concluded, "when you build high-density housing. Density breeds problems" (Anderson 2001).[10]

In an opinion piece for the Saint Paul daily newspaper, Eagan's mayor wrote:

> There is no social justice in a nonelected metropolitan government driving up land and housing costs, and then forcing our citizens to pay for government-subsidized rental housing for formerly self-sufficient workers driven out of the housing market. As Eagan Council Member Paul Bakken said recently, "The city of Eagan will not be a willing accessory to this social crime" (Awada 2001).

The Countermovement

Paradoxically, the Detroit Scenario, in addition to heightening the exclusionary impulses of suburban areas, triggered the development of a strong countermovement. This countermovement used the Detroit Scenario to justify a plan of regional action against growing inequities. To the regionalists, the Detroit Scenario exemplifies the consequences of racial discrimination in housing markets (African Americans' lack of choice), and the legacy of 25 years of government housing policies that facilitated and subsidized white flight to the suburbs (primarily through explicitly racist FHA underwriting principles beginning in the late 1930s[11]) while concentrating subsidized public housing for the very poor in central cities.

Importantly, the Detroit Scenario also highlights a course of action. In order to avoid Detroit's fate, people of color and lower-income people in general cannot be confined to central-city neighborhoods. Barriers to their participation in housing markets outside central neighborhoods must be overcome. The fiscal and economic inequities that emerge within an urban region must be addressed head-on through strong regional action and better understanding of how government funds flow—not to support the existing infrastructure in the built-up core, but instead, to create new infrastructure (schools, roads, sewers, etc.) in outlying, developing suburban areas. The Detroit Scenario in its early stages demands a regional response. Suburban jurisdictions must work to provide affordable-housing opportunities to lower-income families. Lower-income families and families of color must be given the means to move out of the central-city neighborhoods to which they have been relegated. High concentrations of public and assisted housing should be reduced and the families trapped in these living situations should be given a greater choice in housing and neighborhoods. It was exactly this agenda that a young state representative from south Minneapolis brought to the region and the rest of the state legislature early in the 1990s.

The Orfield Phenomenon

State Representative Myron Orfield (DFL), from a south Minneapolis district that encompasses both an affluent section of the "Lakes District" and an area of growing poverty concentration south of downtown, introduced in 1993 a legislative package of regional reform and restructuring to address the Detroit Scenario. Collectively known as the Metropolitan Community Stability Act (MCSA), Orfield's package included six bills that together constituted a comprehensive approach to housing, transportation, and land use policy aimed at reducing regional inequities. The first bill would have created a regional fair-share housing program requiring developing suburbs to open their housing markets to low- and moderate-income households or lose state aid. Though this bill passed both houses of the legislature (after Orfield removed the sanctions for noncompliance), it was vetoed by the governor. Another bill, which would have reformed the Metropolitan Council and made it an elected rather than appointed body, died in committee. Bills on transportation planning and land use planning also were part of MCSA. The transportation bill survived and was signed into law, but only a small portion of the land use bill was enacted. Welfare reform and urban reinvestment bills rounded out the package. The welfare bill was passed but never funded, while the reinvestment bill died in committee. Over the next two years, Orfield reintroduced the housing bill, added a property tax–sharing proposal, and continued to try to reform the Metropolitan Council and reinvestment patterns in the region. The legislature continued to pass the housing legislation, and the governor continued to veto it.

Orfield's legislative achievements were built on a coalition of central-city legislators and lawmakers from inner-ring and less-affluent suburbs whose districts were beginning to show the same problems that the core had been facing for decades. Orfield carefully mapped census and other data to show persuasively that poverty and racial concentrations, property tax stagnation, and low tax capacity were problems that both central cities and inner-ring suburbs shared. The coalition was groundbreaking in American urban politics. Conventional wisdom up to that point stated that the suburbs made up a monolithic entity whose experience was fundamentally different from the central cities. Orfield's ability to change that perception and create a winning coalition was innovative (Cisneros 1995).[12]

Orfield's entire effort received a great deal of media attention and focused state politics squarely on the issue of regional equity during the mid-1990s. His tireless effort at communicating his message to groups across the region was central to his success in the legislature. Orfield became known locally for his traveling show of graphs and tables documenting the growing problems in the region. An energetic and determined public speaker, he used the data very effectively. Between 1993 and 1995, Orfield appeared before virtually any group that would have him, explaining the extent of regional disparities, his understanding of their causes, and his legislative solutions. His was a one-person, public education campaign, and, for the most part, his campaign was effective. Newspapers supported Orfield's efforts and ideas, and community groups began to echo his regional analysis.

Critics, of course, attacked Orfield's agenda, labeling him a socialist and communist for pursuing regional equity. Republican legislators from the developing suburbs opposed his efforts from the beginning, and their influence eventually led to the gubernatorial vetoes of the fair-share housing bill three years running. The media, at times supportive of Orfield's efforts, also were capable of sensationalizing the issue. One television station's coverage of the tax-base sharing initiative opened with, "Some call it socialism . . ." and featured a reporter walking through the streets of the affluent suburb of Edina, "asking homeowners to comment on the possibility of a large local property tax increase that would benefit poor residents of Minneapolis"[13] (Orfield 1997, 145).

Orfield's efforts were supported by research that showed regional inequities in infrastructure subsidies, including the pricing systems for waste treatment and highway services, that systematically advantaged the developing suburbs at the expense of the region's older, more densely populated, core areas (Luce, Lukermann, and Mohring 1994; Lukermann, Snyder, and Luce 1994; Mohring and Anderson 1994).[14]

The Livable Communities Act of 1995

Understanding that Orfield and his legislative agenda would not go away, others in the legislature began crafting a compromise that could satisfy both the legislature and the governor. The result was the Livable Communities Act (LCA) of 1995. LCA, a voluntary, incentive program, provides participating jurisdictions special access to three funds. To receive these funds, communities voluntarily agree to negotiate housing goals with the Metropolitan Council, and subsequently file a housing action plan with the council. The affordable-housing goals for individual communities are set relative to subregional benchmarks. These benchmarks consider the existing market situation and conditions for communities in similar geographic zones and stages of growth. (In 1996, for example, the Metropolitan Council defined housing affordability at a purchase price of $120,000 or less for ownerships units, and $685 or less per month for rental units.)

The benchmarks, however, turned out to be meaningful mainly for those communities that had the best record on affordable housing in the first place. Most communities (80 percent in the case of affordable-home-ownership housing) with less affordable housing than required by their benchmarks were able to negotiate goals that were still below their community benchmarks. As a result of the goal-setting and benchmark processes established by the Metropolitan Council, two-thirds of the communities participating in LCA committed to doing less in affordable housing between 1995 and 2010 than even before. For most communities therefore, LCA, as implemented by the Met Council, legitimates the process of reducing the relative availability of affordable housing.

LCA goals for affordable housing, if fully met, would result in a 13 percent decline in affordable ownership units and 4 percent fewer affordable rental units. The combined effect of LCA ownership and rental projections is a 12 percent deficit in affordable units, compared with continuing the status quo. Put another way, if the LCA-participating communities fully achieved their affordable-housing production goals for 1995 to 2010, the region actually would have a smaller proportion of affordable housing than it did before the program began.

What is most notable about LCA is the political cover it has given communities not interested in increasing affordable-housing options or diversity. From the beginning, communities could point to their participation in LCA as evidence of their cooperation in regional housing efforts, understanding all the while that they actually were being allowed to reduce the relative availability of affordable housing in their jurisdictions. Local officials, glad to incorporate LCA goals into their housing plans, called the affordability levels "a joke" (Goetz, Chapple, and Lukermann 2002b). Other communities, pointing to their affordability indices, claimed they already had done more than their fair share and, therefore, were justified in demolishing some of the affordable units they currently had (Goetz,

Chapple, and Lukermann 2002b; McDonnell 1997). Prior to LCA, the effect of demolishing low-cost housing would have been mitigated by a state law demanding one-for-one replacement of units lost through public action. However, the repeal of this law was part of the price for enacting LCA. Not only were communities again free to demolish affordable housing, but LCA gave many the rationale for doing so.

Ultimately and ironically, LCA's flaw was giving the Metropolitan Council authority to shape the program's implementation.[15] The Met Council's definition of housing affordability for low- and moderate-income families encompassed 69 percent of the region's entire housing stock. The benchmarks themselves were too low (even if they had been fully met by all participating communities, there still would have been a 12 percent reduction in affordable housing compared with continuing the status quo), and not based on need but, rather, on previous practice. In fact, as mentioned earlier, many communities were able to negotiate goals with the Met Council that were below set benchmarks. Through most of the 1990s, the Metropolitan Council was simply not interested in intervening in suburban housing development patterns, even when given the opportunity. As the Maple Grove example was to prove in 1997, the council's chair at the time, Curt Johnson, was more creative in apologizing for suburban exclusionism than in using the council's formal powers and leverage to promote affordability in suburban areas. In this orientation, he simply was reflecting the Met Council members more generally, and the governor who had appointed them. In the end, it came as little surprise that the LCA program, as implemented by the Met Council, posed no significant threat to the status quo.

Postscript: The Regional Housing Crisis

In the mid-1990s, the Twin Cities' housing market began to tighten significantly. Vacancy rates began falling in 1996 and reached 1.9 percent by the fourth quarter of 1997. They continued to fall the next year, bottoming out at 1.1 percent and leveling off at 1.5 percent for much of 1998 and 1999.[16] The market responded to the scarcity in the normal way; prices and rents shot upward. The average rent in the region rose from $566 a month in 1996 to $742 in 2000, an incredible 31 percent increase in just five years—and 11 percent in 1999 alone. Home prices also exploded. In 1998 alone, prices in most Minneapolis and Saint Paul neighborhoods increased by 8 or 9 percent. Though these numbers exceeded the rate of increase in most suburban areas, some suburban communities experienced increases of more than 15 percent (Brandt 1999a). Some of these rapid price increases resulted from too little development for the population growth. In 2000, lenders and realtors began to complain about a shortage of homes to sell, despite a booming construction market (Gendler 2000a, b).[17]

The housing crisis, as is usually the case, was most severe at the lower end of the market. Home prices grew most rapidly for the bottom 10 percent of the market, and thousands of low-end rentals were lost to either price increases or demolition. In 1996 and 1997, more than 2,300 housing units were demolished, most in the central cities (see chapter 5). The low rate of affordable-housing production, combined with large numbers of Southeast Asian and Somalian immigrants, a growing Hispanic population, and growing economic disparities, meant severe housing shortages for low-income households. Low-wage workers were forced to spend more than 50 percent of their income to afford the region's average two-bedroom apartment. Homeownership would have required closer to 70 or 80 percent of a low-wage earner's salary. Workers in 13 of the 25 fastest-growing job categories in the Twin Cities would have had to spend more than 30 percent of their income to afford the region's average one-bedroom apartment (Family Housing Fund 2000; Office of the Legislative Auditor 2001).

The late-1990s housing crisis in the Twin Cities stood out because it crossed over into the mainstream in two ways. First, middle-income families began to feel the crunch; second, businesses began to complain about the lack of housing for their workers and the resulting difficulties in worker recruitment and company development. A 2000 report by the Center for Housing Policy in Washington, D.C., confirmed what many middle-income families in the region had been experiencing for several years: The housing crisis had reached the middle class. In addition to looking at low-income families, the center's study examined families making more than $50,000 a year, and found that 29 percent of those with a housing-cost burden were working, middle-income families, and 73 percent of them owned their homes.[18] Affordability was becoming a more generalized problem in the region, one that threatened the continued economic growth of both the region and suburban locations within it. A survey of Minnesota businesses in 2001 indicated that affordable housing had become the biggest concern among the region's employers. In response to complaints from individual business owners, suburban chambers of commerce formed a task force calling for a combination of public and private action on the issue (St. Anthony 2001; Sherman 2001c).

Housing advocates and providers quickly switched their appeals from social justice to economic development. With financing from a local foundation, a local advocacy group commenced a public relations effort aimed at mainstreaming the profile of a typical family needing housing assistance. Affordable-housing advocates and developers alike declared the necessity of affordable housing for librarians, police officers, and school bus drivers—people (and this was critical in suburban areas) already living in the communities. Under these circumstances, affordable housing in the suburbs was no longer an issue of deconcentrating poverty. When suburban citizens began to question their community's continued ability to grow and their children's ability to eventually afford to live in the community, things began to happen.

In 2000 and 2001, several suburban communities, including Maple Grove and Eagan (though its mayor remained intransigent on the issue in general terms), approved affordable-housing developments. Though developers still regard affordable housing as a challenge in the suburbs, several communities produced high-profile, mixed-income developments during these years.[19]

A Step Backward

From a position of strong regional leadership in affordable housing, the Twin Cities have come a great distance over the past 20 years. Increasing economic and social polarization within the metropolitan area, timid regional officials at the Metropolitan Council, and a growing apprehension about the Detroit Scenario and the spread of urban blight have all taken the region significantly backward in devising and implementing regional solutions to housing problems. Myron Orfield's emergence as a national figure and local leader on these issues results from, in some respects, the growing failure within the region to address increased polarization. Despite Orfield's efforts, little progress has been made in convincing more exclusive suburban areas to take on low-income housing. The rhetoric of deconcentration has proven to be self-limiting, in that it provides a rationale for officials and residents to resist, as they see it, introducing social pathologies into their communities.

The affordable-housing crisis of the late 1990s and the encouraging response of suburban communities only strengthen this interpretation. When affordable housing was de-coupled from deconcentration, and when suburban communities felt more assured that building affordable housing was for "their people" and not the inner-city poor, then progress was made. However, regional action on affordable housing once again picked up only when the severity of the housing crisis overshadowed the deconcentration issue.

NOTES

1. See Leitner (1990); Nickel (1995); and Schwartz and Glickman (1992).

2. Perpich took office in 1977.

3. See Goetz, Chapple, and Lukermann (2002a).

4. See Goetz, Chapple, and Lukermann (2002b).

5. For example, when the 1990 census data became available, the paper ran articles on the distribution of income and employment opportunities in the region. See Leyden (1992). The paper even covered the publication of a book (Rusk 1993) on the issue of metropolitan economic health. See Berg (1993). Other stories included Draper (1993); von Sternberg (1994); and a steady series of editorials in favor of a regional approach to affordable housing.

6. The conference produced a report published by the institute in 1996 (Institute on Race and Poverty 1996). The other public interest group reports focusing on these issues are the Citizen's League (1994); the League of Women Voters of Minneapolis (1992); and the Urban Coalition (1994). At this same time, the former planning director of the City of Minneapolis published a book on regional inequities (Byrum 1992).

7. See Goetz, Chapple, and Lukermann (2002a) and the Builders Association of the Twin Cities in cooperation with the Center for Energy and Environment (2000).

8. Letter from Myron Orfield to Curt Johnson, Chair of the Metropolitan Council, August 15, 1997.

9. By 2000, the Met Council members were the political appointees of then Governor Jesse Ventura, and they were more inclined to enforce the means available to the Council to leverage affordable housing action by local governments.

10. The quote is from a story on the Metropolitan Council's newly appointed chair, Ted Mondale, and his efforts to scatter affordable housing more evenly throughout the region. The quotes set off a reaction among some residents of Eagan and among affordable-housing advocates regionally. Residents of the complex demanded an apology from the mayor and advocates targeted Eagan in subsequent months, organizing intense local support for more affordable housing among the city's residents. See Sherman (2001a, b) and Oseid and Sherman (2001).

11. See, for example, Jackson (1985).

12. David Rusk (1999) calls Orfield the most revolutionary politician in the nation.

13. The story failed to note that as a result of the region's existing tax-base-sharing program, which applies only to commercial-industrial tax base, Minneapolis had been making large net contributions (giving millions more to the pool than it received back) over the previous decade as a result of the city's boom in downtown commercial office space. See Orfield (1997, 145).

14. The three studies are summarized in Lukermann, Luce, and Mohring (1995).

15. The incredible outcome projected for this program, that full compliance by all communities will result in a reduction in the percentage of affordable housing units over time, is the direct result of the manner in which the Metropolitan Council designed the program. The benchmarks for affordability provided to communities were based not on any measure of need but instead on the amount of affordable housing that already existed in the communities and their immediate neighbors. This had the effect of providing lower benchmarks to parts of the region with less affordable housing in the first place, rewarding those areas that had been most restrictive in their development patterns and giving higher obligations to communities that had already done the most. Even given this method of devising the benchmarks, they were set too low in the aggregate. Had the communities participating in LCA merely met the benchmarks provided for them by the Met Council over the 15-year period of the program, there would have been a net reduction in affordable housing as a percentage of all units of 4 percent. But, as mentioned, communities were able to negotiate actual goals that were below the benchmarks, something that occurred most often for those communities that were faced with increasing the rate of affordable-housing production.

The second characteristic of the program that nullified its meaning as an effort to produce low- and moderate-income housing was the way affordability was defined. The Met Council set affordability guidelines at 80 percent of the area's median income for a family of four for homeownership and 50 percent of the median for a family of four for rental housing. The application of the price levels determined through this formula was not adjusted for housing size, however. In the first year of the program, affordable rents were $638, and affordable home prices topped out at $120,000. The fact that this definition meant that 69 percent of the housing stock of the entire metropolitan area was "affordable" would suggest there was no need for the program in the first place. See Goetz (2000).

16. These low rates placed the region third worst among 75 metropolitan areas studied by the Minnesota Legislative Auditors Office in 2001 (Office of the Legislative Auditor, State of Minnesota 2001; Buchta 1998; Buchta and Gendler 1998; Minneapolis Affordable Housing Task Force 1999).

17. The rate of production of rental units in the region, however, declined markedly in the 1990s. More than 62,000 apartments were built in the region during the 1980s, but in the 1990s, production was at less than 50 percent of that figure, reaching only 28,905. See Buchta (2001).

18. The study was reported on the front page of the Minneapolis daily (Hopfensperger 2000).

19. See Goetz, Chapple, and Lukermann (2002a) for the attitudes of developers, and Newberg (2001) for examples of affordable suburban developments.

5

The Neighborhood Politics
of Deconcentration

Anyone who follows the evening news knows Minneapolis has a severe crime problem for which officials have no demonstrated workable solutions. The problems are centered in public housing, where irresponsibility and illegitimacy breed youthful criminals and gang-related murders.

—Resident of suburban Stillwater, Minnesota, 1996

I grew up in that part of Minneapolis, and believe me, Minneapolis is at that point in some neighborhoods where we have to do something or the Minneapolis we knew won't be there anymore.

—Dave Nordmeier, health inspector, city of Minneapolis, 1995

While the language of deconcentration was altering regional politics by simultaneously generating a movement toward regional equity and stiffening resistance to affordable housing in suburban areas, it was also transforming neighborhood politics in the central cities and inner-ring suburbs. The lesson of deconcentration for these neighborhoods was that they had already done their share, more than their share, in fact, and should resist further poverty concentration by opposing concentrated social services and affordable housing. This new understanding of neighborhood objectives altered long-standing relationships between political and institutional actors in the central cities and ushered in a new set of community development strategies. Among the most prominent issues to emerge was the conflict between affordable-housing strategies and the objectives of poverty deconcentration.

Affordable Housing versus Poverty Deconcentration

For three straight years, Myron Orfield had shepherded his housing package through the legislature, only to have it vetoed by the governor. This record only heightened the stature of Orfield and his agenda, and helped to redefine the region's environment for housing and community development politics. While Orfield's efforts failed to convince the afflu-ent and developing suburbs that regional equity was necessary, his ideas were very influential among politicians and citizens of the central cities and inner-ring suburbs.

Neighborhood groups in the central cities of Minneapolis and Saint Paul found Orfield's argument persuasive. Not only was its rationale for reinvestment in their communities attractive, but it also provided a set of guideposts for what that reinvestment should look like. Traditional "com-munity development" efforts, which focused on providing low-income residents with more affordable housing and enhanced social services, were not part of the solution. In fact, it was the very spatial distribution of low-cost housing and social services that was indeed anchoring the poor in central-city neighborhoods. In Orfield's mind, improving conditions for the poor in core neighborhoods was a dead end. Answering the problems of central-city neighborhoods and the poor who were stuck in those neighborhoods meant changing the geography of economic opportunity. Growth and public-sector investments needed redirection inward. The poor needed to be given an opportunity to live in other neighborhoods, other communities, and closer to areas of job growth. The developing sub-urbs needed to do their fair share in providing affordable-housing oppor-tunities. Core neighborhoods no longer required programs that would perpetuate or increase concentrations of poverty.

Orfield (1997) is clear about what central-city investment should look like. His approach to community development is notable, and, because of its influence in the region during this time, deserves to be quoted at length.

> In central cities such as Minneapolis–Saint Paul, a large part of community devel-opment consists of repairing or adding additional low-income units in the poor-est part of the city and regional economy. In a fragmented region, where poor residents are undeniably the sole responsibility of older communities, this is humane and necessary. The buildings are blighted and people need places to live. However, in a regional context, by centering affordable housing in the most desperate neighborhoods, it moves against the grain of a long-term strategy to establish access to opportunity for people and stability for core communities.

After twenty years, even the largest and most successful Community Development Corporation (CDC) initiatives in the country have not changed the basic downward spiral of poor, segregated neighborhoods (Orfield 1997, 77).

This view of local affairs highlights the contradiction between the old strategies of community development (including renovating low-cost housing in declining neighborhoods and providing social and economic services for their poor residents) and the objectives of deconcentrating poverty. In Orfield's construction, the entire edifice of the community development field reinforces spatial inequities. Providing supportive services, including housing, for poor residents in central neighborhoods is at best futile, according to Orfield, and at worst counterproductive. Orfield's focus is on the long term and on the best regional approach to issues of poverty and urban decline. He argues not that the communities should be abandoned, but that the way of helping them lies in a different direction.

The "New" Community Development

Orfield's growing influence altered the region's landscape of community development politics. According to his approach, achieving deconcentration meant that supportive efforts for low-income people in central neighborhoods had to be reduced. While Orfield was making this argument, other circumstances worked in a complementary fashion—not the least of which was the region's obsession with gangs, drugs, and violent crime.

The Militarization of Community Development

From the late 1980s through most of the 1990s, crime prevention and community development were conflated in cities across the country. Faced with rising rates of violent crime, drug use, and gang activity, low-income neighborhoods became the testing grounds for a variety of allegedly community-based, crime prevention strategies.[1] Surveillance cameras and listening devices were installed on city streets in parts of Baltimore, Los Angeles, Portland, and even suburban San Francisco (Egan 1996).[2] Other troubled neighborhoods took to closing off streets, barricading certain blocks in efforts to reduce drive-through traffic and attendant crime.[3] The federal Weed and Seed program, initiated in George Bush's administration, consciously connected neighborhood improvement with crime prevention, integrating law enforcement with social services and economic development.

The emphasis in most of the pilot sites, however, was on law enforcement. In the worst of the urban combat zones, extraordinary measures were called for. A "drug-free zone" in Phoenix, for example, was barricaded and patrolled by police who stopped "suspicious" people. In the summer of 1993, Chicago law enforcement officials conducted weapons searches in the Robert Taylor Homes high-rises—searches that were "technically illegal," according to the Chicago Housing Authority police chief. In fact, the American Civil Liberties Union had been contesting CHA's "Operation Clean Sweep" for several years. More violence at the projects in 1992 and 1993 led to metal detectors and an identification card system for public housing residents (Walsh 1993). In the mid-1990s, as Congress contemplated applying the "three strikes and you're out" rule to a variety of offenses, the Clinton administration went even further with poor families in public housing. The "one strike and you're out" rule—that is, one drug-related offense for any member of a household meant eviction of the entire household—was instituted in March 1996. As the urban poor relinquished more and more of their civil rights in the war on drugs and crime, media images of their communities centered on violence and citizens' valiant but often futile attempts to take back their streets.

Community groups in some neighborhoods welcomed these efforts and enthusiastically participated in community crime-prevention activities. Some communities groups organized "forfeiture coalitions" to try to get a portion of the drug assets seized by law enforcement agencies (Baron 1990). These residents, virtually always in poor neighborhoods, had to choose between reduced civil freedoms or continued carnage in their communities. Residents began to organize against each other. "Neighborhood watch" programs institutionalized mutual surveillance. High-profile, antidrug marches through neighborhoods were refined through something called the Wrice Process. Named after a volunteer anticrime organizer in Philadelphia, the Wrice Process was based on direct confrontation with drug dealers and users. It incorporated chanting mobs of residents in street marches, vigils, and even uniforms, "because every army needs a uniform." The practice spread to other cities in the early 1990s, and endured throughout the decade. Citizen police academies were begun across the country, and police departments busied themselves with block club organizing to increase the "eyes and ears" watching a neighborhood.

Organized community crime prevention and participation in criminal justice campaigns directed by the police, however, typically attract only a small fraction of residents. These residents frequently are property owners and, in mixed neighborhoods, most frequently white.[4] Under these circumstances, community crime-prevention activities usually focus on renters and lower-income residents. Community-based anticrime efforts, thus, pit "respectable" neighborhood residents against the neighborhood's "bad elements."

Minneapolis and Saint Paul also experienced the search for neighborhood troublemakers. Though Orfield very carefully laid the blame for central-city problems on policies that supported regional inequities across a range of public responsibilities, media representations and the fears of residents and local officials moved in a different direction. Slowly, but rather inevitably, the diagnosis for central-city neighborhood problems began to focus on the problematic "elements" within the neighborhoods. If, as the argument went, a concentration of poverty led to increased difficulties for Minneapolis and Saint Paul, then it was but a short step for many people to conclude that their biggest problem was simply having too many of "those people." "Those people" typically were renters and people of color.

In both Minneapolis and Saint Paul, the boundaries between crime prevention and community development policy began to blur. Making neighborhoods better places began to mean ridding them of certain classes of people. Forcing the removal of these people required criminal justice strategies. Saint Paul's antidrug program, Focusing Our Resources for Community Empowerment (FORCE), combined drug raids with housing inspections (typically leading to condemnations and the forced eviction of suspected drug offenders). FORCE operated at a high level for several years in the early 1990s, virtually exclusively in high-minority, high-poverty neighborhoods.[5] More than 92 percent of the raids targeted minority households. Because housing inspectors accompanied police on the raids, the suspect and his or her entire household were typically removed from the premises as a result of an arrest or condemnation. Condemnations could be made even in the absence of an arrest, making this method a foolproof means of moving people out of their homes or apartments.[6] Even when they were not part of a drug raid, FORCE housing inspectors would engage in what they called "knock and talks," announcing that they were from the city there on "consent to search." Though technically the inspectors had no authority to enter the units, they relied upon residents' willingness to permit entry. "People cooperate with these visits; they are not a real intelligent bunch," said the inspector.[7] Once inside, an inspector was able to note conditions that might allow a future raid.

One of this activity's largest impacts was the expanding flow of clients at local homeless shelters. In November 1993, the *Saint Paul Pioneer Press* reported, " 'Condemnation' is more and more listed as a reason families end up in shelters. Ironically, perhaps, one reason is that city housing inspectors now accompany police on crack raids, in an effort to make neighborhoods more habitable" (Baker 1993).

Touted as an example of community crime prevention, the FORCE unit worked hard to make connections with community groups. The Saint Paul police department became the largest community organizer in the city in the early 1990s. In less than two years, the FORCE unit made contact with 881 block clubs, and offered 396 presentations to community groups. The department's community office released a 95-page primer on block club organizing devoted entirely to criminal justice, surveillance of problem properties and suspicious activities, and strategies enabling neighborhood residents to effectively become the "eyes and ears" of the police department. However, the manual offered residents no advice on how to create an inclusive neighborhood group or foster a sense of unity or community within neighborhoods. When officers met with residents interested in creating a block club, they were more likely to deliver the police department's established framework for participation (into which the residents could fit if they wanted to) than respond to whatever local issues residents might present. These organizing efforts were not citizen directed.

The Citizen's Police Academy made up another element of the police department's outreach. This academy was established so residents could learn more about the criminal justice system and police operations, and so they could help the police manage conditions in the neighborhoods.[8]

In Minneapolis, the city's community crime-prevention program, the Community and Resource Exchange (operating under a more benign acronym, CARE) was merged for a while with the city's Neighborhood Revitalization Program (NRP), a comprehensive, citywide neighborhood-planning effort. The city's NRP director suggested that the planning program was a long-term effort at improving neighborhoods, while CARE focused on short-term issues (Pitcoff 1993)—a sort of local ver-

sion of Weed and Seed. A citizen inspection program allowed neighborhood residents to identify potential sites of criminal activity. Though
many neighborhood residents avidly defended CARE, one volunteer (in
a mixed-race neighborhood where more than 80 percent of the residents
were renters) admitted that not all residents were part of the process:
"We don't have enough renters and we don't have enough people of color"
(Diaz 1993). This trend, especially in neighborhoods with a lot of rental
property, was noticed by a number of neighborhood activists. NRP/
CARE Director Bob Miller answered by saying, "Those who have the
highest stake, those who have an investment in the neighborhood, participate more" (Pitcoff 1993).

In 1996, Minneapolis added a formal Weed and Seed program to its
CARE/NRP mix. Some residents were not enthusiastic, however. At a
hearing on this issue, one activist testified, "What Weed and Seed does is
increase law enforcement. And you all know who's going to jail. Those
will be people of color. The government is doing an excellent job of weeding already" (Vogel 1993b). Indeed, both Minneapolis and Saint Paul
were effectively "weeding out" renters and people of color. In the early
1990s, African Americans were, in fact, more than 22 times more likely
than whites to be arrested on drug charges, a figure that placed the Twin
Cities near the top of a national list rating U.S. cities on this measure
(Meddis 1993).

As crime continued to escalate through the middle part of the decade,
the city of Minneapolis introduced the CODEFOR (Computer Opti-
mized DEployment–Focus On Results) strategy—one element of which
was a crackdown on petty crimes in central neighborhoods—in hopes
that more serious crime would be deterred. What this meant, in practice,
was that primarily people of color were being stopped at a high rate for
loitering and similar offenses. The program became a flash point in the
African-American community, which regarded CODEFOR as simply an
institutional form of harassment. The NAACP and a local legal rights
center called the program an unchecked abuse of police power aimed at
people of color. City officials pointed to a decline in crime, however, and
maintained that the program was working (Walsh 1998).

Tenants were also subjects of the area's new neighborhood-
improvement orientation. In March 1993, *The Alley*, the neighborhood
newspaper in the Phillips community of south Minneapolis, reported that
neighborhood landlords, inspired by a police crime-prevention specialist,

had developed a 650-name tenant blacklist. Information included in the list covered "everything from drug dealing, to non-payment of rent, to 'hangs with drug dealers,' to 'complains a lot' " (Vogel 1993a). The list was officially closed when users discovered that much of its information was inaccurate. The Saint Paul police department went even further, endorsing a local tenant-screening service. The service took names from the daily notices of tenants involved in eviction proceedings and added those names to its problem-tenants list. What the service did not do, however, was indicate the outcome of the evictions cases, an oversight that put it in violation of state law. The Saint Paul Tenants' Union shed light on such practices, however, and within three years, the service went out of business.

In April 1990, homeless advocates in Minneapolis claimed that 100 to 150 units of affordable low-cost housing had been lost to condemnations in the previous eight months. Legal Aid attorney Larry McDonough called the stepped-up effort at condemning suspected drug houses akin to "burning down a village to flush out the guerillas" (Hotakainen 1990). The city was condemning entire buildings in order to shut down suspected drug activity in certain units.

Minneapolis health inspectors also became extremely aggressive in condemning properties in high-poverty neighborhoods, though they rarely accompanied the police on drug raids. "You'd be surprised how we can gain access and approval from people to get into their apartments," said one Minneapolis health inspector in 1995.[9] By talking their way into apartments, inspectors avoided the bother of getting a warrant. In fact, according to this inspector, "referrals" came mainly from neighborhood organizations. He went on, "The city ordinance says that we can condemn for cockroaches—it doesn't say how many cockroaches we need to see. The city ordinance says that on a 'straight condemnation' you need to give people between 24 hours and 30 days to move out. But in emergency situations you can press for an immediate vacate. . . . This is what we do with weapons and drug-related cases." The inspector emphasized that very few units were ultimately lost in this process—it was more a strategy for evicting problematic tenants. Concerned about the Detroit Scenario, citizens believed that drastic measures were necessary in the city's central neighborhoods. As the inspector said, "I grew up in that part of Minneapolis, and believe me, Minneapolis is at that point in some neighborhoods where we have to do something or the Minneapolis we knew won't be there anymore."[10]

Reorienting Housing Subsidies

A second element of the new community development was a thorough rethinking of housing policy for core neighborhoods. Neighborhood activists and local officials who had determined that their communities had done more than their fair share and should do no more until the suburbs opened up began to question the CDCs' affordable-housing efforts. Some activists and local politicians decided that their areas contained too much rental housing. In the early 1990s, therefore, council members and neighborhood activists in both cities began to agree that central neighborhoods needed more homeownership opportunities. Minneapolis's new Neighborhood Revitalization Program (NRP), which provided millions of dollars to neighborhood groups that engaged in a planning process to revitalize their communities, demonstrated this shift in thinking. NRP attracted more homeowners and higher-income residents to neighborhood-planning efforts across the city, even in neighborhoods dominated by rental housing. Community plans began to reflect the interests of these residents, interests that were more likely to focus on supporting ownership and reducing emphasis on services to renters and low-income residents. Previously formulated plans that did not reflect this new understanding of neighborhood problems were changed (Goetz and Sidney 1994b). Neighborhood activists were much more likely in this environment to see previous community development efforts as products of a narrow, social service approach, and not necessarily in the best interests of the neighborhood at large. CDC directors felt their previous work in the neighborhoods was being discounted, even criticized, and they complained of being pushed aside by newcomers. As one neighborhood developer said, "It's as if community development didn't exist before NRP."[11]

NRP planning began in many neighborhoods at the very time that the Detroit Scenario was spreading through the region. The neighborhood-planning groups, now more likely to be driven by property owners, began to show a greater concern for mixing incomes. In practice, reaching this goal meant increasing wealth in the community and reducing the role of affordable housing. "We have one of the highest concentrations of low-income housing . . . or actually the highest concentration of low-income housing in the city of Minneapolis. So we don't need more low-income housing," said one neighborhood leader.[12] Others went further, talking about the saturation of low-cost rental housing, connecting blight with rental housing, and advocating "turning the rental around or turning it into home ownership, so we can encourage people to come into our neighborhoods and make an investment." For many neighborhood group members, rental housing meant neighborhood decline, in part because renters were seen as having no stake in the community: "Renters in the inner city generally regard their living as a temporary situation. I know I do, and I'm not that dissimilar from the rest of the human race. And it is that attitude that 'this is only temporary, I'm going to leave,' that means you don't get a person that's committed to doing something to improve the quality of life in that neighborhood."[13] In Minneapolis, the low-income renter was the central client for CDC activities. In the era of deconcentration, however, the low-income renter is a sign of neighborhood problems.

In response to the new environment for community development (and to the specter of the Detroit Scenario in the Twin Cities area), city officials attempted to spatially redirect housing rehabilitation programs. The rating criteria for potential tax-credit housing projects were changed to favor developments outside the impacted core neighborhoods. Newly eligible neighborhoods were often outside CDC service areas, and the new criteria meant that the purchase of potential buildings or sites became more expensive and the completion of such deals more difficult. Minneapolis also began to reorient other housing funds, such as its Rehabilitation Incentive Fund (RIF) program. For years, RIF had been used to shore up declining housing stock in the city's central neighborhood. In 1995, however, the city gave preference to new construction in non-impacted neighborhoods, and a year later required the funds to be used outside poverty areas.

This shift in orientation among grassroots neighborhood activists and city officials running housing-assistance programs caught most community development organizations by surprise. "I don't know how it got construed that nonprofit developers are the enemy," said one former CDC director, "when they have been the primary source of revitalization activity over the last 10 years, and should be an even greater player." In Minneapolis, CDCs had been focusing on rental housing for more than a decade, generally with the support of residents, or at least the tacit approval of local neighborhood groups. In the new formulation, the housing units produced by CDCs were now a substantial part of the problem. Neighborhood groups began opposing CDC efforts and imposing moratoria on new CDC-assisted housing (Goetz and Sidney 1997). As support for multifamily development dried up, a number of CDCs had to reorient their development approaches and begin to focus on homeownership.

Others sharply reduced their development activity, trying to survive on the trickle of multifamily projects they could still successfully market to local funders.

Neighborhood activists had a theory for their new approach—deconcentration of poverty. This theory identified low-cost rental housing as a neighborhood problem, rather than a resource. For example, residents in a largely middle-class Saint Paul neighborhood regarded the neighborhood's only sizable rental building as the source of its concentrated poverty problem.[14] In another case, at a 1995 block club meeting in Saint Paul during which a city police officer presented information on organizing, one neighborhood resident wanted to know what could be done about "the Section 8 residents" down the block (referring to the street's only apartment building, which was not a Section 8 building). Another Saint Paul neighborhood group released the findings of its community survey and summarized "the likes and dislikes" of neighborhood respondents.

> Things residents don't like about their neighborhood: crime and disorder, *renters, other housing problems,* social characteristics and poor aesthetics. . . . Many cited problems with rental properties. Twenty percent of residents surveyed said renters were one of the things they disliked about their neighborhood. . . . Over seventy percent of residents surveyed said the appearance of apartment buildings in their neighborhood was fair or poor (emphasis added).[15]

Public policy in Minneapolis shifted markedly away from supporting rental-housing improvements and toward subsidizing more home-ownership opportunities (Goetz and Sidney 1997), as if, perhaps, all those apartment buildings dotting the central neighborhoods would disappear if ignored. If they did not disappear, both core city governments were more than willing to tear them down.

Demolition and Dispersal in the Central Cities

Most central cities have a lead-paint problem in their older neighborhoods. Minnesota state law gives cities leeway to determine how they will address any lead problems that may occur. Minneapolis, for example, chose an aggressive policy of demolition during the 1990s. City officials suggest it was an aversion to potential lawsuits that drove this policy, but tearing down contaminated units also fit into the city's overall strategy of neighborhood revitalization. Demolitions occurred where the problems were greatest—in the middle of the city's poorest neighborhoods—so the eviction effects and housing stock losses centered on the poor, people of color, and tenants. Minneapolis's lead strategy was much more severe than neighboring Saint Paul's, which chose to fund mitigation and rehabilitation rather than demolition (Hartje 1998).

Even landlords in the central neighborhoods agreed with neighborhood groups, community organizations, and the tenants' union that the city of Minneapolis was too quick to demolish uninhabitable units (see Diaz 1997). In 1998, the city's inspections department monitored 145 boarded units; the city tore down 75. Between 1991 and 1998, demolitions outnumbered newly built units by more than 2,250 (Brandt 2001). In fact, during the 1990s, the city demolished nearly 5,600 housing units.

Though not as active in tearing down low-cost housing as its neighbor, Saint Paul also removed apartments in lower-income neighborhoods. The Concord Square housing complex in Saint Paul's West Seventh Street neighborhood, which was built by a private developer in the mid-1970s with HUD subsidies, exemplifies this demolition strategy. The complex comprised four buildings with 116 apartments that, in 1996, rented for $400 to $500 per month. In 1996, HUD foreclosed on the complex. Occupancy dropped from 68 to 50 units, and the number of households with Section 8 subsidies fell from 40 to 29 as HUD allowed residents to leave without refilling the apartments. As the building deteriorated, the Community Stabilization Project (CSP), a tenant-advocacy group, hired a Spanish-speaking activist to organize the complex's primarily Hispanic and low-income residents. Arguing that the buildings were structurally sound and should be rehabilitated and preserved as affordable housing, CSP and the tenants sued HUD to make necessary improvements. In response, HUD put more than $500,000 into the project for repairs. However, HUD and the city proceeded with plans for the project's demolition, while CSP claimed Concord Square residents were not being included in the community-based process for deciding the project's fate. Though then-Congressman Bruce Vento encouraged the city to preserve the housing (as well as HUD's previous investment), Saint Paul continued to entertain proposals for redeveloping the site. Referring to one proposal to preserve and rehabilitate the buildings, the city council member for the area confessed that "he respect[ed] the . . . proposal to renovate the buildings, but he disagree[d] with the concept of concentrating low-income housing" (Baker and Browning 1996). The intensely fractious public debate over the fate of Concord Square pitted the tenants and their advocates against public officials intent on deconcentrating low-cost housing and community groups advocating demolition for neighborhood improvement. In the end, residents were forced out; two of the buildings were demolished, while the other two were converted into townhomes offering subsidies through the federal low-income housing tax credit program.

Saint Paul's northeast neighborhood is currently the site of the Phalen Corridor Initiative, a multimillion-dollar business and economic development project. Until recently, this area was also home to an eight-building, 136-unit apartment complex called the Lakewood Apartments. The city council (acting as the board of directors of the city's Housing and Redevelopment Authority) voted in 1998 to demolish the apartments and replace them with lower-density, higher-income townhomes. A neighborhood based nonprofit developer, East Side Neighborhood Development Corporation (ESNDC), would sponsor the project, which was to be funded by $3.3 million in federal and city funds. Consistent with the Concord Square project, CSP attempted to organize residents to oppose the demolition. CSP was, in fact, the first to tell Lakewood residents about the city's plan to displace them and demolish their housing.

Several factors led to a wide consensus to tear down the apartments. First, the units were in very poor condition. The city council president called the project "a complete, absolute disaster" (Laszewski 1998). Even CSP admitted the units were deplorable. Second, the project occupied prime real estate, sitting between Lake Phalen and the Phalen Corridor Initiative site. Some project supporters argued that property values around the apartments had been declining despite the lake's appeal and proximity, further demonstrating the need for redevelopment. Finally, ESNDC argued the presence of widespread community support for this type of redevelopment.

CSP, on the other hand, argued that even though the apartments were in bad condition, they still could be rehabilitated and preserved. Consistent with the Concord Square case, the tenants had never been invited to a community planning meeting. CSP also pointed out that the development of new, market-rate homes on property adjacent to the apartments belied concerns over property values. Furthermore, CSP made clear its understanding that the real issue was the community's readiness to use deconcentrating poverty as justification for eliminating 136 affordable-housing units for primarily minority residents. Lakewood tenants and their advocates also used the area's tight housing market as ammunition in their complaints about the proposed demolition and their impending displacement.

The deputy mayor conceded that tearing down Lakewood would cause some "short-term pain." He added, however, that "in the long run, Saint Paul needs the more expensive townhomes to attract middle- and upper-class residents to pay the taxes that will provide more low-income housing" (Laszewski 1998). Therefore, the buildings were demolished during the summer of 1998 and replaced by 30 townhomes, priced between $110,000 and $130,000, and six Habitat for Humanity homes. CSP maintains that most tenants were relocated to housing where conditions were worse than those existing at the Lakewood Apartments.

Demolition and Dispersal in the First Ring

The January 26, 1994, edition of the suburban newspaper, *Brooklyn Park Sun-Post,* featured a picture of several men in suits standing next to construction equipment in front of a large apartment complex. The caption read:

> The Economic Development Authority of Brooklyn Park begins the $6 million renovation of the 396 Wynmor Apartments, a series of three-story buildings built on 20 acres in south Brooklyn Park. The renovation includes the demolition of 54 units. Mayor Jesse Ventura is on hand and joined by other council members and city officials *in throwing ceremonial rocks at the building* before it is torn down (emphasis added).

Brooklyn Park is a first-ring suburb north of Minneapolis. In the 1990s, the city embarked on a conscious effort to upgrade its housing stock by reducing affordability. For example, the Cedarbrooke, a 144-unit apartment building, was converted into senior housing through a $2 million public/private renovation and became the Waterford. In another instance, the city demolished one building in the Groves and upgraded another for higher-income occupancy, renaming the complex "The Cottonwood."

The effort's centerpiece, however, comprised the Huntington Pointe and Huntington Place projects. Originally a single project called the Century Court Apartments, the buildings were constructed in 1969 to meet the housing needs of maturing baby boomers. By the 1990s, Century Court had become just another low-cost apartment complex, experiencing problems of low occupancy, foreclosure, and rising crime. The city's original plan was to demolish the entire complex at a cost of $32 million. In 1996, however, the city's Economic Development Authority (EDA) voted to demolish Huntington Pointe (306 units) and to renovate and raise rents at Huntington Place (834 units). According to the EDA, the city had plenty of affordable rental housing, and eliminating or converting these units would help tighten Brooklyn Park's rental market. After persuading the Minnesota legislature to adjust tax increment financing (TIF) laws, the city of Brooklyn Park was able to issue up to $22 million in TIF funds to finance the renovation and demolition.

Residents for Affordable Housing, a grassroots organization of Huntington residents, soon organized in opposition to the demolition. The organization and its allies pointed out that the 1,140 apartments in Huntington Pointe and Huntington Place represented more affordable rental units than were built in the entire region in a given year.

Under new management, vacancies at the complex fell from 50 to 5 percent in late 1997, and crime also declined. At this point, the official justification for the project switched from crime reduction to lower densities. City officials insisted that most residents supported the demolition and redevelopment plan. One council member reported that in canvassing residents of other city neighborhoods, "well over 90 percent . . . basically said, 'tear 'em all down' " (Kaszuba 1998a). According to the city's economic and housing special projects planner, much of the opposition came from housing advocates who lived outside the city. "They're looking at it from a regional perspective. We're looking at it from a local perspective" (Kaszuba 1998b).

In early 1998, attorneys from Legal Aid joined the tenant group in filing suit to block the city's attempt to use TIF assistance. When the court ruled in favor of the tenants, the city instead proposed using local funds for the demolition. By this time, the proposal was almost three years old, and the price tag had increased to $41.2 million, more than the annual budget of most suburbs. "Though city officials hotly disputed the allegation, critics said the project was a sign of how far a suburb was willing to go to rid itself of low-income housing and tenants" (Kaszuba 1998c).

By the summer of 1998, in the face of continued opposition from residents and regional affordable-housing advocates and a threatened discrimination suit from Legal Aid, the project owner withdrew the proposal for demolition. The owner, instead, has embarked on a more modest remodeling of Huntington Pointe and Huntington Place, carrying a price tag of approximately $6 million but still involving gradual rent increases.

The Mayor's Housing Principles

By 1995, Mayor Sharon Sayles Belton of Minneapolis was working on several fronts to stem the middle-class flight to the suburbs. The city had recently initiated a Neighborhood Revitalization Program (NRP), which, she maintained, was about asking the middle class what they wanted in their neighborhoods (Brauer 1995). Mayor Belton also wanted to end the city's decades-long program of school desegregation. As the city's first African-American mayor, she was uniquely situated to end what had begun as an attempt to equalize the educational experiences of the city's white and black children. In place of desegregation and the system of school choice that had been created in Minneapolis, the mayor wanted a return to "neighborhood schools" because she believed they facilitated greater parent involvement in education, fostered a greater sense of community among neighbors, and reduced long bus trips for students. Furthermore, this system would reassure middle-class families that their children would be allowed to attend schools with their neighbors— the children of other middle-class families.

The effort to return to neighborhood schools, however, had to address the concerns of African-American families, who did not want a return to segregated schools. Therefore, a more equitable distribution of affordable housing throughout the city seemed to be the answer. Indeed, it is often argued that the best school desegregation policy is a housing desegregation policy, and so it was argued in Minneapolis. The mayor developed a short set of housing principles that made dispersal of affordable housing a central tenet for city policy. In May 1995, a month after signing the *Hollman* agreement, Mayor Belton introduced her "housing principles" to the city council.

The response had to be less than she had hoped for. Council members from neighborhoods with few subsidized housing units feared that dispersal would merely spread blight throughout the city. One member suggested that neighborhoods should not have to take more than the metropolitan area's average of affordable units (which then stood at 5.8 percent of all housing units). Another argued that redistribution of low-income units within the city "would take pressure off suburbs to accept their fair share" (Brandt and Draper 1995). The council voted seven to six to return the principles to committee for further refinement. Though the council accepted the principles later that summer, Minneapolis Council Member Joan Campbell called the initial hearing "one of the ugliest council meetings" she had ever attended.

In their arguments, council members simply were adapting portions of the deconcentration story and the Detroit Scenario. They were, in fact, echoing arguments that suggested that the city had already done its share in producing low-cost housing, and that it was time for the suburbs to make affordable housing available in their areas. In addition, council members representing districts within the city were concerned that the blight associated with concentrated poverty would accompany the construction of subsidized housing in their districts. These positions, however, did not help convince suburbanites that they, instead, should accept subsidized housing. As one suburban housing official said, "If they don't want them [the low-income housing units], how can they go out to the suburbs and ask us to take them?" (Brandt and Draper 1995).

The Minneapolis Affordable Housing Initiative

In summer 1997, advocates for the Jobs and Affordable Housing Campaign (JAHC) began to organize throughout Minneapolis around the issue of affordable housing. As described in the previous chapter, the region's housing market had begun to heat up considerably, leading to rapidly escalating housing prices and very low vacancy rates for rental housing. The resulting coalition included Children and Family Services (CFS), an advocacy and service group supporting JAHC; the Metropolitan Interfaith Coalition for Affordable Housing (MICAH), which had long been active in regional affordable-housing efforts; and Jewish Community Action.

The 1997 campaign resulted in a resolution offered before the Minneapolis City Council, sponsored by south side Council Member Jim Niland, to increase the resources the city devoted to affordable housing. In the days prior to the full council vote, advocates felt the need to convince council members that they should act in order to encourage the suburbs to take their fair share of subsidized housing. According to this argument, the suburbs needed to see that the city was willing to do its part. Two other high-profile actors, however, were telling the city council just the opposite. Myron Orfield and Professor john powell (University of Minnesota Law School) both believed the city had been doing its part for far too many years without suburban assistance. Professor powell, director of the Institute on Race and Poverty at the university, had for some time been leading the institute's work on concentration of poverty among low-income urban communities of color. (In 1996, the institute had hosted a national conference on "Linking Regional and Local Strategies to Create Healthy Communities," at which many of the national leaders on mobility and community development spoke about these approaches to concentrated poverty.) Orfield and powell wrote letters to the city council, suggesting that a regional approach to the affordable housing issue was the only way to achieve the necessary deconcentration of poverty, and that the city should be careful to avoid affordable housing policies that would further concentrate poverty.

In the end, the full council so overloaded the Niland initiative with amendments that Niland himself voted against it. The resolution passed anyway and, while failing to enact any of the proposals originally advanced by the advocates, created the Mayor's Task Force on Affordable Housing. The task force was charged with studying the issue of affordable housing and making recommendations to the council.

Mayor Belton appointed powell to head the task force, which was made up of advocates, nonprofit and for-profit developers, and affordable-housing funders. The task force met throughout the rest of 1997 and into the next year, discussing various aspects of the issue and hearing from a number of local experts about the housing situation in the Twin Cities. On more than one occasion, the group took up the issue of deconcentrating poverty. In April 1998, the task force heard Myron Orfield's adamant opinion: The central city and the inner-ring suburbs desperately needed to reduce existing concentrations of poverty and should do nothing that might work to maintain or increase those concentrations.

This approach was not wholly inconsistent with powell's. Actively speaking out in the community, powell felt very strongly that concentrated poverty was the result of a history of residential segregation and discrimination targeted toward African Americans and other people of color. A former Detroit resident, powell frequently pointed to the Detroit Scenario in describing the potential effects of concentrated poverty.

In making this argument, powell referenced, as Orfield had done for several years, the work of a national cadre of social scientists who had convincingly presented four separate arguments. First, poverty in the United States had become very highly concentrated in urban neighborhoods; in fact, the number of neighborhoods in which more than 40 percent of the population lived below the federal poverty level mushroomed between 1970 and 1990. Second, this concentration of poverty stemmed from a range of factors, including residential segregation, changes in the job structure of American cities, and the legacy of American housing policy. Third, concentrated poverty could be reduced only by providing lower-income people with more housing opportunities outside the central city. Finally, research on the only sizable program in the country, the Gautreaux program in Chicago—which systematically attempted to move poor, African-American public housing residents to integrated suburban areas—was producing a range of benefits to those families moving from poorer Chicago neighborhoods.

The Detroit Scenario and the case for deconcentration are both intuitively appealing, and they enjoy a significant level of empirical support. However, the Detroit Scenario and the resultant deconcentration-of-poverty argument appeal to progressives for yet another reason. This argument identifies specific public and private actions that have led to current conditions of poverty and hopelessness in American cities. It also acknowledges the long and grim history of racial discrimination in housing. It provides, in essence, the rationale for a public policy response to urban poverty, an issue lacking any sustained policy attention since the 1960s. Among advocates for the poor, this was not an easy argument to oppose, nor perhaps were its implications fully realized by the mid-1990s.

According to several task force members, deconcentration was among the most difficult issues they faced, and the only one for which the group resorted to mediation. Over time, the task force resolved its internal differences by calling for the preservation of affordable housing in impacted areas and new development in other neighborhoods.

A Change of Focus

All policy approaches invoke a story line of cause and effect, a language that emphasizes some factors and neglects others. The discourse surrounding the deconcentration of poverty accentuates the behavioral pathologies of the poor and places the focus for change on the poor themselves. This language is easily adapted not only by conservatives, who argue that the poor should change their behavior, but also by liberals, who argue that the poor must change their location in order to improve their lot (and, in the end, their behavior will change, too). The deconcentration-of-poverty paradigm has something for both camps. Furthermore, the language of deconcentration has complemented urban policy's criminal justice orientation. The Twin Cities, therefore, have witnessed a dramatic reorientation of community development policy away from more traditional efforts to improve low-income neighborhoods. This reorientation has coincided with important demographic changes in the region, which have also reduced the political foundation of regional efforts to maintain equitable development patterns.

For most of the 1990s, deconcentration of poverty overwhelmed other approaches to the needs of the region's core areas. The most striking example, and the centerpiece of the region's deconcentration movement, was the consent decree in *Hollman v. Cisneros*, a suit originally filed in response to discrimination and segregation in Minneapolis public housing. Chapter 6 examines the roots of the suit, the settlement, and how implementing the decree brought the debate about deconcentration of poverty to the forefront.

NOTES

1. Most community anticrime activity is led and directed by police departments attempting to enlist community members in strategies and efforts that are managed by the department. Buerger (1994) argues that the community role is typically limited to one or more of the following: (1) being the "eyes and ears" of the police, i.e., watching and reporting to the police; (2) cheerleading; (3) providing public support for police activities; (4) "statement-making" activities such as "take back the night" parades.

2. See also Fyfe and Bannister (1994).

3. See, for example, Jordan (1993) and Owens (1994).

4. Buerger (1994); Skogan (1990); and Garofalo and McLeod (1989) argue that crime prevention is a poor means of organizing communities. In their study of "neighborhood watch" programs, they report that residents of poor neighborhoods were concerned that being absent from their homes for a period of time would allow their neighbors a chance to "case" their homes.

5. Similar strategies were in place in 77 percent of the 30 largest cities in the United States in 1995. In San Diego, inspectors enter housing units immediately following a raid to check for substandard conditions. In Dallas and San Jose, the police work closely with housing inspectors, who enter the units immediately after raids. In Columbus, Ohio, a "Building Evaluation Team" made up of fire, police, health, housing inspections, social service, and court workers converge on properties after a raid to evaluate and condemn the unit if necessary. Police sponsorship of tenant screening was also practiced in close to half of the largest U.S. cities in 1995, including classes for landlords on screening and other special support and training. See Goetz (1996).

6. Because most drug raids involve forced entrance, the very circumstances of the raid provide the conditions necessary for a condemnation—a broken-down front door. The drug raids themselves, however, were not always foolproof. One Saint Paul woman testified to her experience with the FORCE unit:

On July the 15th I was in a real bad raid and me and my family was knocked out [of housing] for two weeks. I had from eight year up until a fourteen-year-old. The guns were pulled to their head. They were strip searched on my living room floor. The whole time the police were in there they tore up my house, pulled out, took all my food out of the freezer, cut my mattresses open, everything. Did not find nothing. They used abusive language with my kids. I have a son now, my eight-year-old he is scared to even go to the bathroom at night past the backdoor where the woman police came in with the gun in her hand. They tore out all the windows in my house, kicked down all the doors. . . . And it really left a bad impact on two of my kids. One is now scared of police, and the other can't go to the bathroom at night . . . have to have all the lights on in the house. And come to find out they didn't find anything, it was just people out in the front of my house walking up and down the street selling drugs. And me and my kids are suffering for it (From the testimony of Mary Neal at the Saint Paul City Council Committee on Public Safety, public hearing, August 24, 1994).

In another FORCE raid, the police fired their "flash-bang" device through the window of a 15-year-old girl living with her infant son. The apartment they wanted to raid was next door ("Police Mistake Puts Device in Apartment of Mom, Baby," *St. Paul Pioneer Press*, March 30, 1995, B2). The Saint Paul Tenants' Union alleged that the girl was physically held outside on a cold March night, not allowed to return to her unit for more clothing, shoes, or blankets for her newborn while the police shifted their attention to the unit next door.

    7. Jim Halverson, FORCE housing inspections program, interview by author, February 11, 1994.

    8. Similar police academies were developed in cities across the country. The Louisville academy was touted by President Clinton as a national model for improving police-community relations (Quinlan 1996). Academies, however, are typically a one-way flow of information from the police to the community members, who learn about police techniques. "It's about educating the public," as one police chief said (Clawson 1996). In one case, Cincinnati began a student police academy to repair relations between the department and young people after a widely publicized arrest in which a videotape showed police striking, kicking, and macing a high school student (Weintraub 1996).

    9. Dave Nordmeier, health inspector, City of Minneapolis, interview by author, April 6, 1995.

    10. Nordmeier, interview.

    11. This quote and those that follow are taken from Goetz and Sidney (1994a).

    12. Comment made by a neighborhood organization official during interviews conducted by the author in Minneapolis and Saint Paul during 1993.

    13. Ibid.

    14. After speaking to this neighborhood group about concentrated poverty in 1997, I was approached by several people afterward, one of whom told me that the neighborhood (of primarily middle-class homeowners) also had a concentration-of-poverty problem. Immediately, someone else raised an arm and pointed toward a large apartment building that could be seen several blocks away. The point was clear—the problems in this neighborhood were that building and its occupants.

    15. Flyer from the East Side Neighborhood Development Company (1995), available from author.

6

Hollman v. Cisneros

For over 50 years black people have had their babies, raised their families, and buried their dead in the near north area of Minneapolis. Now, before I meet my maker, I see what it all comes down to: the liberals selling out the only black land we have ever known in Minneapolis to a bunch of development interests, with black leaders from the mayor to our community organizations falling in line.

Shame on the Minneapolis NAACP for participating in this terrible attack on our community. Shame on the NAACP for allowing itself to be used by the City and the other parties to the Hollman "settlement" to make it appear that this theft of our land has the approval of the black people. It does not.

—Nellie Stone Johnson, labor and civil rights activist, 1995[1]

This is not just tearing down a public-housing project. This is an encroachment on the rights of citizens. This is gentrification. This is warfare of the "haves" against the "have nots."

—Reverend Curtis Herron, Mt. Zion Baptist Church, north Minneapolis, 1999

There are people who don't see a problem with poor people being concentrated. Well, I do have a problem with that. I'm on the side that says we must deconcentrate poverty and build strong neighborhoods.

—Minneapolis Mayor Sharon Sayles Belton, 1999

In the 1930s, Minneapolis's near north side, just a mile from the central business district, was home to some of the worst problems in the city. It was a center of crime and juvenile delinquency, suffered from high rates of infant mortality and pulmonary tuberculosis, and endured some of the worst housing conditions in the city. Many buildings lacked central heating, adequate toilet facilities, baths, gas, or electricity (Chapin 1938).

Bassett Creek ran through the middle of the neighborhood (in 1925, however, the creek had been converted to a closed sewer in that part of the city in an effort to control flooding). In 1938, city officials petitioned the federal government to build public housing on the site, thereby clearing it of existing physical and social decay. The resulting Sumner Field project—consisting of 350 rowhouses—was the first public housing project in the state of Minnesota, and among the first built in the country under an experimental program operated by the Department of Interior's Public Works Administration. Sumner Field represented an opportunity to simultaneously revitalize the deteriorating conditions of the neighborhood surrounding the creek, utilize the land under which the creek flowed, and create jobs during the Great Depression.

The medicine did not take, however. Over time, neighboring retail and residential areas gave way to highways and industry, and the site itself became increasingly isolated. Gradually, as the soils shifted, cracks began to appear in the walls and ceilings of homes in the project. Housing and commercial land uses in the surrounding neighborhood continued to decay. The neighborhood remained characterized by dilapidated housing structures, "adverse land use mixtures, a badly designed and inefficient traffic system, and environmental deterioration resulting from the poor drainage around Bassett Creek" (Martin and Goddard 1989, 34). As neighborhood conditions continued to decline, the predominantly white and Jewish population fled to the west, giving way to a growing African-American population.

A second round of redevelopment began in 1959, and between 1959 and 1961, four more public housing projects were built. Together with Sumner Field, these projects occupied a 73-acre site on either side of Olson Memorial Highway in north Minneapolis. The Glenwood project, 220 rowhouse units, and the Lyndale project, 86 rowhouse units, were built side by side south of the highway. The Olson public housing project, 66 units, was located immediately north of the highway on land adjacent to Sumner Field. The Bryant high-rise apartments, set aside for seniors, were built north of Olson and east of Sumner Field. Sumner Field, the largest of the five projects at 350 units, was built in a series of more than 30 two-story buildings directly above Bassett Creek.

By 1961, this 73-acre tract contained more than 900 units of public housing, making it by far the largest concentration of public housing in the city. Its location near the heart of the city's African-American community made it typical of public housing across the United States and eventually became the basis for a desegregation lawsuit (*Hollman v. Kemp*). For the next two decades, city council approval of new public housing sites ensured that new projects would reinforce existing patterns of segregation, argued the plaintiffs. Even when the city initiated its scattered-site program in the 1960s, the council limited it "to the city's three poorest and most highly minority concentrated neighborhoods. In 1969, Mayor Naftalin vetoed the council's limitations, referring to them as 'discriminatory and unwholesome' " (Thompson 1996, 241). Similar siting restrictions were also put upon other HUD-subsidized, non–public housing, until a 1984 citywide task force criticized the process, "noting that concentrating and isolating low income families headed primarily by unemployed single parents intensified social problems" (243). Filed in 1992 by Legal Aid attorneys and the NAACP on behalf of the public housing residents, *Hollman v. Kemp* alleged that after Sumner Field was built, the U.S. Housing Authority deliberately segregated black families by restricting them to the east half of the project, while whites lived in the west half. (*Hollman v. Kemp* was subsequently changed to *Hollman v. Cisneros* with the change of presidential administrations in 1993.)

Settlement Details

The lawsuit named as defendants the Minneapolis Public Housing Authority (MPHA), the Minneapolis Community Development Agency (MCDA), the City of Minneapolis, HUD, and the Metropolitan Council of the Twin Cities. The parties pursued a negotiated settlement through most of 1993 and 1994. Finally, in April 1995, a consent decree was announced and approved by the presiding judge. This decree laid out an aggressive plan of deconcentration and redevelopment, including demolition of the 350 Sumner Field townhomes and the disposition (either by demolition or sale) of the rest of the public housing on site. Whether the other public housing units on site (the Olson, Glenwood, and Lyndale projects) would be demolished also was to be determined later.[2] To enhance the deconcentrating impacts of the agreement, the MPHA also agreed to evaluate for disposition 129 scattered-site units in minority-concentrated areas. Displaced families would be provided relocation assistance to cover moving expenses and counseling in finding a new home. The parties involved would decide the details regarding site redevelopment at a later date. The agreement called for convening focus groups of nearby residents, businesses, nonprofit agencies, members of the plaintiff class, and others affected by the redevelopment in order to provide a basis for this later decision.

In addition, the decree also called for development of up to 770 public housing units to replace those demolished or disposed of in other ways. Some were to be replaced on site; others would be built elsewhere in the City of Minneapolis. The remainder would be built in suburban areas throughout the metropolitan area.

Local officials hailed the settlement as a wonderful opportunity to address significant problems in the community, and welcomed the influx of $130 million in HUD funds at a time when HUD funding was scarce. Jackie Cherryhomes, city council president and the council member for the north side area, claimed, "[The settlement is] the most important thing that's happened in the Fifth Ward and north Minneapolis in the last 30 years. This represents a real opportunity to rebuild north Minneapolis" (Diaz 1995). The MPHA concurred: "There's the potential to dramatically change a part of the city," commented Deputy Director Tom Hoch when the settlement was announced (Washington and Drew 1995).

Though the decree called for a focus group process to provide recommendations for site redevelopment, many local leaders had their own ideas about what a cleaned-up version of the 73 acres might look like. There was talk from the outset of uncovering Bassett Creek and developing a creek/park amenity on site. The *Star Tribune* prominently advocated this alternative, citing a then-current study of city property values that showed a significant spike in home values near the chain of lakes ringing the southwest part of Minneapolis (Mack 1995). Proponents hoped that the near north side would become another link in the chain of greenway paths stretching from the western suburbs, across the entire city of Minneapolis, and well into Saint Paul (Brandt 1995). The *Star Tribune* called it a "once-in-a-lifetime chance to create the kind of amenities on Minneapolis' north side that . . . made the southwest side so desirable" (Mack 1995).

Other community leaders pointed out the site's potential attractiveness and desirability as a location for new housing. The director of the Northside Residents Redevelopment Council (NRRC), the neighborhood organization for the near north, noted the "beautiful sunset views of the downtown skyline" just a two- or three-minute drive away (Mack 1995). This theme was taken up later by opponents of redevelopment, who felt the site's attractiveness was bound to produce gentrification and, indeed, that gentrification was planned. Yet, in 1995, general response to the settlement was the opinion that it offered great hope for solving the city's worst concentration-of-poverty and social problems while simultaneously adding a new and welcomed amenity.

The Planning Process

Plaintiffs and defendants agreed that planning would proceed through the ongoing meetings of two focus groups (later merged into one) charged with presenting a series of recommendations for the site. Once plaintiffs and defendants reached an agreement concerning the form of the planning process, both parties negotiated a planning outline that detailed how the focus groups would operate, which organizations would be represented in the groups, and who would facilitate each focus group. Focus group members included public housing residents, community organization members, low-income residents from developments adjoining the sites, residents of the surrounding neighborhoods, and *Hollman* plaintiffs (represented by the NAACP and Legal Aid), with an emphasis on ethnic and cultural representation.

The focus groups began meeting in late February 1996. Considerable efforts were made to facilitate participation by area residents. Two community meetings, one of which was specifically geared toward the Southeast Asian community, were held. In addition, the focus groups met with individual organizations to highlight the decree's background and inform residents of the planning process.

Meetings were scheduled at convenient times within the respective neighborhoods. Staff provided food, child care, and stipends as well as simultaneous translation services to focus group members. Focus group organizers publicized the meetings in community papers, north side newspapers, and through flyers. All of the focus group meetings were open to the public. In addition to their own meetings, the focus groups also held three community "speak ups" to allow public comment on their work. All of this was arranged in order to maximize community participation. Despite efforts to include all the relevant parties, however, some people still felt left out. In particular, neighborhood representatives and property owners from nearby neighborhoods were upset that they did not have a voice. As it turned out, they would have their say later.

Interviewed two years afterward, many participants agreed that focus group attendance was very good. Language barriers, however, may have hindered Southeast Asian participation. In the beginning, no provision was made for Hmong and Laotian translators. After the plaintiffs complained, the MPHA agreed to provide translation. According to one participant, however, "sometimes the interpreters would not show up, sometimes they would show up and did not interpret very well—or never said anything." Most observers agree that the Southeast Asian community was not very vocal during the focus group meetings. Staffing for the focus groups was provided by the MPHA, the Design Center for the American Urban Landscape at the University of Minnesota, the Minneapolis Planning Department, the Minneapolis Community Development Agency (MCDA), the Minneapolis Neighborhood Revitalization Program (NRP), and the Legal Aid Society of Minneapolis. Focus group staff members met weekly during the process to review the groups' progress and map out possible agendas and strategies for the continuing work. Initially, staff members were heavily involved with establishing the agenda for the group meetings. They presented the lawsuit's history and background and kept the meetings structured, introducing topics for discussion, allowing comment and discussion, and seeking recommendations. Staff also provided speakers to afford focus group members with more contextual information. Law professor john powell of the University of Minnesota, for example, talked about the dire community impacts of highly concentrated poverty. Over time, however, this staff-directed orientation gave way to a more responsive role. As the focus group members gained confidence and information, they were, according to one city official, "less likely to be led in that sort of way. . . . They were more likely to suggest topics on their own that they wanted to talk about, which was fine because what that was doing was creating more ownership over the product that was coming out."

Factions and Fault Lines

Fault lines developed within the focus groups on a number of issues. There was, for example, baseline tension between the two largest ethnic groups living in the units—African Americans, who had long been numerically dominant, and recent Southeast Asian immigrants, who, by 1995, had become the largest ethnic group. One member of the African-American community made this observation: "The tenants who won the lawsuit are really no longer here in large part, and another ethnic group is going to benefit from the results of the lawsuit rather than the people on whose behalf it was originally brought out." Ironically, Southeast Asian residents were much less likely to see relocation as a benefit. As a group, they were much less critical of existing public housing than were African-American tenants.

The focus groups were charged with making recommendations on the disposition of the Glenwood, Lyndale, and Olson projects. Soils data showing extensive instability underneath the site and MPHA insistence that relocation would occur even with rehabilitation swayed the groups toward demolition over rehab. Furthermore, an early estimate by MPHA indicated that correcting just the structural problems at the Sumner Field and Olson projects would cost $30,000 to $100,000 per unit. Such a high cost, argued the housing authority, made rehabilitation impractical.

The configuration of the new housing on site was a major point of contention within the focus groups. Most participants agreed that some income mix was necessary to avoid a reconcentration of very low income residents. Resident participants, however, wanted to make sure there was enough low-income housing on site to ensure that they would be able to move back into the neighborhood. Some participants were concerned that the entire site not be gentrified, but remain hospitable to people of lower income while still offering better housing and employment opportunities. On the other hand, some participants felt that this was an opportunity to introduce higher incomes into the neighborhood, and that development of new public housing, without a significant income mix, would defeat the purpose of the settlement and simply reconcentrate the poor.

Nevertheless, on June 10, 1996, the newly-merged focus group expressed general agreement that as much public housing as possible should be built on the site. The minutes to the meeting indicate there was "not a lot of support for a mixed income [housing] scenario on site" (MPHA 1997, 6). In fact, the group formally voted 12 to 1 for a motion calling for the "maximum number of units of public housing" on site. Yet, the issue of mixed-income versus "maximum public housing" did not disappear. The original motion was brought up several times in subsequent meetings. On July 1, focus group staff brought in James Head of the National Community Development Law Center to speak about the necessity of using a mixed-income approach to make community revitalization work. The issue was revisited on July 20 when a member suggested that city council, which had to authorize the final redevelopment plan, would not accept the "maximum public housing" motion. Two weeks later, MPHA staff provided the focus group with information on mixed-income developments around the country. Finally, on August 19, the group was told by its facilitator that its earlier decision to place the "maximum public housing" on site was inconsistent with a mixed-income approach; the group would have to choose between the two. Aided by Head's testimony and the MPHA data, the August 19 discussion quickly turned to how much mixed-income housing was appropriate. In the end, the focus group passed a motion recommending 25 percent public housing, 25 percent low-income housing, and 50 percent market-rate housing—a position considerably distant from where the group had been two months earlier.

Interestingly, focus group minutes do not reveal any other instance in which an issue, once decided, was reintroduced and reconsidered on multiple occasions. The focus group's June decision to retain maximum public housing on site had surprised the staff. Clearly, in subsequently bringing in James Head, presenting information on other mixed-income projects, and reintroducing the topic, staff members were attempting to shift the group from its original position.

Recommendations of the Focus Group

Ultimately, the group's final plan, finalized in November 1996, stressed the need to create a new community of diverse, mixed incomes, anchored by attractive natural amenities, ethnic/cultural attractions, and educational, job training, and social service institutions. Approximately 28 acres would be available for housing, resulting in 150 to 375 units, depending on density levels. Open space would comprise approximately 40 acres on the existing Sumner Field and Glenwood sites. Institutional use would be allocated approximately 16 acres of development area.

At this point, the lead defendant, MPHA, began the process of writing what would become the Northside Action Plan, an effort that took more than a year to complete. During that year, MPHA officials met regularly with the plaintiffs, primarily Legal Aid, to ensure that the plan would address all the points outlined in the consent decree. In addition, MPHA representatives consulted the other defendants for their input and met with focus group members to update them on the plan's progress. In March 1997, however, the housing authority also released a new soil study indicating an even greater area of unstable soil on the site than the original study had reported. MPHA presented this information to the focus group, pointing out a resulting need to reduce the number of acres of housing that would be built on site. (Throughout their meetings, focus group members had agreed that housing should not be built on poor soils.)

A draft of the plan was completed in late 1997 and presented to the city council for ratification. The plan called for demolition of all existing, family public housing on the site; construction of a mixed-income residential community that would include 25 percent public housing, 25 percent moderate-income rental housing, and 50 percent market-rate housing; a 36-acre open-space amenity to include playing fields, wetlands, and other water features; and a significant new parkway boulevard connection to neighborhoods to the south.

City Council Ratification

In December 1997, 13 months after the focus group had concluded its work, the Minneapolis City Council met to consider the action plan. Under the direction of Council President Jackie Cherryhomes (whose council district includes the site), the council adopted several amendments and then ratified the plan. First, the council changed the housing mix, countermanding the focus group directive on one of its most contentious issues. The council mandated, instead, 75 percent market-rate housing and 25 percent public housing. All references to rental housing were deleted, thereby eliminating any goals related to nonownership housing, other than public housing. Finally, the council insisted that no social services be provided on site.

These were not minor revisions. They were, however, in the words of one informant, "the showing of the muscle of the north side community that lived to the west [of the site] that complained initially that they weren't part of the focus groups." This group, predominantly homeowners, was concerned about the potential reconcentration of poor people; too much affordable housing or on-site social services might "anchor" poorer residents to the area.

The council's amendments did not sit well with focus group participants, attorneys for the plaintiffs, or community members who were beginning to suspect that the elaborate planning process was being used to justify a dramatic reconstitution of the neighborhood. Some community members had already been voicing concerns that redevelopment would lead to wholesale gentrification, and that deconcentration would have the effect of "wiping out" the north side political bases of African Americans and Southeast Asians (Brandt 1997; Diaz 1997; Furst 1996a). The council's moves to reduce low-income housing to 25 percent, and remove social services and rental housing, seemed to confirm those fears.

Any amendments to the action plan, however, had to be approved by the plaintiffs. Legal Aid filed an objection to the council's changes and thus forced a round of negotiations between the plaintiffs and the city council. Ultimately, the plaintiffs signed off on the deal in April 1998 when all parties agreed that a 75 percent market-rate housing target did not preclude developing lower-end market-rate housing or rental housing. It was further agreed that the request for proposals (RFP) describing the redevelopment objectives to potential developers would mention the potential for various market ranges and tenure types among the housing units to be built. In addition, plaintiffs negotiated two seats for themselves on the implementation committee, which was created to carry out the Northside Action Plan. The implementation committee included the mayor, the directors of MPHA and MCDA, the city coordinator, and representatives from the planning department, public works, the park board, the Legal Aid Society, and the NAACP. Cherryhomes chaired the committee.

The implementation committee directed project staff to expand the project's boundaries to the south and southwest to incorporate the rest of the Bassett Creek area. This step was necessary in order to coordinate the action plan with a concurrent study of the Bassett Creek area and with the city's empowerment zone proposal. The Bassett Creek study examined the redevelopment potential for the area south of Glenwood and the land pollution concerns that needed to be addressed to allow development. The city's empowerment zone application (approved by the federal government in early 1999) called for the infusion of millions of dollars in economic development into the greater near north neighborhood (as well as a neighborhood on the city's south side). The city also looked into the possibility of removing other subsidized housing developments adjacent to the 73-acre site.

Then in November 1998, the implementation committee distributed an RFP for redeveloping the project site. It announced the city's official vision:

> A new mixed-income community will emerge—a vital, diverse community in which public housing is interspersed with market-rate housing. This new development will surround a 36-acre park, part of the city's world-renowned park sys-

tem. A new parkway will achieve an historic link between residential communities in north and south Minneapolis, connecting residents of the near north side neighborhoods to the Guthrie Theater and Walker Art Center, the Sculpture Garden, the Loring Park college campuses and to the heart of downtown (City of Minneapolis 1998, 1).

As expected, the McCormack-Baron team (a Saint Louis–based developer that had completed similar public housing redevelopment projects in other cities) was chosen for the project. In January 2000, after demolition of the Glenwood/Lyndale site had begun, the north side redevelopment plan was announced. The final plan called for 800 units of housing, 55 percent of which would be rental units. Two hundred units (25 percent) would be public housing and 200 (25 percent) would be subsidized for moderate-income families. Of the moderate-income units, 110 would be ownership units and 90 rentals. The rest, 250 ownership units and 150 rental units, were set at market rates. Though the number of pro posed market-rate units nearly doubled the initial plan, the proportion remained at 50 percent.

Conflict

Despite the consensus of support in official circles, the scope and nature of the changes wrought by such a "groundbreaking experiment in the deconcentration of poverty," as the *Hollman* agreement was called, generated significant community opposition. The conflict was manifested in two ways. First, a portion of the Southeast Asian community, recent immigrants to the region, opposed the demolition of the community and feared the destruction of support networks so important to their transition to American life. Second, residents contested the model of poverty deconcentration that centered on the loss of affordable housing, the potential for gentrification, and the resulting "redefinition" of the north side neighborhood.

The first argument never became more than a low background hum because the new Southeast Asian community lacked political power. The other argument, however, became a major obstacle for the parties involved in the lawsuit as it engaged representatives of the African-American community on the north side and was swept along by changes in the city and regional housing markets in the late 1990s.

Opposition from Southeast Asians

The opposition to demolition and dispersal from the Southeast Asian community on the north side was based on three complaints: dispersal of families had destroyed their community networks, they had not been full partners in the negotiations process, and the relocation process had not been sensitive to their needs. This opposition to deconcentration had been voiced fairly early in the process. A 1995 study of housing preferences discussed by the focus groups had indicated that close to half the surveyed residents did not want to move out, a sentiment much more common among Southeast Asian families—especially the Hmong—than among other groups. The beginning of Sumner Field relocations in December 1995 triggered a response among some Southeast Asian residents, who hired an attorney to represent them. The focus groups' "Community Speak Up" on April 4, 1996, elicited critical comments from community members about the process. The official minutes from the meeting indicate "the majority of Southeast Asians who spoke made it clear they did not want to move to the suburbs" (MPHA 1997, 3).

LOSS OF COMMUNITY

Southeast Asian families living in north side public housing were more likely than African-American families to like it and to value the community resources and support networks that had been created in the area. Deconcentration opponents among these families argued that dispersal would destroy the networks upon which they, as recent immigrants, depended. These networks existed on two dimensions. First were the formal assistance organizations and service agencies on the north side, including the Hmong American Mutual Assistance Association, the Lao Assistance Center of Minnesota, and the Southeast Asian Community Council. In addition, the north side site was home to an array of social services established over time to assist public housing residents, including a food shelf, adult education, and language services.

The second dimension comprised family networks. According to a report by the Southeast Asian Community Council, dispersal potentially reduced the "influence of extended families and clans on the behavior and values of Hmong teenagers, already at risk. . . . When families must move away from Sumner-Olson, social order will disappear." The report went on to claim that "with the demolition of public housing, young people will be even more isolated. They will be harder to reach, harder to teach" (Inskip 1996).

Additionally, there were concerns in the community that the local housing market did not have enough larger units to accommodate the typically large immigrant family. One Hmong woman commented, "Five-bedroom apartments are virtually nonexistent outside of public housing. I'm worried that I would not find a place big enough for my family" (Washington and Drew 1995). The *Star Tribune* carried dramatic quotes from one Hmong woman who, according to a story, "bought a rope and plans to hang herself if she has to move. 'Here I can see the sky. Here, when I feel sad, I can walk to friends or the park and relieve my sadness.' " The same article quoted another as saying, "It would be better to be dead and be living with the Americans in the cemetery" (Furst 1996b).

"LACK OF CONSENT"

A second complaint voiced by at least some in the Southeast Asian community was that they had not been adequately consulted during the lawsuit negotiations and that the settlement did not represent their interests. Some representatives of the Southeast Asian residents suggested that not enough members of the plaintiff class were included in the focus group process (Bauerlein 1996). Another claim suggested that the many Southeast Asian residents who could not read even in their own language were unable to benefit from any of the notices that were sent, regardless of the language used. "It was a class action suit without the involvement of the class," claimed the director of the Minnesota Tenants Union. The ex-director of the Hmong American Mutual Assistance Association added, "There's no consent. It was a misnamed consent decree" (Furst 1997).

TROUBLES IN THE RELOCATION PROCESS

A third area of concern for the Southeast Asian community was the process of relocation. In April 1996, the director of the Lao Assistance Center of Minnesota reported that a number of families moved without relocation assistance because they did not understand the process and were not given enough information about it (Bauerlein 1996). An Urban Coalition study of the Sumner Field relocation supports that notion. The study documents that a portion of those relocated felt they were not given enough information about the process or were hurried through it. In most cases, it was Southeast Asian families that reported these responses.

The report found that "more than half of the Hmong respondents did not want to move" from their north side units (Urban Coalition 1997). One in five (22 percent) respondents felt they had been pressured and rushed out of the Sumner Field apartments. All of the respondents so reporting were Hmong. "Hmong households reported much greater difficulty finding new housing than members of other ethnic groups," according to the report. Hmong respondents were less likely to report having been assisted with transportation during the relocation process, having received necessary relocation information, or having been treated respectfully.

THE FIRST PROTESTS
In May 1996, members of the Southeast Asian community protested their relocation in the first public opposition to the *Hollman* redevelopment. A group of 30 marched through the Sumner Field project, carrying signs announcing their complaints about being rushed out of their units and being widely scattered and isolated as a result of the process (Bauerlein 1996). A group of the protesters pleaded their case to the mayor, and in early June, the then-president of the Minneapolis Urban Coalition announced he was joining them to request a delay in the relocation of residents who did not want to move (Furst 1996b). This effort generated little momentum, however, and no delay in the redevelopment.

More than a year later, in July 1997, more than 100 Hmong submitted a formal request to presiding U.S. District Court Judge James Rosenbaum, asking that the case be reopened because of dispersal's negative impacts on their community. Judge Rosenbaum declined their request, and the relocation and demolition continued. In time, reaction from the Southeast Asian community died away, as more of their members were relocated away from the site.

Beginning the Debate on Deconcentration

Despite the scope of the *Hollman* decree and the brief resistance of some in the Southeast Asian community, for many months the redevelopment plan remained below the radar screen of many community activists. While the focus groups were deliberating, and for most of the period during which the action plan was being created, the project did not receive much media attention. There was, in fact, not much for the media to report; families were being moved out, but the site itself remained untouched, and there were no visible signs of change.

Sumner Field residents were relocated in the summer of 1996, the last family moving out in September. Then the Minneapolis Public Housing Authority decided in late 1996 to demolish the nearby Bryant High Rises, two buildings containing 188 units for elderly public housing residents and located on the east side of the 73-acre project site. MPHA had estimated that the rehabilitation cost for the Bryants was within 10 percent of their replacement cost. Under new, federal HOPE VI guidelines, the local housing authority could in such cases move for demolition and partial replacement combined with a shift in subsidies to tenant-based Section 8. This is what MPHA proposed for the Bryants: replacement of about 100 units and conversion of 88 subsidies into tenant-based certificates and vouchers (Brandt 1996). In January 1997, HUD approved the demolition, and relocation of households from the Bryants began. The buildings were empty by June. Demolition of the Olson Townhomes began September 16; the Bryants were torn down a week later.

Opponents delayed demolition of the empty Sumner Field units, however, by requesting historic preservation. As mentioned earlier in the chapter, Sumner Field was one of the earliest public housing projects in the nation, completed under a temporary initiative that actually preceded the public housing program established in 1937. The National Advisory Council on Historic Preservation ruled that some of the Sumner Field buildings could and should be reviewed for possible preservation. (The others, located on poor soils, were excluded from the council's ruling.) In the end, historic status was denied, but demolition was delayed for several months while the request was being considered.

The Affordable-Housing Crisis

In the summer of 1997, as MPHA staff was finalizing the draft Action Plan, the city's affordable-housing crisis began to emerge. Advocates organized around the issue and their efforts led to City Council consideration of the Niland resolution (see chapter 5) and formation of the Mayor's Task Force on Affordable Housing.

The mayor's task force was the scene of a protracted debate about deconcentrating poverty. A sizable number of participants saw a great need for affordable housing in Minneapolis and were motivated to meet that need. State Representative Myron Orfield, who spoke to the task force, argued against more affordable housing in the city precisely because he felt it would further the centralization of resources that leads to a concentration of poor families in the central city. Orfield and powell continued to argue for a strong statement by the city in favor of a regional approach. This episode is important for the unfolding *Hollman* story because a group of low-income housing advocates, previously muted before the appeal of the deconcentration of poverty argument and the Detroit Scenario, began to find its voice on this issue.

Opposition to Poverty Deconcentration

Advocates in the affordable-housing campaign had been fighting rearguard actions against the demolition of existing affordable housing for several years. They began to put together this experience with the growing acceptance by local officials and neighborhood groups of the concentration-of-poverty argument. Housing advocates attributed the loss of two apartment buildings in Saint Paul, the threatened demolition of more than 1,000 units in the inner-ring suburb of Brooklyn Park, and the growing reluctance of Minneapolis neighborhood groups to create affordable housing to the logic of deconcentration of poverty. Central-city neighborhood groups had begun talking about how they had provided their share of low-cost housing and how it was time for the suburbs to do more. Inner-ring suburban communities moved to demolish affordable units, arguing that they, too, had an over-concentration. Housing advocates came to see *Hollman* as another example of a loose and uncoordinated, but no less threatening, movement to reduce affordable housing in the city in the name of deconcentrating poverty. They felt that in the midst of what was becoming a severe affordable-housing shortage, the *Hollman* decree meant the loss of several hundred more units of low-cost housing. As one of the organizers later wrote, their "goal was not only to organize the community to stop or delay further demolition, but to make affordable housing a public policy priority, by exposing the devastating effects of demolition and the lack of affordable housing on real people" (Watson 2000, 1). In other words, it was time in their minds to wed the affordable housing campaign to the *Hollman* issue.

North side service agencies and other interested parties began to meet in September 1998, several months after the plaintiffs had approved the action plan. This group, the Hollman/North Minneapolis Human Development Coalition, met "to ensure meaningful community participation in the planning, implementation, and evaluation of the community development of the Near Northside of Minneapolis."[3] This coalition included representatives from several community centers in the neighborhood, the Harrison Neighborhood Association, two Southeast Asian community groups, Summit Academy, and the Jobs and Affordable Housing Campaign.

One of the issues the coalition discussed was how the *Hollman* redevelopment fit into other city plans for the larger community. The city's planning documents envisioned a larger-scale remake of the north side community. Plans included the possible removal or renovation of four nearby low-income apartment buildings that did not "fit in with the proposed mixed-income housing to be built" on the *Hollman* site (Brandt 1998).

NORTHSIDE NEIGHBORS FOR JUSTICE
In December 1998, a new group grew out of the coalition meetings. The Northside Neighbors for Justice (NNJ) was created through the efforts of organizers at Children and Family Services, and joined with organizing efforts being undertaken by MICAH. Jewish Community Action, another partner in the affordable-housing campaign of the previous summer, also became involved in the NNJ effort. Shortly after NNJ was formed, MICAH organized the Northside Pastors group to gain its perspective on the *Hollman* issue.

NNJ's position evolved over time from general demands for living wages, affordable housing, and "meaningful involvement in decisions that affect our lives" to very specific demands about the north side public housing projects. As its position evolved, NNJ did a very effective job of communicating its opinions throughout the north side community and to city officials (primarily Council President Jackie Cherryhomes and Mayor Sharon Sayles Belton). Coalition members were aided in this by one of the African-American newspapers with wide circulation on the city's north side, the *Minnesota Spokesman-Recorder*. The *Spokesman* began running a regular column called "The *Hollman* Forum," which was not so much a forum as the direct mouthpiece of NNJ. It was written by a housing advocate who had been active in the JAHC campaign and was also part of NNJ. Thus, from the end of December 1998 and for several very active months thereafter, the paper carried prominent articles on *Hollman* that outlined the NNJ position in great detail. The accuracy of the claims in the forum did not always match the enthusiasm with which they were made, as Legal Aid attorneys felt compelled to submit corrections on more than one occasion.

The other main African-American newspaper, the *Insight News,* also based in the north side, was just as self-consciously supportive of the city. Throughout the next 18 months, the *Insight News* carried prominent articles on the redevelopment issue by the mayor and Council President Cherryhomes. It also carried articles describing the families' positive experiences in relocating to better neighborhoods. The volume of supportive stories in the *Insight News,* however, came nowhere near to matching the regular barrage of criticism carried by the *Spokesman.*

NNJ and the opposition movement also benefited from exposure through KMOJ, the north side community–based radio station. KMOJ, though not as editorially explicit about its opposition to redevelopment as the *Spokesman,* did provide various opportunities for critics and supporters alike to discuss their perspectives. Council President Cherryhomes appeared several times on the station's public policy forum throughout 1999 and 2000, as did john powell and several members of the NNJ coalition.

The *Insight News* and KMOJ together sponsor a community forum at the popular north side restaurant Lucille's Kitchen, located just over a mile from the heart of the redevelopment site. This location serves as yet another venue for community discussion. A portion of each forum is aired live over KMOJ. Throughout early 1999, the *Hollman* redevelopment and the deconcentration-of-poverty argument were regularly discussed at Lucille's Kitchen. Typically, the crowd at the forum tipped in favor of the NNJ position.

NNJ engaged the *Hollman* process from a series of positions that questioned virtually all aspects of the consent decree and the redevelopment. NNJ fought the underlying principle of deconcentration, suggesting that it undervalued the assets that existed in poor neighborhoods and embodied a discredited, "urban renewal" approach to problems of urban poverty. Second, coalition members organized against the forced displacement and relocation of families living in the Sumner Field and Glenwood units. In this, NNJ was reacting to reports of continuing problems in the relocation process and the negative experiences of some of those families that were being forcefully moved. Finally, NNJ opposed the further demolition of units on the north side as an ill-conceived venture in the midst of a severe housing crisis.

Deconcentration and Gentrification

Most significantly, NNJ became the first group to publicly question the deconcentration-of-poverty approach and the Detroit Scenario. Coalition members found what the plaintiffs' lawyers had agreed to in the consent decree to be insulting. The consent decree identified neighborhoods as "minority-concentrated" if more than 29 percent of the population was nonwhite. As one African-American activist asked, "Are they telling me that I shouldn't live in a neighborhood where 30 percent of my neighbors are like me?" For its part, NNJ looked around the north side and saw a neighborhood with a great deal of diversity and a number of community assets that were worth protecting, rather than a monolithically poor and devastated community. NNJ saw an African-American community with a long tradition and history, rather than a neighborhood needing to be remade by the city. The very first "*Hollman* Forum" in the *Spokesman* expressed this view about deconcentration: "Is this a wise strategy for reducing the residential segregation or is it a convenient way to get these people off that property? Who is the *Hollman* enterprise really for?" (*Minnesota Spokesman-Recorder* 1998).

The distrust of deconcentration motives among opposition groups was tied to a concern that the redevelopment of the project site was the first wedge in the city's gentrification strategy. To these groups, the effort to demolish the Sumner Field and Glenwood homes and replace them with mainly market-rate housing was a land grab, an effort to expand the renaissance occurring in the adjacent warehouse district that stood between the project site and downtown. In effect, NNJ and other groups began to assert that they wanted the north side to remain hospitable to middle- and lower-income families of color; they believed the redevelopment plans would not permit this. One of NNJ's organizing sheets inviting people to a 1999 meeting quoted directly from City Council President Jackie Cherryhomes, before adding its own twist (see figure 6.1).

Concerns for gentrification and displacement of current residents increased when news spread that the city was considering the demolition and disposition of other subsidized housing projects surrounding the redevelopment site. The CityView, Park View, and Cecil Newman apartments, accounting for close to 600 units of affordable housing, sit just north and west of the project site. As 1999 came, it became clear that the city envisioned the north side redevelopment as part of a larger plan for the entire Bassett Creek area, and potentially a new gateway to downtown

*Figure 6.1. Excerpt from Northside
Neighbors for Justice Community Flyer*

"Five years from now the drive down
Olson Highway will look much different
than it does today.

New parks, ponds and playfields. . .
Mixed income housing . . .
Jobs and training . . ."

**TOO BAD YOU WON'T BE
HERE TO ENJOY IT.**

Minneapolis from the west. NNJ quickly called the alarm in an effort to protect these other affordable units and to expand its organizing base. The quick response by NNJ and other groups forced the city to beat a hasty retreat from those demolition plans.

The Problems of Relocation and Displacement

NNJ also wished to publicize more widely the adverse experiences of many displaced households. By the end of 1998, more than 300 families had been relocated from the project site, and NNJ felt that many had been disadvantaged by the process. The Urban Coalition study of relocation, which had been released in 1997, provided some evidence of problems. Some families felt they had been rushed out of their units; others felt they had not been given enough information about their options.

NNJ used these experiences to attempt to undermine public confidence in the entire deconcentration strategy. By documenting significant dysfunction in relocation, NNJ could raise more concern about the intrusiveness of the north side redevelopment process. Problems in relocation also helped symbolize how poor families (those for which the lawsuit was filed in the first place) had, in NNJ's view, come to be pawns in a much larger conflict over land and the future of the city's near north side.

NNJ's biggest impact occurred in February 1999 when organizers obtained an MPHA interoffice memo tracing the relocation experiences of the 17 plaintiffs in the original *Hollman* complaint. The memo indicated that several of the plaintiffs were homeless, and that MPHA had lost contact with others.

The messages from NNJ and other opponents of redevelopment gained their greatest currency in the context of the city's growing affordable-housing crisis. As the crisis developed, it became the focus of these organizers and, ultimately, the focus of legal efforts to stop the demolition. In fact, halting further demolition of public housing on the site became the principal objective of NNJ and the other activist groups. Stopping it would achieve a series of objectives for the opponents: It would halt the need for continued relocation of residents, it would stop further depletion of the affordable housing stock, and it would stall the redevelopment process in general. The activists came to realize that once the units came down, most of their fight would be lost, and any leverage they might have over the city would be gone.

The Minneapolis NAACP

The Minneapolis NAACP's shifting position on the issue was the unlikeliest aspect of the political battle over deconcentration. A co-plaintiff and partner with Legal Aid in the original lawsuit, the NAACP abandoned its support of the north side redevelopment and moved to stop the demolition of the public housing on site before the issue was finally resolved. The political contortions performed by the Minneapolis NAACP clearly illustrate the tensions over this issue within the north side and African-American communities, and symbolize the larger political divides generated by the deconcentration-of-poverty approach.

In 1992, the Minneapolis NAACP, under the leadership of Matt Little and Bill Davis, longtime allies of Mayor Sharon Sayles Belton and established leaders within the African-American community, decided to join the *Hollman* lawsuit as co-plaintiffs. The suit and negotiated settlement addressed an issue of central concern to the African-American community in Minneapolis and countless other cities—the history of segregationist and discriminatory housing policy pursued at the national and local levels. The mayor herself was a longtime member of the Minneapolis branch and the ties between her political machine and the local NAACP were strong. For many years, the Minneapolis organization had been dominated by insiders and maintained powerful connections with the mayor and the local Democratic party.

In 1996, Bill Davis lost the Minneapolis branch presidency to Leola Seals, a job counselor on the north side and an outsider to the established NAACP power structure. Seals came to office promising to take a new look at several positions the NAACP had previously taken. In the end, she oversaw a dramatic change in organizational strategy. Under Seals, the NAACP directly confronted and challenged the mayor on three important fronts. First, it continued to advocate a 1995 school desegregation suit against the state that had been filed under the previous regime. Seals's NAACP broadened its attack, however, to include the city's policy of returning to community schools. The organization packed several school board meetings throughout 1996 and 1997 and loudly disrupted the proceedings, demanding that its issues be addressed. This change in tactics was controversial for an organization that previously had pursued its objectives in a lower-profile, behind-the-scenes manner.

Second, the NAACP under Seals's direction was vocal in its reaction to the Minneapolis Police Department's CODEFOR program. The NAACP labeled this computer-directed, anticrime initiative racially discriminatory because of its focus on minor offenses committed by African-American males in core city neighborhoods. Finally, under Seals, the organization modified its role in the *Hollman* lawsuit. Initially, the Seals-led NAACP focused on channeling redevelopment resources to the community. Seals's lieutenants, who were watching the redevelopment process, were anxious to monitor the flow of funds. Their objective, at least initially, was to see that local residents benefited. The organization openly questioned whether the city could be trusted to spend the settlement funds in the best manner. Citing the need to ensure that redevelopment benefits reach the families directly affected, the NAACP in 1998 requested $23 million from the settlement funds that it would put into housing and employment efforts aimed at the site's public housing residents and neighbors (Brunswick 1999).

These three visible and controversial stands put the NAACP in direct conflict with two of the most prominent African-American officials in the city—the mayor and newly appointed school superintendent Carol Johnson. The NAACP's new position also triggered an opposition slate of candidates for the branch's November 1998 election. Because of disputes over the eligibility of some of the challenging candidates, the election was postponed until January 1999, at which time Seals lost to Minneapolis firefighter Rickie Campbell by 16 votes. The state NAACP then suspended the results because of disputes over the eligibility of candidates and some of the votes. Seals remained president until the dispute was resolved in Campbell's favor.

During this time, Seals began writing articles for the *Spokesman-Recorder's* "*Hollman* Forum" in which she made a series of strong claims about the settlement and how it was being implemented. Her articles dramatically escalated the NAACP's criticism of the decree. Seals claimed that the NAACP's co-plaintiff, Legal Aid, had effectively abandoned its representation of the class, and "bent over backwards to accommodate city officials" during the implementation process (Seals 1998). In various articles in the column, Seals sounded the alarm on gentrification, wrote about the potential loss of additional subsidized housing in projects surrounding the *Hollman* site, and returned to the organization's main theme during her tenure—channeling settlement resources back into the community. She complained that although the plaintiff class was "99 percent people of color, white people controlled all the money and the community planning process." Seals also wrote about the absence of people of color from the planning process and about the money set aside for training site residents for jobs produced by the project and businesses formed in the redevelopment process.

While the NAACP's internal dispute became an ever-greater preoccupation in early 1999, it disappeared for a time from the public debate over *Hollman*. The national NAACP sent an administrator to monitor branch operations while the election dispute was resolved. Thus preoccupied, the NAACP was absent when the opposition campaign took off in February, unrepresented when the implementation committee interviewed three competing developers in March, and missing from two important demonstrations opposing redevelopment in June and July.

The Anti-*Hollman* Campaign

On February 16, 1999, Lucille's Kitchen was packed with people to hear the forum on the north side redevelopment. With Council President Jackie Cherryhomes and MPHA Executive Director Cora McCorvey in the audience, the panel included one spokesman from NNJ, another from JAHC, and an attorney for Legal Aid. The growing controversy over relocation and redevelopment had put the Legal Aid attorneys in an unexpected position. They had entered into the suit almost a decade earlier in an attempt to force redress for decades of housing discrimination that the Minneapolis African-American community had experienced. As noted earlier, Legal Aid attorneys had not originally sued with the intention of deconcentrating poverty. In the end, however, they had a settlement that was, essentially, a poster child for national deconcentration efforts, and one that they felt included significant benefits for the plaintiff class as well as the north side community. When the redevelopment issue blew up in 1998 and 1999, Legal Aid's position in the political terrain shifted significantly, even though it had not changed its views at all. Instead of being viewed as a defender of the community, and the organization that had helped make the city, the Met Council, and the federal government accountable for past transgressions, Legal Aid—in the eyes of the redevelopment opponents—was perceived as partnering with the city, MPHA, and HUD in trying to foist an anti-community, resettlement, and gentrification plan upon unwilling residents. Redevelopment protesters questioned even the fees charged by Legal Aid and speculated about whether the organization was actually representing the city and the developers instead of its low-income clients.[4] Thus, it must have been with some trepidation that Tom Streitz, a Legal Aid attorney involved in the suit, took his seat as a member of the February 16 panel at Lucille's Kitchen.

Opponents focused on the gentrification issue. As one attendee asked, "Have you noticed the beautiful view of downtown from where the rowhouses used to be? Who do you suppose will enjoy that beautiful view when this project is completed?" (*Minnesota Spokesman-Recorder* 1999c). In many respects, this was a logical focus for such a meeting. The public policy forums at Lucille's were and continue to be a north side tradition. Lucille's and the *Insight News*/KMOJ Community Forum are institutions within the city's north side African-American community. They recall for all who are present or listening on the radio the decades-long claim that the African-American community has to that part of Minneapolis.

The focus on gentrification also made sense because relocation issues had receded as the 1996 Sumner and Olson resettlements became more distant, and scheduled demolition of the remaining units in the Glenwood and Lyndale projects was still several months away. Thus, Travis Lee, a panelist and member of NNJ, claimed, "It's still a mystery to most people just who will benefit most from the millions invested in this project" (Brandt 1999e). To a neighborhood subjected to massive urban renewal and redevelopment projects for 60 years, the meaning of this statement was perfectly clear. It expressed residents' two major fears in the face of large-scale redevelopment. First, as voiced by NAACP officials in the Seals faction, community members feared that outsiders would control redevelopment, do all the work, and receive most of the benefit of the millions of dollars dedicated to redevelopment and the jobs and new business opportunities it created. Even more central was the second fear—a fear that when the dust cleared, anyone looking around at the residents of this brand new development, with its park amenity, its link to the Guthrie Theater and Loring Park neighborhoods to the south, and its $200,000 homes, would see the faces of outsiders.

For his part, Streitz defended Legal Aid's position. He noted that the organization had threatened to take the city back to court when the city council had attempted to reduce the percentage of affordable housing in the redevelopment (*Minnesota Spokesman-Recorder* 1999c). He also assured the crowd that Legal Aid was continuing to monitor the relocation process and see that all families were provided adequate services. No accommodations between the parties were made that morning at Lucille's. Council President Cherryhomes and MPHA Director McCorvey sat silently in the audience. The battle lines, as it were, were becoming ever more clear.

From this point forward, the campaign to alter redevelopment plans hit high gear, and the city became embroiled in front-page controversy that lasted for many months. In February, NNJ leaders came upon that internal MPHA e-mail outlining the status of the original 17 plaintiffs. According to the memo, three plaintiff families were homeless at the time, and at least two others, and possibly a third, had been evicted from their new homes. Two additional plaintiffs were no longer in communication with MPHA, their status unknown. MPHA later claimed the memo was an erroneous draft, and city officials accused affordable-housing advocates of stealing the document (Furst 1999). Nevertheless, it refocused advocates' attention on relocation. Furthermore, the advocates made great use out of the memo, as well as a Legal Aid statement about the status of the original plaintiffs and a subsequent statement by MPHA, each of which offered different details about the fate of the original plaintiffs.

The campaign in the *Spokesman* picked up momentum, with multiple stories in each edition. In March 1999, the *Spokesman* devoted an entire edition to the *Hollman* redevelopment, in which it reprinted previous stories and added some new ones. In it, a letter from eight Hmong residents of the Glenwood and Lyndale projects called the redevelopment another "Secret War" against their people, a reference to the secret U.S. bombing of Hmong territory in Laos during the Vietnam War. Referring both to the wartime barrage of U.S. bombs and the city's redevelopment plans, the writers asked, "Why did we find ourselves in the middle of all this? Because we were living on strategically important land, land that other people wanted to take from us" (Vang et al. 1999).

The special edition also contained statements by NNJ, reprints of the articles written by Leola Seals, and a statement from residents of the nearby Park Plaza apartments opposing the potential demolition of their building as part of the city's larger plan for the north side area. A small item under the headline, "*Hollman* Cover-up Alleged," summarized the controversy over the e-mail memo. A letter to the editor from Jackie Cherryhomes defended the redevelopment plans. Contrary to the *Spokesman*'s normal circulation procedure of newsstand distribution only, thousands of copies were distributed door to door throughout the north side.

In April, NNJ organized a march outside MPHA headquarters at which about 50 to 80 protesters decried the displacement of families from the north side. The Reverend Curtis Herron, pastor of Zion Baptist Church in north Minneapolis and a member of the Northside Pastors group, likened the resettlement to the "ethnic cleansing" that had been receiving worldwide attention in 1998 during the Bosnian conflict. The protesters again mentioned the MPHA memo and produced one of the original plaintiffs, who described her housing travails after relocation. The plaintiff, Earline Robinson, reported she had been periodically homeless after leaving the north side projects, and had only recently found an apartment (Furst 1999). Robinson, in fact, had left the projects well before the relocation services were in place, and thus did not receive any assistance in her moves. NNJ called for an independent investigation of family relocations.

In response to the protesters' claims, the lead attorney for Legal Aid explained, "At the time we settled the lawsuit, in 1995, the vacancy rate [for apartments in the Twin Cities] was 6 or 7 percent, which was quite healthy, and no one could have anticipated that we would now be dealing with a vacancy rate of 1 percent" (Furst 1999). This was acknowledgment of perhaps the single most vexing problem for those shepherding the north side redevelopment. The growing acuteness of the affordable-housing crisis over the next few months would throw their efforts to demolish public housing into a completely different and much more difficult context. The affordable-housing shortage and the difficulty relocatees were experiencing in using household-based Section 8 certificates in the suburbs (a Legal Aid attorney at the Lucille's Kitchen community forum in December had likened the certificates to confederate money

[*Minnesota Spokesman-Recorder* 1999c]) brought together all three of the opposition's issues. Relocation and assistance for displaced families were of prime importance in a market so difficult for low-income house- holds. The demolition of more than 300 more units of subsidized low- income housing in the Glenwood and Lyndale projects, on top of the more than 350 already demolished on the site, seemed to make much less sense in light of the region's critical shortage of low-cost housing. Concerns over the possible gentrification of the site also gained potency when combined with the affordable-housing crisis. Where, if not on the north side, were these low-income families going to live? And, given rapidly escalating housing prices in the region and on the north side itself, fears of gentrifi- cation were much more realistic in 1999 than they had been even two years earlier.

The housing crisis also handed redevelopment opponents yet one more issue in their fight—the excruciatingly slow pace of replacement-housing construction. This was an issue on which Legal Aid readily agreed with the redevelopment opponents. Though the defendants had moved quickly to demolish the Sumner and Olson projects, though they were emptying the Glenwood and Lyndale projects and relocating those families as well, and though they were proceeding to identify a developer to manage the north side site redevelopment, they were making very little headway in con- structing the more than 700 units of replacement housing called for in the settlement. By June 1999, more than four years after the signing of the consent decree, only 47 replacement units had been built, and 8 of them were in a non-impacted part of north Minneapolis. At that rate, the replacement units would not all be in place until roughly 2050.

For all that, progress in replacement housing was slow for several com- pelling reasons. MPHA had no authority to build outside of Minneapo- lis, and had to rely upon the voluntary cooperation of other agencies. The consent decree limited the number of "*Hollman* units" within a given housing development to no more than 10 percent, a provision that, while designed to prevent further concentrations, effectively required many separate developments and agreements. Many suburban jurisdictions were not anxious to take these units; many had no housing development agency in place to carry out such development. The Metropolitan Coun- cil had agreed to step in and facilitate the development of *Hollman* units in suburban areas without a housing development agency, but dragged its feet for more than a year before mounting a serious effort (see chapter 7). As valid and vexing as each of these obstacles was, they were relatively unimportant in the overall political conflict erupting over the north side redevelopment. The pertinent facts for many people were that the defendants had moved swiftly to displace and relocate low-income families from the north side, but seemed to be making almost no progress in building suitable replacement housing for these families elsewhere. "Wouldn't it have made more sense," argued one advocate, "to build new units and then demolish? Wouldn't it have shown more consideration for these families if they could have moved right from their Northside homes into *Hollman* funded replacement housing? Instead, they have been relocated into apartments other people desperately need in a rental market so tight it's about to bust" (*Minnesota Spokesman-Recorder* 1999b).

Redevelopment efforts suffered more public relations difficulties when the city's major newspaper, the *Star Tribune*, ran a story on Lucy Mae Hollman, the plaintiff by whom the entire lawsuit and redevelopment effort was known (Brandt 1999f). Hollman had originally been relocated into scattered-site public housing. She moved from there with a tenant-based Section 8 voucher. Unable to keep that apartment, she purchased a home in the north side Hawthorne neighborhood. In that transaction, however, she became the victim of a "flip." A flip is a real estate swindle in which the scam-operator purchases a home and immediately resells it at an inflated price to an inexperienced homebuyer. In Hollman's case, the seller had held the property for two years. However, he had paid only $7,000 for it and had taken out permits for $3,600 worth of improvements. The assessor valued the property at $43,000. Hollman, who said she never saw an appraisal, paid $80,000 for the house. After an illness, she fell behind on her inflated payments. In May 1999, when the story was printed, she was in the process of losing her home through foreclosure. Had Hollman kept current on her home payments, however, she still would have been displaced, because the city was in the process of demolishing all the homes on her block to build a new school. The story illustrated for the opponents virtually all of what they wanted to say about the deconcentration efforts. Hollman, the person for whom the suit was known, and therefore the personification of the displaced low-income resident, had bounced around the housing market for years after being displaced from public housing. Her inexperience and earning power (made fragile by both her low-wage job and her health problems) had exposed her to a housing market that was without mercy.

As summer came, enough families had been moved out of Glenwood and Lyndale that demolition there could begin. The imminent demolition brought the controversy to its peak. On June 8, demolition crews arrived and began working. Sensing that the demolition would attract protesters, the MPHA had not announced the date. Learning of the planned demolition only the night before, opponents quickly assembled at the site and attempted to stop the bulldozers. Fourteen protesters were arrested, including eight prominent ministers from north side churches. After the arrests, a group of protesters went to city hall and demanded a halt to the demolition. Upon hearing their arguments, Mayor Sayles Belton agreed to a temporary interruption. By this time, however, one building already had a gaping hole through it, the width of a bulldozer. Further demolition had stopped when workers discovered that the hydraulic hoses on a backhoe had been slashed. After a quick arraignment and release on bail, the protesters gathered at Lucille's Kitchen where an *Insight News/ KMOJ* Public Policy forum was in progress. As the *Spokesman* later reported, "The events of the morning had already been broadcast by KMOJ and the Lucille's crowd gave a warm welcome to those who had volunteered for arrest. . . . A collection on the spot was taken to pay their fines" (*Minnesota Spokesman-Recorder* 1999a).

The mayor halted the demolition so the parties could begin to discuss alternative scenarios for the Glenwood/Lyndale units (Diaz 1999i). The African-American Leadership Summit and the Council of Black Churches, two groups with stronger ties to the mayor, entered the fray with their own plan for redevelopment. Their recommendations, entitled "The Whole Man Way," called for a moratorium on demolition pending more progress on replacement-housing development. The plan also called for more affordable-housing units to be put back on the north side site than the city council had agreed to.

Meanwhile, NNJ and others began to urge the temporary reuse of the vacated Glenwood/Lyndale units and even, possibly, their permanent rescue from demolition. At this point, the NAACP came out of its shell. Its long internal leadership dispute had finally ended, and, although Leola Seals's term was over, the momentum of community opposition to the *Hollman* demolition was too great for the organization to ignore, even if it had wanted to. Furthermore, there is evidence that even despite the election of a more conciliatory NAACP governing board, a majority of active members had come to view the *Hollman* redevelopment with misgivings. In the NAACP's first official statement about *Hollman* in months, the group's attorney expressed his concern with "the disruption and the gutting of the North Side's black community" (Diaz 1999h).

By unilaterally stopping the demolition, the mayor, who had stepped into the middle of this conflict with her June 8 action, had actually put the city in violation of the decree and thereby made it legally vulnerable. Furthermore, it became clear early on that she had little power to force the other defendants to change their actions and resolve the dispute that was raging in her city and within her constituency.

The mayor did, however, pledge more aggressive city action in developing replacement housing within the city limits. The decree had called for at least 88 units to be built in non-concentrated neighborhoods in Minneapolis, but, with the exception of a single development on the north side, nothing had been done in the four years since the agreement had been signed. Shortly after halting the demolition, the mayor announced that the city would create 74 new, scattered-site public housing replacement units by April 2000 (Diaz 1999h). Combined with the 14 units that were already up or in advanced planning, the city would thus fully meet its obligation of 88 units. While affordable-housing advocates welcomed this action, it did not do much to ameliorate the political crisis. This was the one issue, after all, about which everyone agreed—the pace of replacement-housing development had been far too slow. The mayor's announcement broke no new ground and did not address the critical issue—the fate of public housing at Glenwood and Lyndale, and the future of the entire 73-acre north side site.

On the issue of saving, even temporarily, the remaining public housing, the prospects of achieving an agreeable resolution were slim. Most of the units were vacant by June 1999 and, in preparation for demolition, many had been systematically stripped of their internal systems and amenities. Furthermore, all forms of regular maintenance had been suspended for months. All this had left the units uninhabitable without significant rehabilitation.

Mayor Sayles Belton had strong ties to the Clinton administration and a close relationship with HUD officials. Thus, advocates held out some hope that she might be able to use that influence to wriggle rehabilitation funds from HUD—funds that would make Glenwood and Lyndale habitable again, at least in the short term. However, HUD had been pursuing similar strategies of demolition and redevelopment all across the country, and the *Hollman* way was HUD's way. HUD quickly indicated that it would not provide funds to rehabilitate the Glenwood/Lyndale units.

On July 9, the city's north side implementation group recommended a large increase in the number of housing units to be rebuilt on the north side site—from the original 450 to 750. The implementation committee also capped the market-rate units at 50 percent. This action significantly increased the number of low- and moderate-income housing units planned for the site, and was a bow to both pressure from the housing advocates and the realities of the housing shortage. This move, supported by housing advocates, was called a "retreat from the *Hollman* mandate of deconcentrating poverty," by one planning commissioner, who worried it might "choke off demand for the market-rate housing" to be built on site (Diaz 1999c).

Meanwhile, pressure from the redevelopment opponents drove the mayor to make a trip to Washington, D.C., and appeal personally for rehabilitation funds to save the remaining public housing units. Once again, HUD officials turned her down. The mayor returned saying that the agency would put no new money into the projects and had given her 60 days to find new funding to save the Lyndale units. Even if she were successful, according to HUD, the Lyndale units still would have to be demolished nine months later, by April 2000. It is unclear under what authority HUD could have given the mayor such a deadline, since the district court, and not HUD, had the final say in *Hollman*-related activities. HUD did agree to continue providing operating and rent subsidies until the units were demolished, an obligation so fundamental that it did not qualify as much of a concession.

The trip to Washington, however, did give the mayor some needed political cover. She was able to demonstrate her efforts to save the units and point to the intransigence of her federal partners as the chief obstacle. She came back with a short deadline, however ambiguously claimed, and the news that, even if successful, reoccupation of the units would only last for nine months. In addition, the mayor was reminded that demolition of the Glenwood units was necessary under any scenario to allow the redevelopment plan to go forward. As a result, the Glenwood units were taken off of the negotiating table, leaving only the 86 Lyndale units. Days later that number was reduced to just 70 units, based on an assessment of the actual number that were salvageable at that point. In a very short time, the mayor had managed to redefine (and in the process reduce) what was possible in relation to saving the Glenwood and Lyndale projects. Reoccupation would only be temporary, if it occurred at all; no HUD funds would be made available to restore the units; and only 70 out of more than 300 units still standing were even under consideration.

Opponents kept up their pressure, nonetheless. By the end of July, the mayor announced her plan to seek $300,000 in city money to save the 70 units. She called it a "short-term strategy based on the fact that there [was] no place for some families to find decent shelter" (Diaz 1999a). No one liked this strategy. The city council's Ways and Means Committee rejected the proposal, while the Reverend Herron of the North Side Pastors commented that "saving only the Lyndale units would not meet our needs" (Diaz 1999a). Two days later, the *Hollman* 14 appeared in court, providing another opportunity for north side protesters to rally. Close to 150 people marched outside of the Hennepin County Government Center, calling for an end to the demolition.

As July came to a close, the protesters saw few possible avenues for saving the remaining public housing units. Though the affordable-housing crisis had provided them with a platform from which to argue against demolition, the mayor by August had maneuvered so that any answer to the protesters' demands would be short-term and limited—a response to the existing difficulties of finding replacement housing for families displaced during the demolition. Overwhelming concern over the availability of affordable housing for the displaced had pushed aside the larger issues of gentrification, the future of the north side site, and the greater legitimacy of deconcentration. There were still discussions about these larger issues, to be sure. Reverend Herron continued to talk about the "immorality of gentrification," and about deconcentration as "ethnic cleansing." The policy discussion, however, centered rather narrowly on the then-current lack of affordable housing.

At an August 15 rally for the *Hollman* 14, the NAACP announced that it would begin legal action to stop the demolition. For the first time, the NAACP was participating in a public action protesting the redevelopment. Interestingly, the NAACP's reentry into the fray coincided with NNJ's decline as a major player. NNJ had inexplicably diverted some of its slender resources by combining efforts with a group opposing the expansion of Highway 55 through southeast Minneapolis, an issue of little relevance to NNJ's constituency. As NNJ faded, the NAACP became the focal point for opposition activities.

The NAACP's announcement of impending legal action was a major development, considering the organization's standing as a co-plaintiff in the suit and existing status with the court. With this petition, project opponents escalated their struggle—from political efforts to legal attempts to stop demolition. Up to this point, protesters' successes had always been subject to the court's ultimate approval to the extent that any new features modified already-agreed-to elements of the consent decree. The NAACP's move would take the issue directly to the judge. The irony is all too clear. The NAACP, a plaintiff in the original suit, was getting ready to ask the presiding judge to stop the defendants from carrying out the remedy.

In August 1999, the *Star Tribune* presented the various political positions participants had staked out. Herron and others decried the forced relocation of the poor. Bill English, leader of the African-American Leadership Summit, called for the revitalization of the north side, not a complete redevelopment. English was invoking the larger debate over whether deconcentration or community development was a better strategy for dealing with concentrations of poverty. Another north side pastor argued against the presumption that a concentration of African-Americans was, per se, a problem to be corrected. Pastor Paul Robinson of the north side Community Covenant Church was quoted as saying, "Folks of color have never had a problem living with folks of color. Somebody outside the community decided that" (Diaz 1999g).

On the other side, the mayor and council member Cherryhomes reiterated the deconcentration-of-poverty argument. The mayor suggested that deconcentrating poverty and building strong neighborhoods were legitimate policy objectives, while Cherryhomes submitted that the "hard-working people" she represented supported deconcentration (Diaz 1999g). The *Star-Tribune* itself editorialized in favor of deconcentration, noting that "plowing every dollar into affordable housing would only further concentrate poverty and perpetuate the image of Minneapolis as a client city" (*Minneapolis Star Tribune* 1999). "Plowing every dollar into affordable housing," of course, characterized none of the proposals being suggested by any of the parties. But the rhetorical effect is clear. It places the pursuit of affordable housing at odds with the pursuit of a healthy community, and states explicitly what many proponents of deconcentration sometimes find difficult to say—that deconcentrating poverty and affordable-housing strategies are, at some level, opposed to each other.

Meanwhile, events moved on, and the higher rhetoric of the deconcentration debate dissolved into an increasingly desperate and more narrowly defined attempt to save several hundred affordable-housing units to ease the city's shortage. Demolition was scheduled to resume on August 18. The day before, however, the mayor and Cherryhomes agreed to delay the demolition so the NAACP could prepare legal motions to save the remaining 200 units (Diaz 1999b). While preparing their motion, NAACP leaders met with city officials in an effort to convince these officials to reconsider their position. City officials would not change; they tried instead to get NAACP leaders to accept a "compromise" position allowing Lyndale to be saved and Glenwood torn down. As it was, the mayor had said that even if all parties agreed on this position, she did not know where the $300,000 would come from to complete the rehabilitation.

On August 28, just days before the U.S. District Court in Minneapolis was to hear the NAACP's motion, the Minneapolis branch's members voted to reaffirm their position that both the Glenwood and Lyndale units be rehabilitated (Diaz 1999e). With this vote, the members explicitly rejected the compromise that the Glenwood units be torn down. The vote made what happened several days later all the more inexplicable.

On September 2, with a crowded courtroom awaiting the hearing, attorneys from Legal Aid, the NAACP, MPHA, and HUD met in Judge Rosenbaum's private conference room and agreed to exactly the same deal that the NAACP had earlier rejected in talks with city officials, and that NAACP members had rejected five days earlier. The NAACP lawyers suggested, in announcing the agreement, that it contained several concessions they had been seeking—an accelerated pace of replacement-housing development, provisions for extended use of Section 8 vouchers by displaced families, and stronger guarantees for minority participation in the redevelopment.

Regarding these as concessions, however, is a generous interpretation. City officials, and especially the mayor, had been aware for many weeks of the city's vulnerability on the replacement-housing issue. In fact, the city had pledged to step up the rate of replacement-housing development immediately after demolition had been halted in June. Essentially reiterating the same pledge almost three months later was not much of a concession. Furthermore, allowing displaced families more time to use their Section 8 vouchers was a minor administrative move easily accomplished. In fact, in such a tight housing market, it was unlikely to make much difference. Finally, stronger guarantees for minority participation, while a laudable goal and perhaps shared by many redevelopment opponents, were in fact a primary objective only for the NAACP. Minority participation in the redevelopment was not of principal interest to NNJ, MICAH, or the Northside Pastors. In fact, there was something ironic about this item because it regarded the demolition and redevelopment as a *fait accompli*, and merely allowed for the community's participation in the action. NNJ and the Northside Pastors had been looking to, in some sense, "save" a portion of their community, something quite different from assuring that "the community" would be allowed to participate financially in its own dissolution. The lawyers emerged from the judge's office announcing that the deal had to be ratified by HUD, the Met Council, the City, and the NAACP before it became effective.

As for the embarrassing fact that NAACP members had already voted down essentially this same agreement, proponents of redevelopment within the organization questioned the validity of both the vote (the vote had been 15 to 10 in an organization with just over 1,000 members) and the meeting at which it was taken (both the mayor and Council President Cherryhomes, members of the NAACP, claimed they had never received notice of the meeting). Furthermore, it was unclear to NAACP members whether the general membership or just the executive council had the right to approve or reject the deal (Diaz 1999e).

On September 18, the city council ratified the agreement; it reversed its earlier position and voted to spend $300,000 to temporarily renovate the remaining Lyndale units (Diaz 1999d). Two days later, however, the NAACP's executive committee rejected the plan. In the span of three weeks, the organization had managed to reverse itself twice. The recently elected president of the Minneapolis branch, who had 16 days earlier called the deal "acceptable," now signaled his willingness to oppose it by saying, "It's time to rumble" (Diaz 1999f).

At the eleventh hour, according to the *Star Tribune*, the NAACP offered in secret to settle (that is, to accept the demolition of the Glenwood units) if the city provided the NAACP with $500,000 annually to finance an NAACP-based organization to track *Hollman* residents, assist them in relocating to the new housing to be built on site, and help them "adjust to the new community" (Brandt 1999d). City officials rejected the idea, noting that these functions were already being provided.

One week later, Judge Rosenbaum heard the arguments. The NAACP attorneys had decided that they would make the severe affordable-housing crisis the basis of their motion. They argued that in the midst of the region's tight housing market, the demolition of Glenwood and Lyndale would add to homelessness in the city. This strategy was peculiar in that it did not allege that the defendants violated the decree, but instead asked the judge, in essence, to amend the decree on the basis of changed conditions. Judge Rosenbaum wondered out loud whether he had the power to address these "new issues." Though the NAACP lawyer assured him he did, the judge moved on to another argument. Rosenbaum asked the MPHA lawyer about the lack of progress on replacement housing. While the MPHA could not well defend the slow pace of replacement-housing development, the lawyer did point out that the NAACP motion did not address the issue of replacement housing, a point with which Legal Aid attorneys agreed.

Replacement housing, a requirement of the consent decree and an obligation of the defendants, was an issue on which the defendants were vulnerable. Furthermore, as a requirement of the consent decree, the city's record on replacement housing was something about which the judge could rule. NAACP strategy, however, did not address replacement housing; it argued instead that the judge should save Glenwood and Lyndale because the city now needed those affordable units. As the city's lawyer said to the judge in summation, "The NAACP wants you to take over the city's affordable housing program. With all due respect, your honor, you don't have that authority." In the end, Rosenbaum agreed.

After the hearing and prior to the judge's ruling, the NAACP—perhaps sensing its weak legal position and belatedly realizing the judge's incli-nations—offered the city yet another deal. This time it suggested that 140 units be temporarily saved, instead of the 70 units that the city had pledged. The city rejected this deal, too.

Unsurprisingly, Judge Rosenbaum ruled on September 30 to reject the NAACP motion to stop demolition. Reacting to the NAACP's focus on the lack of affordable housing, the judge wrote, "The NAACP's motion asks the court to order changes in the consent decree because of a changed economic environment. But the lawsuit before the court, and the decree that resolves that dispute, are not based on questions of rental economics" (Hawkins 1999). He added, "The court cannot be a social and community planner empowered to solve all of the community's ever-changing problems" (Brandt 1999c).

On October 26, 1999, four and one-half years after the decree was signed, three years after the focus groups had called for the demolition of the north side units, and four and one-half months after the *Hollman* 14 had stood in front of the bulldozers, the remaining units of the 39-year-old Lyndale and Glenwood public housing projects began coming down. About half the units came down that very day, with "about a dozen sub-dued opponents gathered outside the fences to watch" (Brandt 1999b). Several families still lived in some of the other units. The last family would be moved out in April 2000, and the last unit razed the follow-ing week.

In January 2000, the developer of the north side project, Richard Baron, announced his plans for 800 new housing units on the site. As mentioned earlier in the chapter, 55 percent (440 units) would be rental units, including 200 public housing units, 90 subsidized units for low- to moderate-income households, and 150 units rented at market rates (between $835 and $1,225 for two- and three-bedroom apartments). Of the 360 home-ownership units, 250 would be sold at market rates, ranging from $90,000 for smaller two-bedroom homes to as much as $200,000 for some four-bedroom homes. Another 110 homes would be subsidized for sale to income-qualified buyers. The percentages worked out to exactly what the focus group had recommended three years before—25 percent public housing, 25 percent subsidized housing for low- and moderate-income families, and 50 percent market-rate housing. The only concession to the events of the intervening years was the number of units to be built on site, which had increased from 450 to 800.

An Uneasy Consensus

The debate over the *Hollman* redevelopment in Minneapolis helps demonstrate the issues in efforts to deconcentrate poverty. Opponents of redevelopment worried about the gentrification of the neighborhood. It was, after all, located adjacent to several transportation corridors, only a mile from the city's downtown core, and, as many observers pointed out, afforded wonderful views of the city's skyline. In many respects, the fight was over who could lay claim to the neighborhood. One portion of the city's African-American community felt it had a claim, based on decades of settlement. Furthermore, opponents valued the community that they believed the parties to the lawsuit saw only as an "impacted" area. Spokespeople from the community questioned the assumption that the north side poor wanted to be integrated into other communities, and that a concentration of people of color was in fact a public policy problem. A different portion of the African-American community, however, felt that deconcentration was a legitimate way to reverse decades of housing discrimination that had trapped many of them in that community. Homeowners from adjacent areas, and the "hard-working" constituents referred to by council member Cherryhomes, wanted less poverty in the neighborhood. The class-based nature of this divide within the African-American community is difficult to miss.

Another issue evoked by the *Hollman* redevelopment is the coercive nature of demolition and displacement. At the time of demolition, virtually half the residents who were asked indicated they did not want to move. Reluctance to move was centered in the Southeast Asian community and based on both a fear of the dissolution of its social-support networks and its lack of dissatisfaction with its current situation. The sight of low-income people demonstrating to save their housing from being bulldozed in the name of revitalization is distressingly reminiscent of urban renewal. That the fate of several displaced families included subsequent evictions, homelessness, and further residential instability heightened opponents' sense of injustice. That the displacement and demolition were carried out so quickly—so much more quickly, in fact, than the rate at which replacement housing was built—reinforced opponents' notion that deconcentration of poverty was less about the residents of the north side public housing than about clearing the way for redevelopment of a prize parcel of land near the city's center (another image distressingly reminiscent of urban renewal).

The Minneapolis case highlights the tension between deconcentration of poverty in older urban neighborhoods and efforts to increase housing affordability for poor families. The demolition of more than 300 public housing units that took place at the height of an affordable-housing crisis served only to make more acute an inherent characteristic of forced deconcentration—the removal or conversion to other uses of previously low-cost housing. Even in a community with a rental vacancy rate hovering at 1 percent, the logic of deconcentration mandated that hundreds of the city's most affordable housing units be demolished.

Perhaps the outcome might have been different had opponents organized themselves earlier. By the time the opposition coalesced, all the important decisions already had been made. The focus groups had made recommendations, and the defendants and the plaintiffs had agreed to a plan of action. The redevelopment had gained a momentum and legal legitimacy that could not be stopped. On the other hand, such second-guessing by opponents might underestimate the extent to which officials in the city (and at HUD) wanted the redevelopment to occur, and the power of the deconcentration argument and the Detroit Scenario. The *Hollman* consent decree was an expression not only of HUD policy, but also of Minneapolis city policy as well during the 1990s. Large segments of the city's policymaking structure embraced it, and earlier or better community organizing could easily have proved just as ineffective against this official consensus.

NOTES

1. This letter to the editor appeared in the weekly newspaper *City Pages* (November 25, 1995). Nellie Stone Johnson was 89 years old at the time she wrote this letter. For most of her life, she was among the state's most influential labor and civil rights activists. She was active "organizing hotel workers into unions in the '30s; working with Hubert Humphrey to form the DFL in the '40s; winning a seat on the Minneapolis Library Board as the city's first black elected official; helping write employment and civil rights legislation in the '60s; standing with low-income renters whose homes were being demolished during the '80s and '90s." She died on April 2, 2002 (*Minneapolis Star Tribune* 2002).

2. As a high-rise for elderly residents, the Bryants were not part of the lawsuit settlement. Legal Aid attorneys felt the demolition and dispersal model was not appropriate for seniors.

3. From the Coalition minutes of September 2, 1998, available from author.

4. In a letter to the *Minnesota Spokesman-Recorder*, Jeremy Lane, executive director of the Legal Aid Society of Minneapolis, explained the fees it had received as a result of the legal work done on the decree. See Lane (1999).

7

Implementing Deconcentration

Moving Families and Building Replacement Housing

We're living with it. They're a separate entity, though. They are not a part of our neighborhood. There is no interchange. There's no coming to my house for tea, or me going to your little abode for a cup of coffee. They're on their own.
—White resident of Yonkers, New York,
on deconcentrated public housing families, 1998

For deconcentration of poverty to work as a strategy, it must be accepted in the "receiving" community as well as in the "impacted" neighborhood, and it must represent a viable mobility option for the poor. This chapter examines the efforts to implement the deconcentration elements of the *Hollman* decree: the relocation of north side residents, the operation of the voluntary mobility program, and the production of replacement public housing units throughout the Twin Cities region.

The *Hollman* deconcentration strategy comprised both involuntary and voluntary phases. Family displacement and relocation represented involuntary dispersal in that the families had no choice but to move out. Families that moved into the replacement housing and participated in the mobility program, however, voluntarily agreed to use the resources made available by the consent decree to move from a poverty or minority neighborhood to a non-concentrated area. The involuntary aspect of deconcentration proceeded quickly in Minneapolis and, despite the considerable political resistance described in the previous chapter, was essentially completed by the end of 2000. The voluntary phases, however, proved more difficult.

The Relocation Process

The relocation of families from the Sumner Field and Olson projects began in August 1995 and was substantially completed a year later. Relocating families from the other two projects, the Glenwood and Lyndale townhomes, began in August 1998 and continued until May 2000. Families at all four sites were provided access to the same set of benefits and supports. Three of the lawsuit defendants, HUD, the Metropolitan Council, and the Minneapolis Community Development Agency (MCDA), provided funds for mobility counseling for all displaced families, as well as families using the special "mobility certificates" called for in the decree. North side residents who wanted to purchase a home during relocation also had access to funds for moving expenses, closing costs, and down-payment assistance.

The mobility services did not reach all the displaced families, however. Those that moved out prior to the commencement of mobility services did so without assistance, in most cases.[1] In addition, those that violated their lease terms while awaiting relocation assistance also were denied services, and some units were vacant. In all, official relocation assistance was provided to 440 families in the four projects, which contained a total of 720 units.[2]

Southeast Asian families were most reluctant to leave. About half the relocated residents did not want to move, and most of these were recent Hmong immigrants or non-Hmong families from Laos or Vietnam.[3] These families were also more likely to report problems in relocating. Many said they did not know why they had to move, and close to one in four, interviewed in 1996, reported that they had not been given enough time.[4]

Those families that did receive assistance obtained information on available units along with help in viewing potential residences and signing leases. Counselors helped some residents prepare to meet their prospective landlords, paid rental application fees for people using Section 8 vouchers to relocate, and assisted families with paperwork. Relocation agencies arranged child care, transportation, and translation assistance for some families. Mobility counselors worked on site at the public housing projects. When the relocation of families from the Glenwood/Lyndale projects began in 1998, the line outside the relocation office (located in a vacant public housing unit at the edge of the Glenwood project) began forming at 7:30 A.M. and stretched around the corner at one point. Many families brought their children in to serve as translators.

Families in the early round of relocation were steered into Section 8 units, reflecting the lawsuit's deconcentration objectives. By the second round of relocation in 1998, however, the housing market was so tight that most families were relocated into other city public housing. Families interested in purchasing a home were screened for income eligibility and, if eligible, referred to a homeownership counseling agency designated to help families deal with credit and application issues and to find lenders with experience in the low end of the real estate market. During the first round of relocation, some families maintained they were unaware of some of the services that the mobility counselors provided.[5] Nevertheless, most families receiving the services found them helpful, and most reported no significant problems. Dissatisfaction was centered in the Southeast Asian community.

In general, relocation proceeded quickly at first. More than 200 families were moved out of the Sumner and Olson projects in just over 12 months. The second round took longer because a tighter housing market made it more difficult to find comparable units for families to move into. Wedging close to 200 families into the Twin Cities housing market of 1998 and 1999 was not easy, and as a result, many families moved to other public housing. The Special Mobility Program, mandated by the consent decree, demonstrates the difficulty of deconcentrating families when housing is scarce.

The Special Mobility Program

The Special Mobility Program (SMP) began in 1995 with 600 certificates and 300 vouchers. A voluntary program, SMP provides Section 8 assistance and counseling for moves to nonpoverty- and nonminority-concentrated neighborhoods throughout the region.[6] Priority for SMP vouchers goes to the named plaintiffs, residents of MPHA projects in concentrated areas of the city, and families on the MPHA waiting list (with priority to those living in areas of minority or poverty concentration). Participants are given at least 180 days after receiving housing counseling to enter into a lease agreement for a rental unit in a non-concentrated area.

The very tight Twin Cities housing market that prevailed between 1996 and 2001 hindered implementation of the Special Mobility Program, however. Low vacancy rates meant greater competition. With many applicants from whom to choose, landlords could avoid Section 8 applicants if they did not want to submit to unit inspections or program paperwork. At the same time, escalating rents resulted in fewer units qualifying for the subsidy (HOME Line 2000). There were indications, too, that the problem was more than just a shortage of housing units or low fair market rents (FMRs). The Met Council reported that 60 percent of those on its waiting list were members of minority groups, but only 40 percent of lease-ups were minority. Most of the public housing agencies in the region were having difficulty with their Section 8 programs during this period. Six of every seven households given a Section 8 certificate by the Met Council in 1998 were unable to find an apartment that qualified and a landlord who was willing to rent to them. The success rate for vouchers was somewhat better, but still limited to one in four. In 1999, the rate of Section 8 success in the Twin Cities was among the lowest in the nation.[7]

MPHA attempted to get HUD to increase the area's FMRs (the upper limit on eligible rents under the Section 8 program) as a way of increasing the number of eligible units from which families could choose. HUD declined in 1998 and again in 2000. Minneapolis officials also investigated the possibility of converting Section 8 certificates into Section 8 vouchers to take advantage of the higher lease-up rates among voucher holders.[8] Congress facilitated this in 1999 with a merger of the certificate and voucher programs that retained the mobility advantages of the vouchers. Even when units could be found, though, many families still were denied housing because of their rental history and credit records. Thus, in 2000, with the approval of the Legal Aid attorneys, MPHA revised SMP's eligibility criteria to limit participants to families that had no more than three unlawful detainers (evictions) and no criminal record.

Program Demand

From the beginning, the program has attracted less interest from eligible families than many had expected. Over six years, from 1996 to 2001, MPHA directly contacted an estimated 4,500 families about the availability of special mobility vouchers. Yet only 285 families (roughly 6 percent) were interested enough to contact the mobility counseling agencies and engage the process enough for the agency to open a file on them.[9] Several possible reasons may account for this lack of interest. First, the majority of families in the priority groups may have been satisfied with their existing housing situations. This is more likely to be true of those in the public housing priority group than those on the waiting list. Families joined the waiting list, after all, because they were dissatisfied with their existing housing. Second, the quality of the waiting list that MPHA used for five years was questionable. Many of the notices the agency sent to families on the list were returned as "undeliverable." Yet, from 1996 through 1999, MPHA continued to use the list, not updating it until 2000. Third, the tight housing market may have discouraged those with acceptable housing from risking a move when competition for units was so high. However, participation was risk-free in the sense that participants did not have to surrender their existing housing in order to join the program and look for a new unit. Whatever the reasons, the lack of demand for the program proves that the opportunities represented by the special mobility vouchers were not a compelling alternative for the vast majority of the plaintiff class.

Program Performance

Between January 1996 and March 2002, 80 families successfully leased a unit through the program. Most of the program's success has occurred since mid-2000 and has accelerated each quarter since then. Over the first four years, fewer than 30 families actually used SMP vouchers to move from concentrated neighborhoods. In the fifth year, less than 10 additional families moved, and until 2001, the program saw no significant progress in getting families to move. In fact, more SMP families were leased up during 2001 than in the first five years of the program combined. This increase coincided with a loosening of the rental market in the Twin Cities area generally. In fact, the Section 8 program in general has been easier to implement since early 2001.[10] The program's rate of success also increased after MPHA updated its waiting list in 2000. Both factors undoubtedly made it easier for MPHA and the counseling groups to identify interested families and assist them through the process of searching for and leasing rental properties. Overall, the program has a 28.1 percent lease-up rate. That is, just over one in four families engaging in the counseling process have been able to utilize the subsidy successfully. This is slightly higher than the rate generated by the Gautreaux program in Chicago, but far below rates produced at the Moving To Opportunity demonstration sites.

Facing the Obstacles

The *Hollman* consent decree called for the replacement of all public housing units demolished or taken out of service, up to a maximum of 770. Replacement units were to be built in non-concentrated parts of the metropolitan area. Some units were to be replaced on site, as determined by the planning process described in chapter 6. In order to facilitate the decree's deconcentration objectives, at least 380 units were to be placed in suburban areas. The decree prohibited any replacement units from being placed in Saint Paul, or in poverty- or minority-concentrated neighborhoods anywhere in the region. In anticipation of difficulties in developing suburban units, the consent decree offered an incentive to suburban housing agencies. Those that built replacement housing could offer 30 percent to families from their own waiting lists, leaving 70 percent for Minneapolis families. This policy diluted the deconcentrating effects of the replacement-housing effort, but was offered in an attempt to get the units built. The incentive meant, in effect, that HUD and MPHA would be providing public housing units to help suburban communities partially meet their own demands for subsidized housing and, in return, these communities would be accepting *Hollman* units reserved for the plaintiff class. The plaintiffs expected the replacement units to constitute a net addition to the region's affordable-housing stock, which precluded light rehabilitation of existing affordable units, or converting existing subsidized units to public housing.

The difficulties in building replacement housing were two-fold. First, public housing faced political resistance in suburban areas and non-concentrated neighborhoods in Minneapolis. Second, MPHA lacked the authority to build public housing anywhere but in Minneapolis, even though the decree called for the housing to be built throughout the region. Completing the consent decree's replacement-housing requirements depended on the voluntary cooperation of other metropolitan communities.

Technical Obstacles

In the United States, public housing is administered by a local agency under contract with HUD. This agreement between HUD and the local agency, the annual contributions contract (ACC), is the means through which operating and management funds are transferred from the federal government to the local agency. In the beginning of the replacement-housing effort, MPHA simply agreed to hold the ACCs for projects built in suburban areas. Early on, however, MPHA found that its costs in operating these suburban units in scattered sites were higher than the operating subsidies it was receiving through the ACCs. The agency was losing money on each suburban unit it managed.

MPHA first attempted to deal with this problem by asking the Metropolitan Council to hold the ACCs for suburban units. The Met Council refused. Though the council operated a housing and redevelopment authority (HRA, the Minnesota equivalent of a public housing authority), it offered only tenant-based Section 8 subsidies in suburban areas not served by an HRA. While authorized under federal law to build public housing, the council as of 1995 was not interested in expanding its role to directly provide subsidized housing.

Outside of the Met Council, few suburban agencies had the capacity to operate public housing units. In 1996, two of the five suburban counties lacked well-functioning local agencies. A third, with perhaps the most capable agency in the region, refused to participate. This left the Carver and Scott County housing authorities, located on the far southern and southwestern periphery of the metropolitan area, as the only two options at the county level. Some suburban municipalities had housing authorities that might have become involved in replacement housing. However, they generally were smaller operations that, because of their size, did not qualify for HUD's public housing modernization funds, which were reserved for agencies that owned and operated more than 250 units. Without guaranteed access to ongoing capital subsidies, smaller agencies were very reluctant to commit to building replacement units. This obstacle was removed in 1998 when the Capital Fund Program was created and made available to all local housing authorities. From 1995 through 1998, however, successfully implementing the decree's replacement-housing requirements in the suburbs meant locating an agency with the administrative capacity and willingness to hold the ACC and sufficient units to qualify for modernization funds. No agencies outside the two central cities fit this profile, however.[11] With suburban public housing a losing proposition financially for MPHA, and no other likely agency stepping forward, progress on construction of *Hollman* units in the suburbs was extremely slow in the decree's initial years.

Political Obstacles

Technical challenges notwithstanding, political opposition was the most enduring and widespread obstacle to fulfilling the replacement-housing objectives of the consent decree in its early years. This was the case even in Minneapolis. As already mentioned, the city made little progress on its allocation of replacement housing for the first three years. Outside of a single eight-unit project several miles north of the project site, the city took no steps to even begin the process of finding non-impacted areas within its boundaries in which to place housing. In part, this situation was the result of MPHA's decision to focus its efforts on getting suburban units built, because, it felt, they would be the greatest challenge. In addition, Minneapolis manifested little political will to build more public housing.

Just a month after the decree was signed, Minneapolis public housing officials found they would have trouble convincing even their own council members from wards with little subsidized housing that dispersal was a good idea, let alone suburban officials who historically had opposed low-income housing. In May 1995, the mayor presented the city council with her "housing principles," which made dispersal of affordable housing a central tenet for city policy. The council as a whole did not respond favorably (see chapter 5). And the council's negative reaction to the suggestion that non-impacted neighborhoods take on a greater share of affordable housing was not lost on suburban officials. Just as Minneapolis council members objected to the placement of subsidized units in their wards, suburban officials resisted taking a greater share of the region's low-cost housing. The mayor's difficulty in gaining acceptance of her housing principles illustrates the chief political contradiction in deconcentration strategies—when subsidized housing is identified as the problem in one community (or neighborhood), it becomes hard to convince other communities that they should accept more subsidized housing.

Indeed, *Hollman* units in the suburbs were a hard sell. As one suburban official said early in the process, "Public housing is simply not an acceptable strategy in many places. Elected officials simply won't go for it, and it is not on the table for discussion."[13] Suburban officials were concerned that they would be asked to participate in a legal remedy to which they were not a party. Some community leaders objected to the interference in local control that was embodied in such a dispersal plan, while others voiced concern that if they accepted such housing and other communities did not, then their communities would become "dumping grounds" for low-cost housing. One MPHA official who had spent almost two years working with suburban areas commented on the difficulty of placing public housing in the suburbs: "You have to spend some time dealing with the stereotypes of poor people" (Diaz 1997).

The mid-1990s witnessed fierce suburban resistance to subsidized housing of all types (see chapter 4). Part of the opposition resulted from the public discourse generated in the deconcentration debate. Suburban residents and public officials were no more anxious to subject themselves to the perceived dangers of accommodating poor people than were central city officials willing to continue dealing with concentrations of disadvantaged residents.

One of the earliest suburban projects to include *Hollman* units, developed in Minnetonka, exemplifies such opposition. Suburbanites fought the development not because a small percentage of the units were *Hollman* units, but rather because the project as a whole would be "affordable" and involve developing a wooded lot at the edge of an area of single-family homes. According to the developer, opposition focused initially on concerns about parking, traffic, and density. Once the development's projected rent levels became known, however, opposition focused on affordability. The developer received threatening phone calls at home. Elected officials required the developer to meet repeatedly with neighbors and endure multiple reviews by city agencies. The entire approval process took more than a year, including "several months of ugliness," according to the developer.

In this particular case, city development staff members were supportive, and the Metropolitan Interfaith Coalition for Affordable Housing (MICAH) organized support. In the end, the city council approved the project, six to one. According to the developer, the fact that the project contained *Hollman* public housing units had not worsened the situation; the neighbors simply were opposed to affordability at any level.

In other places, the fact that proposed units would house Minneapolis public housing residents was exactly the focus of opposition. In September 1996, residents of the eastern suburban county of Washington voiced their opinions. As one commented, "We shouldn't contaminate our county with these people." Another stated that if he had wanted to live in a diverse neighborhood, he would have moved to a low-rent area of Minneapolis. "This idea of everybody having to be equal is absurd. Equally miserable is what they want" (Broede 1996). Later that year, the northern suburb of Mahtomedi voted down a project with *Hollman* units during a meeting at which one resident was applauded for declaring, "We don't need a Phillips neighborhood in Mahtomedi!" (Lynch 2001). (Phillips is a largely poor and nonwhite neighborhood in near south Minneapolis.)

The Funding Gap

Even if MPHA could find some entity to develop the suburban housing, and even if the political resistance to such housing could be overcome, it soon became clear that HUD had not allocated enough development money to build all 770 units. The funds provided by HUD in the consent decree agreement would have allowed roughly $93,000 per unit, if all 770 replacement units were built. The first few replacement-housing projects, however, had been more expensive. Furthermore, it was likely that construction costs would be even higher because of higher land costs in many of the other developing suburbs in which MPHA wanted to build. In fact, the estimates suggested that the existing pot of money would produce only 630 units, a gap of about $28 million.

The *Hollman* Implementation Group

By June 1998, the Sumner and Olson projects had been demolished, more than 250 families had been relocated, and planning for site redevelopment had been completed. Yet only 19 units of replacement housing had been built, and financing had been established for only 48 others. Like the mobility program, development of replacement housing was clearly lagging. Three years into the effort, MPHA still lacked a workable strategy for producing the units in suburban areas. It was at this point that a new informal group calling itself the *Hollman* Implementation Group (HIG) was formed.[14] HIG was initiated by the executive director of the Family Housing Fund of Minneapolis/Saint Paul, a nonprofit organization whose board comprises public officials from across the region. (The Family Housing Fund is the largest nonpublic source of affordable-housing capital in the metropolitan area, and, therefore, a major actor in the regional housing arena.) In the summer of 1998, its executive director began to convene monthly meetings of officials from the agencies that were defendants in the lawsuit, and from other organizations that were active in producing affordable housing in the region. HIG's goal was to assist in implementing the replacement-housing objectives and the Special Mobility Program.

Over the next two-and-a-half years, HIG strategized about how to get the replacement units built in suburban areas. The group expanded in the summer of 1999 when participants realized they also would need representatives of both the suburban agencies responsible for affordable housing and the plaintiff groups. By 2000, close to 20 people representing 12 local governmental bodies were meeting regularly each month to discuss progress on the development of *Hollman* units. Its wide representation allowed the group to deal with a range of factors that inhibited the timely implementation of the consent decree's replacement-housing requirements. Participation by local officials did not necessarily mean, however, that local political obstacles had been surmounted. Though the director of the Dakota County housing authority was an active HIG member, for example, his board of county commissioners still refused to accept *Hollman* units. Similarly, the official from Ramsey County attended HIG meetings despite opposition from that county's commissioners over participation in *Hollman*-related developments. Nevertheless, HIG provided a forum for discussing the political and technical obstacles that had brought the replacement-housing effort to a halt.

In the summer of 1998, the HIG strategized on three issues: making Section 8 certificates and vouchers more effective in the region, converting some of the 900 special mobility certificates into project-based subsidies, and getting replacement units built more quickly in the suburbs. The first related to the slow rate of progress in the Special Mobility Program authorized by *Hollman*. Each year, hundreds of the Section 8 subsidies HUD had committed to the region as a result of the decree went unused because of lack of demand and difficulties certificate holders had experienced in using tenant-based assistance in the Twin Cities' tight housing market. HIG worked with MPHA to get HUD to increase the region's FMR and/or convert the Section 8 certificates into vouchers.

"Project-Basing" Section 8 Subsidies

The prospect of converting some of the *Hollman* tenant-based Section 8 subsidies into project-based subsidies was aimed at solving two problems: It was a way to utilize subsidies that were going unspent as a result of the failing mobility program, and it would be a source of funds to help eliminate the funding gap. Project-basing Section 8 subsidies would also help solve the production problem because units produced with this kind of subsidy would not be subject to the same constraints as public housing units. The cash-flow concerns about ACCs and the capacity of local agencies to qualify for improvement funds would both be avoided with project-based Section 8 subsidies.

Other attempts to address the funding gap, including a HOPE VI grant application to HUD, and the possibility of more moderate rehabilitation of existing units (to bring down development costs), proved unworkable. The HOPE VI application was not funded, and the plaintiffs objected to moderate rehabilitation because it could result in displacement and, more important, would not constitute a net gain in affordable housing. The Hennepin County Commissioners, though unwilling to participate directly in the development of *Hollman* units, created in late 1999 a $2 million subsidy fund for *Hollman* units, a fund matched by $1 million from the McKnight Foundation. This funding helped reduce but did not eliminate the gap. Increasingly, it seemed that the only option for filling the gap lay with converting tenant-based Section 8 subsidies into project-based assistance.

The problem, and the irony, was that converting Section 8 subsidies would fly in the face of more than a decade of HUD policy. Since the 1980s, HUD had been shifting its subsidized housing efforts in the other direction, away from project-based assistance and toward more portable, tenant-based subsidies. In fact, such an objective was central to the *Hollman* settlement in the first place. HUD provided 900 tenant-based subsidies to members of the plaintiff class for the very purpose of furthering the shift in federally subsidized housing away from project-based subsidies. Converting them back to project-based subsidies would constitute a step in the opposite direction. Accomplishing the conversion, moreover, would require not only plaintiff approval, but also HUD approval, which seemed unlikely at best.

As it turned out, even plaintiff approval was problematic. Legal Aid attorneys did endorse the proposal, but the other plaintiff party, the NAACP, did not. At the time, NAACP leaders were in the midst of a struggle that precluded any coherent policy development. In the end, even after its leadership struggle was resolved, the NAACP was not supportive. A formal proposal to HUD never was made.

However, in 2000, HIG and MPHA settled on another way to shift the subsidies to project-based funding. MPHA proposed that HUD return to the region some of the millions of dollars that had been unspent in previous years because the Special Mobility Program was used so little.

Technically, this was not a request to "project base" existing subsidies; it was a request for additional production subsidies from a pool of funds that HUD at one time had devoted to tenant-based assistance. The difference seems slim, but it was enough. This proposal had a much better chance of receiving HUD approval and did not require an amendment to the consent decree (and subsequent approval by all parties, including the NAACP). In February 2001, HUD in fact approved the proposal, and $28.5 million became available for development funds.

The Tide Turns

Initially, HIG focused on identifying an agency that could hold an ACC in suburban areas where no local housing authority existed. It explored the idea of creating a new multijurisdictional entity that could be formed through a state law allowing joint powers agreements (JPAs) among local governments. Ultimately, however, the JPA approach faced the same political buy-in problems as any other approach. Local communities were uncertain of the financial commitment required by participation in a JPA, and, more important, a great deal of opposition to public housing in its own right still existed.

As the likelihood of a JPA faded, HIG focused on other strategies. One was to place some *Hollman* units in Saint Paul. In the summer of 1999, the Saint Paul PHA had expressed a willingness to accept up to 100 such units. Doing so, however, required an amendment to the consent decree. Passed in May 2000, the amendment allowed up to 300 units of replacement housing to be constructed in Saint Paul (subject to the same restrictions as other replacement housing—that it be in non-concentrated neighborhoods and that 30 percent of the units be filled by persons on the Saint Paul waiting list).

Another HIG strategy involved revisiting the possibility of the Met Council holding the ACC in smaller communities. When MPHA first approached the council with this idea in 1995, it was rejected. In December 1998, however, the council signaled its willingness to hold the ACCs in suburban areas, but not to own the units (preferring to partner with nonprofits or other public agencies). Both the Family Housing Fund and MPHA offered to assist in hiring a development coordinator, and the Saint Paul HRA provided additional technical assistance to the Met Council, which had never developed affordable housing before. The election of a new governor and the appointment of new Met Council commissioners temporarily derailed progress, however, on the council's *Hollman* strategy. Ten months passed before the council hired anyone to direct the effort. By January 2000, the council also agreed to own the public housing it developed. The council did indicate, however, that it would develop *Hollman* replacement housing only in communities where the local government agreed to it.

This important caveat meant, in practice, that the council would need the approval of each individual community where it wanted to develop public housing. In contrast, the Washington County housing authority in 1999 had gained approval from its county board to implement individual *Hollman* projects without separate cooperation agreements with each city. Using this strategy, the Washington County housing authority could avoid public hearings on each development, a key factor in evading the political resistance of residents and officials. Met Council staff and officials, however, did not pursue such a blanket authority because, as a regional agency, the council's authority could come only from the state legislature. Council staff felt the possibility of success in the legislature was too low and, in any case, would require an expenditure of political capital they did not want to make. The absence of blanket authority, however, essentially negated any political advantage that came from having a regional body develop the housing. The Met Council's entry into the development effort may have solved the technical problems of creating *Hollman* units in the suburbs, but it did nothing to solve the political problems.

Meanwhile, other developments helped the replacement-housing effort. Public housing modernization funds were made available to all housing authorities, guaranteeing agencies the long-term capital improvement funds necessary to maintain the units. The Washington County housing authority solved some internal problems and, with the help of the Family Housing Fund, hired staff to develop public housing. The affordable-housing crisis in the region was also coming to a head, and suburban officials were beginning to acknowledge the need for more affordable housing in their own communities (see chapter 4). By the beginning of 2000, there were agencies willing and able to develop public housing and hold the ACCs, the funding gap had been filled, and the opposition to subsidized housing had been eased, somewhat, by the severe crisis in affordable housing.

Building Replacement Units

Minneapolis

Minneapolis had an allocation of "at least 80" *Hollman* units in non-impacted neighborhoods. After four years, though, only one development with eight units had been completed. In fact, the city made no concerted effort to develop any additional *Hollman* units until the protest actions of 1999, when the mayor held up demolition of the Glenwood and Lyndale projects in the face of resistance from affordable-housing and north side activists (see chapter 6). Only in the context of the severe shortage of affordable housing, the protests of community activists, and the impending demolition of the remaining 300 units of public housing on the north side did the city begin its efforts to meet its replacement-housing obligations. In some respects, its pledge to increase the rate of replacement-housing development was the price the city had to pay to continue the demolition and redevelopment of the north side site. During the summer of 1999, the mayor promised to have all 88 units ready and occupied by April 2000, a year earlier than the deadline established in the consent decree. The MPHA created an allocation formula for determining how many units would be acquired in each of the city's non-impacted neighborhoods. Officials met with neighborhood groups to explain the policy and ease concerns about a reconcentration of public housing, announcing that scattering 88 units across the city meant that no one neighborhood would see a large concentration. MPHA planned to purchase individual units on a site-by-site basis and lease them to public housing residents (as in the city's regular scattered-site program). By October 1999, MPHA had acquired 30 units, but only 34 were actually occupied by the end of April 2000. By year's end, 75 units were occupied, and the city met the consent decree deadline by having all units occupied by April 2001.

Washington County

Though agreeing in principle to accept 60 *Hollman* replacement units, as of 1999, the Washington County housing authority had made no progress in actually following through on the agreement. The agency had encountered some internal difficulties rendering it incapable of developing new units. By year's end, however, new personnel were in place, including a consultant (funded by a grant from the Family Housing Fund) hired to develop the replacement units. The agency received blanket authority from the county board of supervisors to acquire units on a scattered-site basis in all the county's municipalities. Therefore, the agency did not have to seek approval of individual city councils for the units it purchased, which helped speed the process dramatically. The agency's first purchase was a single-family home in the southeastern suburb of Cottage Grove. The homeowner already had received renovation funds from the agency, but was in default and facing foreclosure. Purchased in July 1999, this home became the first of 46 single-family and townhome units acquired in a nine-month period. By purchasing homes that were already on the market, or HUD foreclosures, the agency avoided displacing families and eliminated relocation costs. Even so, it was difficult to purchase and reha-bilitate units for the amount allowed by HUD. Because HUD had not yet agreed to release the unexpended Section 8 subsidies, the Met Council and the Family Housing Fund made gap financing available. The Washington County agency's quick work was the area's first sizable and sustained suc-cess in developing suburban *Hollman* units. As the affordable-housing crisis worsened around the region, other successes soon followed.

Carver County

The Carver County housing authority had purchased a few units as early as 1998. The county's allocation from MPHA, however, was 50 scattered-site units. Progress was slow, not only for political reasons, but because the agency was having difficulty finding property for which the purchase and rehabilitation costs did not exceed the amount allowed by HUD. In fact, the agency calculated that it would be fortunate to get 40 units com-pleted with the resources that were originally allocated. Nevertheless, HUD's agreement to fill the financing gap allowed the county agency to fill its allocation. The housing authority ended up spending an average of $160,000 per unit for purchase and rehabilitation.

The agency also attempted to avoid competing with first-time home-buyers, so it pursued only single-family homes and duplexes that had been on the market at least six weeks. Unlike the Washington County housing authority, the Carver County agency had to seek approval of individual communities before proceeding.[15] Some cities required a for-mal vote by the city council, while in others, staff passed on the agency's proposals.

County staff indicated that some communities were quite receptive to the housing as long as the housing authority could show it would not be reconcentrating the units within a city. In other places, according to agency staff, "some of the council meetings [were] very difficult to go through. It was incredible what would come out of people's mouths" when they opposed this type of housing. Housing authority staff noted: "Some places would have loved this housing had their own residents been placed in the units."[16] The consent decree's mandate that 70 percent of the replacement housing be held for Minneapolis families was an obstacle in many places; community officials wanted their own residents to occupy all the units. Other public officials expressed concern about lost tax revenue if the housing authority owned the property. Still others expressed concern over the additional burdens such housing and the families that lived in it would produce for the local schools.

Finally, local leaders definitely tended to want the housing authority to purchase their "bad" units, according to agency staff. That is, local officials would approve the purchase of homes by the housing authority only if they were blighted properties. Such an approach would produce more tangible benefits, reasoned these officials, by improving the city's worst properties, and also would generate less opposition from neighbors. By 2002, the agency had purchased property in every community it had originally targeted. Over time, older city officials who opposed public housing would retire; elections would change the face of some councils; new city managers would be hired; or, as happened in at least one case, the most vocal opponents would simply miss the public meetings at which the issue was decided. The affordable-housing crisis had eased the political resistance, but not eliminated it. As one elected official in the county privately urged the housing authority, "Do more, just don't tell me about it."

Met Council Strategy

Through the last half of 2000 and well into 2001, Met Council development staff met with individual cities. Working only in suburban areas that did not have their own housing authorities, and limited to negotiating with communities for their consent to develop public housing, Met Council staff made little progress at first. The council began by bargaining with communities, offering them deals that included senior housing if they accepted *Hollman* units. A change in council staff, however, led to a reduction in what the council was willing to promise. Instead of offering two senior housing units for every *Hollman* unit accepted, council staff now promised only to give high priority to any Section 8 proposal involving senior housing that it received from a community accepting *Hollman* units.

Met Council staff also committed to a conservative strategy, avoiding public confrontations on the issue of accepting *Hollman* units. Staff members negotiated with city staff behind the scenes and set up "work sessions" with city council members to discuss *Hollman* and public housing. Met Council staff never brought a project to a public vote unless they were confident of victory, trying to "avoid a momentum of opposition," as one Met Council staff member described it.[17] In practice, this meant that the Met Council did not move to a vote in any community for several months.

Council staff began their efforts in the first-ring suburbs north of Minneapolis. The communities' initial response was to offer the Met Council the worst units in their housing stock or impose conditions that would make the development prohibitively expensive, or both.[18] As in Carver County, many community officials objected to the loss of property tax revenues, despite Met Council staff efforts to show that the reduction would amount only to about 0.2 percent annually. One Met Council staff member claimed that these demands and concerns were simply "another way of saying, 'no.' " Several northern suburbs (in a region with relatively less-expensive homes) suggested they already had enough affordable housing and that the Met Council should spend its time building *Hollman* units in Edina, Minnetonka, or Eden Prairie—more affluent suburbs to the south and west. Met Council staff, however, avoided the wealthier suburbs because their high housing prices would mean acquisition costs in excess of what the program could afford.

After several fruitless months in the northern suburbs, Met Council staff shifted their strategy, enlisting the help of regional, affordable-housing advocacy groups in making the case for *Hollman* units. This was a somewhat ironic alliance, since previously these groups had loudly criticized the council's lack of initiative. Still, by February 2001, the Met Council had not closed a single deal in the suburbs. MPHA began to publicly express its concern that the council would not fulfill its agreement on developing units, and considered reallocating some Met Council units to the Saint Paul PHA (Brandt 2001).[19] The Met Council's efforts finally paid off, however, and several weeks later, the council announced its first agreements. Four suburban communities including, notably, Maple Grove agreed to accept a total of 75 units. Soon after, other communities concurred, and the council began to develop its full allocation of 150 units in the suburbs of Minneapolis.

"Progress"

Implementing the deconcentration of families as called for in the consent decree proved quite difficult in most cases. The most expeditious efforts occurred in the involuntary relocation of north side families. This process was necessary in order to facilitate the demolition of the four public housing projects and the redevelopment of the site. The voluntary aspects of the deconcentration effort, however, were more difficult to implement. The Special Mobility Program stumbled along for many years, hampered by a lack of demand and adverse housing-market conditions that thwarted the successful use of tenant-based subsidies.

Building replacement housing also proved difficult, as it had in virtually all other desegregation lawsuits across the country (Popkin, Galster, et al. 2000). Unlike the other cities, however, officials in the Twin Cities found a way to get the units built. In many respects, the *Hollman* Implementation Group represents the best of what the Twin Cities region is known for regarding regional cooperation. A weighty, foundation-based non-profit brought together all the parties to the lawsuit, as well as all the other public parties relevant to affordable-housing development, to work together and fashion a strategy to deal with the challenges of developing *Hollman* units in the region's suburbs. Technical obstacles were solved, each in its turn. It is impossible, of course, to determine whether these solutions might have emerged anyway; however, without HIG's involvement, it is highly unlikely these solutions would have emerged so quickly.

Political opposition from receiving communities was substantial, and delayed implementation of the program for several years. Significant resistance occurred even within Minneapolis. The city expedited its efforts only when forced to by opponents of the north side demolition. Both in absolute terms and measured against the ultimate goal of 770 replacement units, little progress was made in the first four years after the decree. But as MPHA and HIG solved the technical problems, the region's escalating affordable-housing crisis resolved enough of the political hurdles to make the program work. Suburban companies and chambers of commerce began to note publicly that the lack of affordable housing was inhibiting economic development and growth. The extremely low vacancy rates and escalating housing costs made the crisis apparent to all. Ironically, then, the same housing-market conditions that made the mobility program difficult made the replacement housing possible.

While MPHA and HIG were casting about for solutions to the replacement-housing problems, the temptation to amend the consent decree was evident repeatedly. Several specific amendments were discussed, some more seriously than others. Virtually every one would have softened the deconcentrating effects of the decree. The consideration of and, in some cases, the adoption of these amendments illustrate the trade-offs between dispersal or integration objectives on the one hand, and affordable-housing objectives on the other.[20] For example, shifting Section 8 certificates to vouchers made the subsidies easier to use (vouchers being more flexible), recognizing the difficulties inherent in using tenant-based Section 8 subsidies in the very tight regional housing market of the time. Such a shift, however, lowered the level of affordability for the typical family. The desire to "project-base" some of the Section 8 subsidies represented an attempt to sacrifice the enhanced "choice" of tenant-based assistance to the objective of getting subsidized housing built. Next, lawyers for the plaintiffs also were asked whether they would waive the 70 percent set-aside of replacement units for Minneapolis families, something they would not agree to. This would have facilitated a faster rate of development but compromised the decree's deconcentration effects. Finally, the consent decree's orders that units could not be placed in impacted census tracts, or in Saint Paul, were both relaxed in order to get a development completed on the south side of Minneapolis and allow Saint Paul to contribute to the replacement-housing effort. Technically, these were steps backward in the effort to deconcentrate poor families, but were made in recognition of the difficulties of meeting the decree's production goals.

What became clear to those involved in the replacement-housing effort was that the consent decree could not, by itself, change the dynamics of the regional housing market. Affordable units were easier to build where costs were lower and political opposition less vocal. Yet these areas, too, would not provide the greatest amount of geographical and socioeconomic dispersion.

In the end, however, Minneapolis officials have been able to implement successfully each element of the deconcentration effort. Families have been relocated; the mobility program, despite its limitations, is up and running, and, as of early 2002, even expanding; and the replacement housing is built or committed to be built. The next questions thus become how well these efforts have actually achieved deconcentration, and impacts they have had on the families involved. Chapter 8 takes up both.

NOTES

1. Several families that moved before the Glenwood/Lyndale relocation received their benefits retroactively.

2. Most of the attrition in the second round of relocation occurred prior to the commencement of mobility services. Only 213 families remained in the Glenwood/Lyndale projects when relocation began, and 193 of these received relocation assistance. See Goetz (2002b).

3. This is a consistent finding across three studies at three points in time, including the pre-decree study of public housing families by Zeisel (1997) done just prior to the focus group process, the 1996 interviews completed by the Urban Coalition, and 1999 interviews done with a sample of 196 relocated families (Goetz 2002a).

4. All of those that felt rushed in the process were Southeast Asian families. This information taken from Urban Coalition (1997).

5. Almost two-thirds of Sumner-Olson residents interviewed in 1996 reported that they received transportation to view housing units, and only 6 percent used the child care assistance. One third of the respondents with children reported that they were unaware that such assistance was available (Urban Coalition 1997).

6. The definition of minority and poverty concentration is the same as for all other aspects of the consent decree: census tracts in Minneapolis and Saint Paul with more than 33.5 percent of the population below poverty, census tracts in the suburbs with more than 12.2 percent below poverty, and census tracts throughout the region with more than 28.69 percent minority population.

7. A HUD study in 1999 indicated that the "successful leasing level [in the Twin Cities] is perhaps the lowest in the nation, except for the Bay area of San Francisco, California" (Bast 1999).

8. Households with vouchers could use them for apartments that rented for more than the FMR if the household was willing to pay the difference in rent out of their own pocket. This made the typical voucher more costly for a family (necessitating their paying more than 30 percent of their income for rent) but also made it easier to use because it increased the number of potential apartments accessible to the family.

9. There are 10 named plaintiffs who have priority for the mobility vouchers. In addition, MPHA manages 3,611 units of public housing in concentrated areas. These families were notified of the program as early as 1996. Beyond that, 700 families are on the agency's current waiting list and were notified of the program in 2000. The previous waiting list contained a roughly similar number of names, though a large portion of them had moved and could not be contacted by the time MPHA attempted to notify them of the availability of SMP vouchers.

10. MPHA's overall utilization rate for its regular Section 8 program increased from 86 percent to more than 100 percent during this period. MPHA officials report that during the lean years, when agencies throughout the region were having difficulty with the successful utilization of their Section 8 subsidies, a number of *Hollman* special mobility families were "absorbed" by suburban public housing agencies. When a family executes a lease for a unit outside of Minneapolis (a case of "porting out"), the MPHA must notify the housing authority in the other municipality in order to schedule an inspection of the property and for the preparation of the lease agreement. The receiving community's housing authority can choose to administer the voucher and bill MPHA for it, or it can choose to "absorb" the voucher and count it against its own stock. In times when demand outstrips the supply of vouchers, there is no incentive for the receiving community to absorb a voucher that has been ported in. On the other hand, when the housing market is extremely tight and housing authorities are experiencing low lease-up and utilization rates, as was the case in the Twin Cities for most of the time between 1996 and 2001, there is an incentive for receiving communities to absorb the voucher (pay for it out of their own unused stock of vouchers) in order to increase their own utilization rates. According to MPHA officials, this practice has occurred with the SMP vouchers. The rate of absorption, however, would not affect the lease-up rates of the Special Mobility Program because absorption occurs after the lease-up is counted by MPHA.

11. Some suburban communities had existing HRAs with the authority and the capacity to hold ACCs, but not the number of units to qualify for modernization funds. The Scott and Carver County (southwest suburban) HRAs participated in some early projects, but lacked the size to make the HUD threshold for improvement funds. The Washington County HRA (operating in the suburbs to the east of Saint Paul) lacked the administrative capacity in the mid-1990s to run a public housing program. The Dakota County HRA had both the administrative capacity and size to participate but not the political desire. The Dakota County commissioners simply refused to participate in the *Hollman* program because they wanted their own residents to have access to all of the units produced, not just the 30 percent provided as an incentive.

12. Sharon Sayles Belton in public remarks at the Hubert H. Humphrey Institute, April 23, 2002.

13. This quote was recorded by the author at a meeting of the *Hollman* Implementation Group, a volunteer group of officials who met between 1998 and 2001 to improve the implementation of the decree, April 8, 1998.

14. This group, the HIG, should not be confused with the official *Hollman* Implementation Committee set up to work on the redevelopment of the north side site. The *Hollman* Implementation Committee is made up of officials from the City of Minneapolis primarily, and coordinates activities related to the north side redevelopment. On the other hand, HIG is a group of public officials from around the region concerned with the development of replacement housing. The *Hollman* Implementation Committee was set up by the City of Minneapolis, while HIG emerged on its own as a cooperative effort generated by actors outside the group of plaintiffs and defendants.

15. Though the Board of Supervisors gave the HRA blanket authority, it did require the agency to go to the individual cities before proceeding. This gave the cities the option of pursuing a less formal means of reviewing the project and approving it.

16. Carver County Housing and Redevelopment Authority staff, interview by author, March 1, 2002.

17. Metropolitan Council official, interview by author, September 14, 2001.

18. Some communities demanded that the council purchase units that did not exceed 80 percent of the community's median value, or to make improvements equal to 30 percent of the value of the house.

19. The council did agree to relinquish part of its allocation of 300 units in February.

20. See the classic treatment of this dilemma in Calmore (1980). See also Wilen and Stasell (2000).

8

Being Deconcentrated

It's not just a change of neighborhood, it's a change of lifestyle and a change of culture.
— Moving To Opportunity mobility counselor in Los Angeles, 1997

We had to become extra vigilant in tenant screening and property management.
We have to be careful about setting these families up for failure. Their neighbors are
looking for anything to complain about. They live in a glass box out there. Depending
on where they are, their neighbors are terrible to them.
— Scott County, Minnesota, housing official, 2002

The *Hollman* consent decree deconcentrated poor families in three ways—by demolishing public housing units and forcing hundreds of families to relocate from the north side, by moving families into replacement housing built in non-concentrated parts of the metropolitan area, and by providing mobility certificates to families enabling them to move out of concentrated neighborhoods in Minneapolis and into low-poverty and predominantly white areas in the region. Displaced families were involuntary participants in deconcentration. Forced to move because their homes were demolished, they resemble those families that lose their homes through HOPE VI demolitions or vouchering out. The other two groups of *Hollman* families are, however, voluntary participants, having willingly moved out of their previous residences, either to occupy replacement housing or to use a special mobility certificate in another neighborhood. In this respect, then, they resemble Gautreaux or MTO families that make an affirmative decision to deconcentrate. The *Hollman* case allows us to compare voluntary and involuntary dispersal methods within a single housing market, something not previously done.[1] This chapter looks at how these methods dispersed families and examines families' experiences in their new neighborhoods.[2]

Moving to a New Home

Mandatory Relocation

The families of the Sumner Field, Olson, Glenwood, and Lyndale public housing projects lived in the most concentrated pocket of poverty in Minnesota. Despite inhabiting the most disadvantaged 73 acres in the entire metropolitan area, with their worn old buildings and dreary surroundings, most residents (60 percent of those interviewed) did not want to move. As mentioned in chapter 6, the desire to stay was greatest among Southeast Asians, residents whose first language is not English, and those who had been on public assistance the longest. The reluctance of recent immigrants is understandable, of course, given their desire to maintain supportive networks. Yet, close to half the African-American residents also indicated that they had not wanted to move. The mandate to move was widely accepted only by the (very small) white population.

Nevertheless, as discussed previously, all households eventually made way for the north side redevelopment. They were moved in two waves. The first, in 1995 and 1996, involved families of the Sumner Field and Olson projects. The second, occurring from 1998 through 2000, emptied the Glenwood and Lyndale projects. Relocation counselors attempted to facilitate a move to a neighborhood and type of housing preferred by the relocatees. As a rule, poor families from minority racial groups, and especially those with language barriers, face difficult housing prospects in most cities. Lacking the purchasing power to choose from a range of different neighborhoods, they face routine discrimination in most housing markets. Further constrained by the need to be near public transit, friends and family (for help with child care), or social services, these families are unaccustomed to expressing "true" preferences in housing. In the face of these multiple constraints, mobility programs run the risk of defining these families' preferences as much as facilitating them. Well over half the families relocated in the first wave, for example, indicated a preference for Section 8 housing; only 14 percent wanted to remain in public housing of any kind. Three years later, however, more than half the Glenwood and Lyndale families expressed a preference for public housing.

Why such a difference? There were no important demographic differences between the groups. In fact, what shaped the families' "preferences" were the relocation officials themselves and the market conditions they faced. During the first round of relocation, the consent decree was still new and fresh. It was based on the assumption that tenant-based assistance offered greater choice and, ultimately, led to greater locational dispersion than public housing. The old public housing paradigm, in fact, was what the consent decree hoped to replace. As a result, relocation officials who supervised the first round of displacement stressed greater deconcentration through the Section 8 program. Three years later, however, a different relocation agency, brought in several years after the consent decree was negotiated and signed, managed the displacement process for Glenwood and Lyndale residents. Agency staff worried less about the deconcentration mandate and more about the logistics of quickly moving 200 families into new housing. Therefore, staff members consciously steered people into public housing units, rather than the Section 8 program, which held a less-certain outcome for many. This shift in relocation strategies was reinforced by changes in the housing market. The second wave of displacement occurred in the middle of the region's affordable-housing crisis, with rents rising precipitously and vacancy rates stuck below 2 percent. In such a market, Section 8 vouchers became extremely difficult to use, and this was reflected in *Hollman* families' "preferences."[3]

To a great extent, displaced families had little desire to move far away. Most wanted to stay in Minneapolis, and Southeast Asian, elderly, and larger families generally wanted to remain on the north side.[4] Those families that wanted to leave the city typically indicated a desire to move only to the inner-ring suburbs, directly north of the city. Fewer than 10 percent targeted a destination outside the central city or inner-ring suburbs. Reflecting these preferences, most displaced families focused their housing search in neighborhoods within Minneapolis; in fact, 70 percent looked only in the central city.[5] Though these families theoretically had unlimited choice, their actual housing searches reflected a very narrow set of alternatives.

These families were, in fact, as unlikely to look outside Minneapolis for housing as a comparison group of Section 8 and public housing residents. Furthermore, they were as likely as the public housing comparison group to say that they had "no choice" in determining the neighborhood to which they moved. Public housing residents, of course, must go where there are public housing vacancies, and so have quite little choice in their locational decisions. Displaced families, however, had no similar programmatic restrictions on where they could relocate. That they reported feeling as constrained as public housing residents suggests they did not experience the greater choice made available to them in the displacement process.

RELOCATION OUTCOMES

Almost three-quarters (71.2 percent) of the participants ended up in the type of housing they preferred, though the likelihood of matching preferences was related to the type preferred. Almost all families that preferred public housing were able to match it (88 percent), compared with only 70 percent for those preferring Section 8, and 55 percent for those desiring homeownership. Overall, 15 percent of the relocated families became homeowners, 42 percent moved to different public housing (mostly to scattered-site housing), and 36 percent used the Section 8 program.[6]

Displaced families, in fact, ended up more heavily concentrated in the central city than even their stated preferences would have suggested. More than half simply wound up elsewhere on the north side of Minneapolis, and seven out of eight (87 percent) ended up somewhere within the Minneapolis or Saint Paul city limits. Another 10 percent relocated to inner-ring suburbs north and west of Minneapolis, and just 3 percent moved beyond the inner ring.[7]

Figure 8.1 shows the dispersal of displaced families throughout the metropolitan area. The most obvious pattern is the high concentration of relocatees within Minneapolis, and light scattering into other communities. In fact, 20 percent relocated to an address within a one-mile radius of the center of the north side public housing site, 39 percent relocated within a two-mile radius, and 58 percent relocated within three miles. Figure 8.2 shows the actual location of relocatees within these radii, and beyond. Most families moved to other areas in the north and near south sides of Minneapolis or, in other words, to the other core neighborhoods of the city.

Though, on the whole, most families were able to move to their preferred location, the relocation process did not serve as well those families that wanted to move out of the central cities.[8] Among the displaced families, however, some locations were easier to match than others. Of those families that preferred the central city, 80 percent were able to match that preference. Of those that preferred north Minneapolis, 84 percent matched their preference. For households that wanted to move to the inner-ring suburbs, however, only 56 percent actually ended up there. For

Figure 8.1. Location of Twin Cities Families after Displacement from the North Side Site

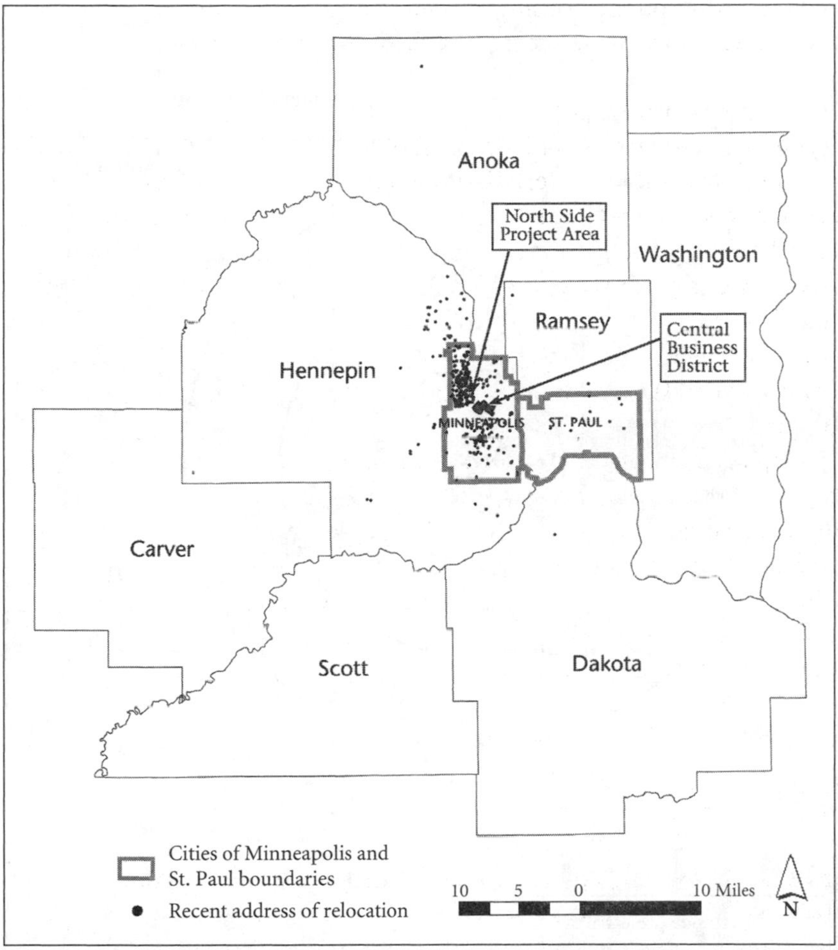

Source: Minneapolis Public Housing Authority relocation files.

those identifying a location outside both the central cities and inner-ring suburbs, only 32 percent matched that preference.

NEIGHBORHOOD ANALYSIS

What are the displaced families' new neighborhoods like? Did these families, on the whole, improve their neighborhood conditions? Were they able

*Figure 8.2. Location of Twin Cities Families Relocating Near the
North Side Site*

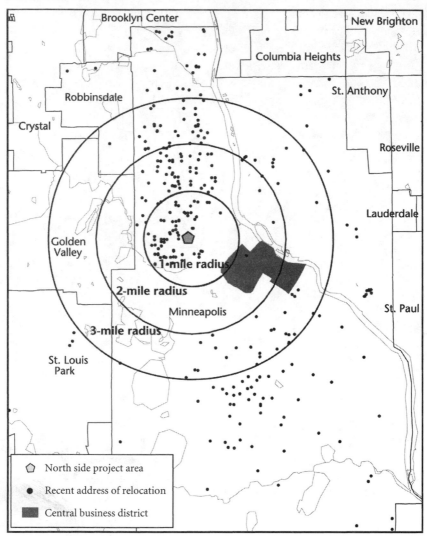

Source: Minneapolis Public Housing Authority relocation files.

to move out of concentrated poverty or neighborhoods of concentrated minority populations?[9] Considering that the neighborhood from which they moved had no match in the metropolitan area for poverty and other measures of disadvantage, their new neighborhoods, not surprisingly, look quite a bit different on a number of dimensions. The new neighborhoods enjoy significantly higher median household incomes, for instance, far fewer residents receiving public assistance, and much less poverty. Relocation neighborhoods also exhibit fewer female-headed households and a greater percentage of their labor force employed.[10] They are home to significantly fewer African-American and Asian residents. The percentage of black residents fell by half, and the Asian population, on average, is one-eighth of that residing in the north side site. Furthermore, families that moved out of the central city have experienced greater changes than those that moved elsewhere in the city.[11]

Though relocatees have seen significant differences in their new neighborhoods, these neighborhoods are, in fact, little different from those inhabited by the regular Section 8 control group. They are similar, for example, in terms of minority population, percentage of the population employed and on public assistance, and overall poverty rate. These neighborhoods have higher minority populations than other city neighborhoods, and their poverty rates are still twice as high as the rest of the city. This outcome is consistent with most research on the Section 8 program in the United States. Overall, Section 8 allows a rate of dispersal greater than that of project-based assistance, but still tends not to disperse families any more broadly than the low-income population at large. So it is with the relocation effort in Minneapolis. Displaced families improved their neighborhood conditions, but still remain in neighborhoods of higher poverty relative to the city and the region at large.

"RECONCENTRATING" POVERTY THROUGH RELOCATION?
The relocation pattern generated by *Hollman* families raises the distinct possibility that most are experiencing "re-concentration" rather than deconcentration. Three factors contribute to this assessment: Half of the families moved directly to other neighborhoods that meet the court's definition of minority or poverty concentration; most moved to neighborhoods that are in the process of adding more minority and poor residents; and those that moved more than once subsequently moved back into neighborhoods that demonstrate not only higher poverty rates than

the initial relocation neighborhoods, but are also evolving toward even greater poverty and minority status.

One-third of the families (32.6 percent) moved to neighborhoods that were both minority and poverty concentrated, according to the decree's thresholds. Being white, however, significantly reduced a family's odds of relocating to a concentrated neighborhood.[12] Families that moved into Section 8 housing (as opposed to purchasing a home or moving into public housing) were more likely to move to minority- or poverty-concentrated neighborhoods. Remaining in the central city also increased residents' odds of moving to a concentrated neighborhood.[13] The data also show that the neighborhoods to which families relocated were increasing in poverty and minority residents at a rate 50 percent faster than other city neighborhoods and four times faster than the rest of the region.[14] Twenty percent of the relocated families had moved out of their relocation home by the time this analysis was done (more than 5 percent had moved twice). Typically, subsequent movers lasted about a year in their relocation neighborhood, though some moved much earlier. These movers, on the whole, moved back toward neighborhoods with lower incomes and greater poverty.[15] Finally, the rate of increase in poverty and minority populations is greater in neighborhoods into which families have moved subsequent to their initial relocation neighborhoods. Furthermore, for these families, subsequent neighborhoods have witnessed increases in poverty and minority populations twice the overall increases in Minneapolis.[16]

Voluntary Relocation

Families in the Special Mobility Program (SMP) and in replacement housing are likely to have an experience different from displaced families. There are, in fact, bases for expecting the pre- to post-move differences to be both greater and less for those in the mobility program and replacement housing. On the one hand, not all Minneapolis families that participate in SMP, or moved into replacement housing, came from the north side site. In fact, most did not.[17] The conditions of the neighborhoods from which they moved, therefore, are not as extreme as at the north side site. Thus, less improvement could be expected. On the other hand, the replacement housing is located in non-concentrated neighborhoods (as required by the consent decree), and those families that used SMP vouchers also must move to non-concentrated neighborhoods. Both make the average neighborhood to which these families voluntarily moved less distressed than most neighborhoods where displaced families relocated. On this basis, greater differences could be expected.

SPECIAL MOBILITY PROGRAM

Some important differences stand out between families that voluntarily participated in the mobility program created by the *Hollman* decree and displaced families that participated involuntarily. Almost three out of four SMP participants between January 1996 and March 2002 were African Americans. Only 15 percent were Southeast Asian.[18] In contrast, African Americans made up only 39 percent of the displaced families, while 57 percent were Southeast Asian. This difference is predictable, given the higher rate of resistance to relocation among Southeast Asian families. Voluntary mobility participants were more likely than displaced families to be single-parent households (80 vs. 51 percent). They also were younger, on average, and had slightly smaller households. Finally, they were more likely to be employed than displaced participants, and had a higher average monthly income.[19] The *Hollman* experience, then, suggests that voluntary programs attract somewhat different participants than do involuntary deconcentration programs.

SMP participants were more likely than displaced families to want to move to the suburbs. Though staying in Minneapolis remained the preference for about half the SMP families, they were more likely to direct their search toward the suburbs, and were interested in a wider range of suburbs than displaced families. African-American and white participants were more likely than Southeast Asians, American Indians, and Hispanic families to favor suburban locations.[20]

Program "success." Program success is defined as leasing a unit with an SMP certificate. Overall, the program had a 28.1 percent lease-up rate over its first six years. That is, slightly more than one in four families that went through the counseling process were able to successfully use the subsidy and rent a unit.[21] There were no great differences in counseled families' ability to lease successfully, based on income, automobile ownership, household size, or employment status. Those that wanted to move to the city were no more likely to succeed in using the subsidy than those that wanted to move to the suburbs.[22]

Location outcomes. Most SMP participants that succeeded in leasing a unit moved to a neighborhood in one of the central cities (54 percent stayed in Minneapolis, 5 percent went to Saint Paul; figure 8.3). Almost 90 percent of Southeast Asian participants remained in the central cities,

Figure 8.3. Location of Twin Cities Families That Used Special Mobility Certificates

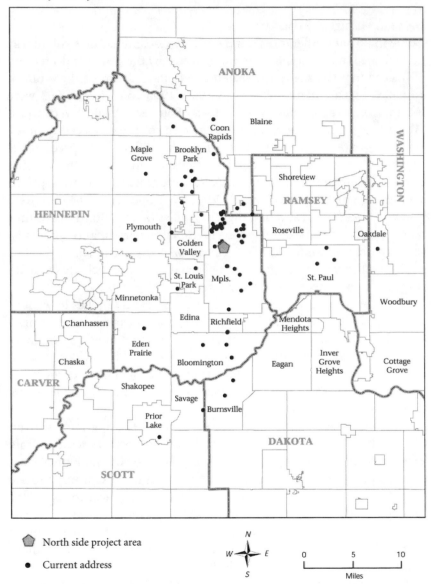

Source: Minneapolis Public Housing Authority Special Mobility Program participant files.

compared with less than half the African-American families. African-American families were the only ones to move outside the inner-ring suburbs. Interestingly, higher-income families (albeit within the rather constrained income range of SMP participants) were most likely to stay in the central cities (75 percent, compared with 50 percent for other families). Most families that leased units (59 percent) were able to move to the community of their choice. As with involuntary relocation, families that wanted to stay in the central cities were more likely to achieve their goal than those wishing to move to the suburbs.[23]

The neighborhoods to which SMP families moved showed consistently lower levels of distress than the communities from which these families came. The degree of change is not as dramatic as for those residents who were moved out of the north side project site. Nevertheless, the new neighborhoods had higher median incomes, fewer low-income residents, fewer residents on public assistance, and lower poverty rates.[24]

In a pattern that also mirrors the experience of the displaced families, the fact that an SMP family's new neighborhood was located in the suburbs had a large effect on the neighborhood's characteristics. Suburban neighborhoods exhibited more white residents, more college-educated residents, fewer low-income households or children or people in poverty, higher median incomes, fewer people receiving public assistance, and so on, across every statistical category examined (except percentage of households headed by a female).[25]

Replacement Housing

GEOGRAPHIC DISPERSION OF REPLACEMENT UNITS
As of February 2002, 416 replacement units were completed and ready for occupancy. Twenty-one percent (88 units) are in Minneapolis; the rest (328 units) are located in various suburban communities across the metropolitan area. Figure 8.4 shows the geographic distribution of completed units and significant spatial dispersion. Most replacement units are located in developing suburbs outside the central city and inner ring. None appear in Dakota County (south and east of Minneapolis), however, because that county refused to participate in response to the requirement that Minneapolis families account for 70 percent of the replacement units produced. Units can be found in many of the fastest-growing and dynamic suburbs in the region, including Woodbury (east of Saint Paul); Eden Prairie, Maple Grove, and Minnetonka (west of Minneapolis); and Chaska

Figure 8.4. Location of Replacement Housing in the Minneapolis–Saint Paul Region

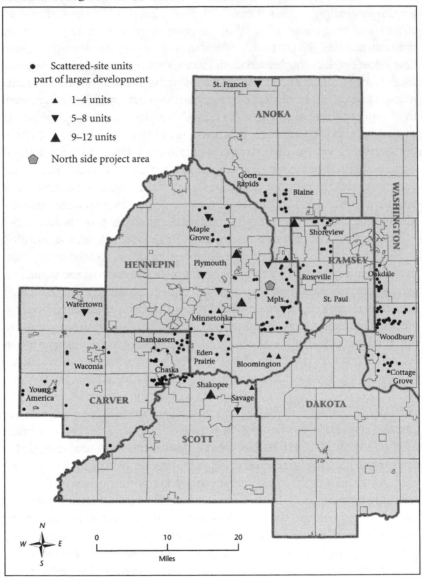

Source: Minneapolis Public Housing Authority.

and Chanhassen (far southwest). Within Minneapolis, there is a scattering of units throughout the city, including the more affluent southwestern neighborhoods.

NEIGHBORHOOD PROFILE
Not surprisingly, neighborhood characteristics for replacement housing are extremely different from those found in the north side site. Most dramatic is the poverty profile: Only 8.2 percent of children and 5.6 percent of all residents live below the poverty level in replacement neighborhoods, compared with 79.7 percent of the children and 72.8 percent of the entire population on the north side prior to demolition. Even more impressive, perhaps, is that the neighborhoods of replacement units compare favorably to the entire metropolitan area: They have a higher percentage of population with a college degree, fewer very low income residents and residents below the poverty level, fewer female-headed households, and a greater employment rate than does the metropolitan area as a whole.[26]

Eighty-four of the *Hollman* replacement units were built in smaller, mixed-income or subsidized projects. Others were developed in a scattered-site fashion, with public agencies purchasing single-family homes or townhomes and subleasing to public housing families. The scattered-site model produced units in neighborhoods that contained marginally higher income and fewer very low income families and persons below the poverty level than did the other development model. In addition, there were fewer residents on public assistance and more employed residents in neighborhoods where scattered-site units were located.[27]

In general, the record of developing replacement units in predominantly white and low-poverty areas throughout the metropolitan area has been extremely good, especially in comparison with what has happened in many other cities subject to similar consent decrees.

HOUSEHOLD PROFILE
The initial experience suggests, however, that despite the success of the Minneapolis effort, these replacement units will not deconcentrate the city's public housing families as envisioned by the plaintiffs or defendants. Despite the 70 percent set-aside for Minneapolis families, only 57 percent of the occupied suburban replacement units were actually inhabited by Minneapolis families as of February 2001. The consent decree requires only that the units be offered to Minneapolis families. If no families can be found to fill the units, then the suburban agencies are free to go to their

own waiting lists. In suburban Washington County, for example, only 5 of the first 36 *Hollman* units went to Minneapolis families. Between July 1999 and March 2000, the Washington County housing authority purchased 46 single-family and townhome units. Significant difficulties arose, however, in marketing the units to Minneapolis families. First, the waiting lists the county received from MPHA were out-of-date and inaccurate, creating difficulties in contacting families that were still eligible for and interested in suburban *Hollman* units. Second, even for those interested in suburban units, living in Washington County homes was not very attractive. Located many miles from the north side of Minneapolis, on the other side of Saint Paul, the county is virtually unknown to Minneapolis public housing families. For those individuals without a car, these units were out of the question. Even for those with personal transportation, moving to Washington County meant moving to a community about which most people knew nothing.

These problems are not limited to a single county. By early 2000, officials worried that some of the *Hollman* replacement units were being built too far away. Even the small town of Saint Francis, 42 miles north of downtown Minneapolis, had *Hollman* units. Getting central-city poor families interested in moving to a small town that far from the city was proving difficult. The drive to the Carver County housing authority southwest of the city is 25 minutes from the north side of Minneapolis. According to one staff member, arriving families comment about the distance:

> They say, "Wow, that was quite a drive." Then we take them another 20 minutes out to look at the house. This is just too far away for many families. The one thing that keeps some of them is the house itself. They look at the house and the thought of living in a single-family home would bring them to tears, and make them think that maybe they could live out here.

In other developments, Minneapolis families were not making it past the tenant-screening procedures used by private management firms. MPHA tried to get the firms to apply a less-rigid set of criteria, but it was not always successful.

Implementation of the consent decree was constrained by the dynamics of the regional housing market. Affordable units were easier to produce where costs were lower and political opposition less vocal. Yet, these areas would not provide the greatest geographical and socioeconomic dispersion. In the Twin Cities region, local officials learned that getting the units built, as difficult as that had been, was not the only hurdle in deconcentrating poor families through replacement housing. Once the units were up and operating, officials then had to find families that were willing and able to move in. Through the beginning of the replacement-housing effort, officials were successful less than half the time. Replacement units served to eliminate only the constraint of monthly housing costs from the mobility choices available to Minneapolis public housing families. These families continued to function with all the other limitations poor families bring to the housing market, including lack of transportation in some cases, need for informal support networks, and lack of familiarity with large portions of the regional market. In the end, though many families expressed a desire to move to suburban areas, few actually chose to.

Differences in Degree of Deconcentration between Voluntary and Involuntary Participants

The relocation outcomes of *Hollman* families across all categories show significant differences in the degree to which they were dispersed, and differences, too, in the profiles of their new neighborhoods. Displaced families that were involuntary participants were much more likely to end up elsewhere in the central city. They were more likely to limit their housing search to the central city than were voluntarily participating families that moved into replacement units or used the special mobility subsidies. Voluntary participants reported feeling less constrained in their housing search, and were more likely to mention the positive attributes of their new neighborhoods as factors that appealed to them. Involuntary participants, in contrast, frequently indicated that they moved to their new communities because of market and personal constraints.[28]

There are differences between the neighborhoods to which displaced families and voluntary participants relocated.[29] Neighborhoods to which displaced families relocated had higher minority populations, more female-headed households, and poverty levels two to three times higher than those in the neighborhoods of voluntary participants. More than half the involuntary participants moved to neighborhoods that met or would soon meet the consent decree's definition of poverty or minority concentrated. Of course, this would be expected, given that program rules obligated voluntary participants to relocate to neighborhoods with both minority and poverty concentrations below the thresholds set by the consent decree.

Living in a New Neighborhood

This section focuses on how *Hollman* families have reacted to their new neighborhoods.[30] It is based on in-person interviews with a stratified random sample of more than 600 families, including people displaced from the north side site, participants in the Special Mobility Program, families that voluntarily moved into replacement housing, and two comparison groups—participants in the regular Minneapolis Section 8 program and public housing residents living in concentrated neighborhoods.[31] *Hollman* families typically had lived in their new homes for more than a year when the interviews were conducted, though some had been there for as long as three years.

Children's Experiences

Previous research in Chicago and other cities has shown that children of poor families benefit from mobility programs that take them out of high-poverty neighborhoods. Changes are especially noticeable in children's school environments and socialization patterns. The experience of *Hollman* families, however, is not consistent with these findings. In contrast, there were no statistically significant differences between *Hollman* families and the comparison groups on a series of survey items about their children's school experiences. *Hollman* parents were no more likely than comparison group parents to report that their children liked their new schools, were doing well in school, or were receiving enough attention from teachers. In addition, *Hollman* parents were no more likely to report improvements in any of these after moving, compared with before moving. Multivariate analysis, controlling for demographic differences across the groups, confirms the lack of program effects.[32]

The social experience of *Hollman* children shows a more complicated pattern. Parents who volunteered to be deconcentrated reported better social outcomes for their children, after moving, than did the involuntary group. Furthermore, the children of families that were involuntarily displaced were less likely to play with others in their neighborhoods than were children in the voluntary and comparison groups. Southeast Asian families were most likely to report greater social isolation among their children (though this was in addition to, not in place of, the effect shown for the involuntarily displaced group).[33]

Social Interactions

Among the hypothesized benefits of moving to lower-poverty neighbor-hoods is the advantage their greater levels of social capital offer to lower-income families. As Briggs argues, there are two types of social capital that can benefit families: the type that helps them get by on a daily basis (e.g., a ride somewhere, a cup of flour, or 30 minutes of informal child care), and the type that helps them get ahead (e.g., job tips, references, and con-nections) (Briggs 1998). In neighborhoods of concentrated poverty, both can be limited. High crime levels can keep people behind their doors, lim-iting social-capital exchanges. Furthermore, research has shown that in very poor neighborhoods, people's social networks are often smaller and more redundant than they are in middle-class neighborhoods, thus limit-ing the formation of the social capital that allows people to better their sit-uations. Therefore, deconcentration can potentially increase the social capital of poor families. These types of social-capital exchange, of course, require people to talk to their neighbors.

The pattern of social interactions and neighboring behaviors among *Hollman* families in their new neighborhoods is complicated and defies easy summary. Fewer than one in four *Hollman* families reported getting help from neighbors when moving into their new home or apartment (with no differences between the voluntary and involuntary groups). Sim-ilarly, mistreatment by neighbors also seemed relatively rare, with just over one-quarter of *Hollman* families reporting being treated badly by a neigh-bor in their new neighborhoods. Families that moved into suburban homes were no more likely to report mistreatment than were those who moved elsewhere in the central cities.[34]

On a number of items, significant differences appeared between fami-lies that were moved involuntarily and those that participated voluntarily. For example, voluntary participants were more likely to have made friends in their new neighborhoods, though they were no more likely to have a "close friend" living nearby.[35] Voluntary participants also exhibited more "neighboring behaviors" in their new communities than did displaced families, being more likely to say hello to neighbors and more frequently stopping to talk. In addition, displaced families were significantly less likely to engage in these neighboring social interactions after moving than before, a pattern not seen with voluntary participants.[36] The decrease in neighboring was greatest among Southeast Asians. Finally, voluntary participants were more likely than displaced families to be involved in vol-unteer activities in their new communities.[37]

The racial dynamics of *Hollman* deconcentration were complicated because of the large number of recent Southeast Asian immigrants among the displaced families. They, by and large, reported better racial dynamics in their new communities than they had experienced at the north side site. Specifically, displaced families were more likely than any of the other groups to be satisfied with the racial makeup of their new communities, and less likely to report problems of racial intolerance. The displaced group, of course, typically made short moves away from the north side public housing site, but remained within the city limits and frequently relocated elsewhere on the north side. It appears as if these short moves resulted in reduced racial tension between the Asian and black communities, while not exposing the displaced families to the potential of new tensions in predominantly white neighborhoods.[38]

Comparison of *Hollman* families with the regular Section 8 participants and the stay-in-place public housing residents also reveals a somewhat complicated pattern. *Hollman* families were no more or less "neighborly" in their new communities than were the comparison groups. More important than program status in determining these neighboring behaviors was whether the family was Southeast Asian (these families were less likely to report neighboring across most of the items), and the age of the respondent (older respondents reported less social interaction). The length of time a respondent had lived in his/her current home was not significantly related to any of the social-interaction items when *Hollman* families were compared with control groups, but was important in explaining the change from pre- to post-move levels among *Hollman* families. The longer a family had been at its new location, the more likely it was to report an increase in neighboring, compared with its previous neighborhood. On the other hand, *Hollman* families were less likely to be involved in volunteer community activities than were the comparison groups.

It could be argued that an increase in social activity is too much to expect of a program that moves people out of their familiar communities and into new ones, communities that are often quite distant geographically and socially. Some might argue that the lack of a negative program effect for most social-interaction items is the most that could be expected, and is actually encouraging. What is discouraging, however, is that many of these families, especially the displaced group, did not move great distances geographically or socially. Furthermore, the social-capital argument assumes some level of meaningful contact between the deconcentrated families and their new neighbors.

Some evidence exists that the type of housing into which *Hollman* families relocated had some impact on subsequent social interactions. For example, families that moved to replacement units reported higher levels of neighboring on most items than did those families that used mobility certificates to move into scattered-site housing. Although the replacement units were located in nonpoverty- or nonminority-concentrated parts of the metropolitan area, they were, at the time the survey was conducted, in fairly large subsidized projects. The voluntary group members in replacement units, then, were living in mini-environments that mirrored (at least in income profile) the communities from which they had come. Social interactions they reported were unlikely to be with higher-income residents because their immediate neighbors also were in subsidized housing.[39] Thus, the social interactions necessary to activate the social-capital effects described above may not be occurring for these families after all.

Neighborhood and Housing Satisfaction

The impact of deconcentration on families' satisfaction with their neighborhoods is mixed. Only sporadic and inconsistent evidence exists that *Hollman* families are more satisfied with the characteristics of their new communities. The deconcentrated families were no more or less satisfied than the comparison groups with the availability of child care in the neighborhood, or the proximity of their new neighborhoods to their place of worship, or to friends and family. *Hollman* families were actually less satisfied with the bus service in the neighborhood, the schools in the neighborhood, and their proximity to health care. Finally, *Hollman* families were more satisfied than the comparison groups with the grocery stores, and the parks and playgrounds in their new environments.[40] Taken together, these items indicate that neighborhood satisfaction is not a monolithic concept, especially for families recently relocated from very poor neighborhoods. Program participants saw significant improvements in some elements of their new neighborhoods, but registered less satisfaction with others.

There was more uniform satisfaction, however, among *Hollman* families with respect to their new housing. Both voluntary and involuntary participants were more satisfied than were the comparison groups. However, displaced families, many of whom moved out of public housing and into Section 8 units, reported being less satisfied with the cost of their new housing than did the public housing comparison group.[41] Among *Hollman* families, the magnitude of improvement in housing satisfaction was greater among voluntary families than among those involuntarily displaced.[42]

Neighborhood Problems

Hollman families that moved out of neighborhoods of concentrated poverty reported a significant reduction in a range of visible, problematic neighborhood conditions. They reported significantly fewer problems of graffiti, public drinking, drug use, and abandoned buildings in their new neighborhoods than did the control groups. Furthermore, there were large reductions in these reported problems for both the voluntary and involuntary groups.[43]

Crime

There is similarly good news from *Hollman* families related to their sense of safety and rate of crime victimization in their new communities. Compared with the Section 8 and the public housing comparison groups, they felt safer in their current neighborhoods, they reported that their children felt safer; and they reported being more satisfied with the level of safety in their new neighborhoods. *Hollman* families also experienced significant improvements on all these items from pre- to post-move.[44] They were also less likely than the two comparison groups to report that they, their children, or their neighbors had been recent victims of a crime. They also reported significant reductions in victimization after moving.[45]

The findings for neighborhood problems and safety and crime victimization represent the most positive outcomes for *Hollman* families, and demonstrates the pattern of experiences hoped for by those advocating the deconcentration of subsidized families. *Hollman* families experienced consistent and significant improvements in their reported living conditions relative to where they used to live and to the comparison groups.

Employment

Supporters of deconcentration argue that moving the poor out of disadvantaged central-city neighborhoods positively impacts their ability to get jobs—a direct result of the greater availability of jobs in less-disadvantaged neighborhoods and an indirect result of social-capital effects.[46] Thirty-six percent of the displaced respondents were employed at the time of the interview, compared with 48 percent of the voluntary respondents, 45 percent of the Section 8 control group, and 39 percent of the public housing control group (none of the inter-group differences are statistically significant). Though slightly more than 15 percent of the treatment group members gained a job after moving, about 15 percent did not have a job at the time of the interview, though they had one before moving.

In fact, *Hollman* families in general, and each of the groups (voluntary and involuntary participants) specifically, show no differences pre- to post-move, and no differences from the comparison groups on a range of employment outcomes. They are no more likely to be employed, for example, or to work more hours a week. The quality of employment is no different across groups as well, as measured by wage rates, commute, and opportunities for moving up.

What Deconcentration Has Meant to *Hollman* Families

The Minneapolis case provides some evidence for the difficulties of actually deconcentrating poverty through either voluntary or involuntary means. Families that were involuntarily displaced from the north side public housing site overwhelmingly chose (87 percent) to remain in the central city, and more than 55 percent stayed within a three-mile radius of the site. Half moved to other poverty- or minority-concentrated neighborhoods (using the consent decree's definitions). One in five moved again less than two years after initial relocation, generally to neighborhoods with higher measures of "distress" than the original relocation destinations. This raises a concern over whether families will, over time, return to the types of neighborhoods from which they have been displaced.[47] Finally, the neighborhoods to which relocatees were moved, though significantly lower in levels of poverty and non-white population in 1990, had experienced the greatest growth in poverty and non-white population during the previous decade. That is, most families moved to neighborhoods that apparently are themselves moving in the direction of greater concentrations of minorities and poverty.

The *Hollman* decree did result in the movement of displaced families out of the city's single most distressed neighborhood, and broke up the region's largest concentration of poverty. The neighborhoods that relocatees currently inhabit show significantly lower levels of "distress" on every category we measure: less poverty, more homeownership, higher employment rates, fewer people on public assistance, and so on. These indicators provide great support to those who see the demolition of highly concentrated public housing and the relocation of families as improving their neighborhood conditions. The deconcentration effort's ability to move a majority of families out of areas of minority and poverty concentration entirely, however, has not been demonstrated.

At the same time, implementing the voluntary aspects of the *Hollman* decree was quite difficult. More than four years after the decree was signed, fewer than 50 replacement units had been built (out of a required 770).[48] Formidable technical and political obstacles hindered MPHA officials as they attempted to scatter public housing units throughout the region. Once a sizable number had been developed in the suburbs, it became clear that more than half were being rented by families from suburban waiting lists rather than families from central Minneapolis. At the same time, an extremely tight housing market, which had rendered the mobility vouchers as useful as confederate money in the suburbs, suppressed demand; fewer than 50 mobility certificates (out of more than 700 available) were successfully used during the first five years of the Special Mobility Program.

Families' post-deconcentration experiences offer a mixed assessment of voluntary and forced mobility. For example, there is only sporadic support for the hypothesis that participants (either voluntary or not) will report improvements in their living conditions, and better conditions than a comparison group of similarly situated, but not dispersed, public housing residents.

Positive outcomes tend to be largest and most consistent on issues related to personal safety and neighborhood incivility. That is, when asked about their own sense of safety and the safety of their children, both displaced and the voluntary group members reported significant improvements relative to their own pre-move residence, and to the control groups. This pattern was repeated for items related to the existence of "street problems," such as public drinking, drug use, and graffiti. What deconcentration has done unequivocally for these families is allow them to feel more at ease about these issues.[49]

At the same time, few effects of deconcentration appear where they could have been expected—on neighborhood satisfaction and employment experience. Neighborhood satisfaction was highly variable, with respondents reacting favorably to some aspects of their new communities and unfavorably to others. For the majority of items, however, there simply was no effect either way. Research on MTO and Gautreaux also has shown that dispersed families register lower levels of satisfaction with some public services, such as transportation and access to health care, after moving. Yet, previous research indicates dispersed families' much greater overall satisfaction with their new neighborhoods. The survey instrument in Minneapolis, however, did not include an overall question on neighborhood satisfaction, focusing instead on a number of specific elements related to neighborhood environments. The findings in Minneapolis reinforce the conclusion that neighborhood satisfaction is multidimensional, parts of which may be enhanced by dispersal, while others are damaged.

Similarly, there were no employment effects from the moves. The Twin Cities economy during the interview period was extremely strong, yet deconcentration did not translate into significant improvements in labor force participation or the quality of jobs held by these families. For the involuntarily displaced—most of whom did not move out of the central city—relocation did not, perhaps, put them in any greater proximity to areas with job growth. However, voluntary group members—many of whom relocated to suburban areas—did not seem to gain any employment benefits either.

The lack of program effects for some items is not necessarily a failing. With measures of social isolation, for example, it is perhaps too much to expect that dispersed families will actually increase their neighboring behaviors. In fact, that families transition to new neighborhoods without reporting significantly less social interaction is good news for the program. As argued earlier, however, the social-capital justifications for deconcentration require some level of social interaction between program families and their new neighbors.

Finally, evidence was fairly consistent that families forced into deconcentration reported fewer benefits. This pattern emerged on items related to the social interaction of children, and neighborhood and housing satisfaction. In these areas, the voluntarily mobile reported a happier scenario.

Mixed Reviews

The findings reported here indicate somewhat less-widespread support for the existence of deconcentration benefits than has been reported for

MTO, Gautreaux, or other mobility programs. Several explanations are possible. First, Minneapolis results are based on short-term family experiences. Most families dispersed as a result of *Hollman* have lived in their new neighborhoods less than two years. This may account for the lack of program effect in some areas. Employment provides a good example. It is unlikely that the only barrier to employment faced by *Hollman* families is spatial mismatch. Merely relocating to where jobs may be more plentiful may not be enough to generate substantial increases in employment rates. Even if it were, the majority of those displaced did not, in fact, move to suburban locations. Most stayed within a three-mile radius of their old addresses. If more indirect neighborhood effects (such as new role models, greater access to employment and training, or benefits from different social networks) are to generate greater levels of employment, then they will take more time to work.

Nevertheless, many treatment-group members had, at the time they were interviewed, been in their new apartments for several years. When length of residence was taken into account in the multivariate analysis, however, it had no effect on the degree of social interaction or on employment efforts.

Second, most previous studies examine voluntary mobility or scattered-site programs. Thus, the very fact of program participation for families in these studies suggests selection bias. Families in these programs were more motivated, less dysfunctional, or more dissatisfied with their previous living conditions than were nonparticipants. Including involuntary participants, on the other hand, is bound to reduce the level and scope of program effects. While this may account for fewer overall program effects, it does not explain that Minneapolis program effects, even among voluntary participants, are more sporadic than reported in other studies.

Third, the *Hollman* deconcentration includes a sizable immigrant population atypical of other dispersal efforts, which have been targeted at largely African-American populations. The many Southeast Asians living in Minneapolis public housing strongly criticized demolition and relocation. For the most part, they did not want to move, and their post-move experiences have been less positive than those of others. Like the previous explanation, however, this one also does not account for the more sporadic benefits experienced by voluntary participants.

Fourth, neighborhood conditions in Minneapolis were perhaps not as bad prior to deconcentration as those in other cities. The degree of central-city neighborhood problems, for example, is simply not as severe in

Minneapolis as it is in Chicago, Baltimore, and other cities where mobility studies have been conducted. As a result, the change in environment for deconcentrated Minneapolis families might not be as great, resulting in fewer dramatic changes in perceived living conditions. While this is possible, it must be kept in mind that, at least from a statistical standpoint, the north side site from which the displaced families were moved was by far the most distressed in the region, exhibiting poverty and income characteristics far different from any others to which families might have moved.

What is probably most meaningful in Minneapolis is the distinction between voluntary and involuntary deconcentration. All of the involuntarily deconcentrated families came from the hyper-disadvantaged north side neighborhood. Even though they were less likely to go to suburban areas, and even though they relocated to areas with greater disadvantages than did the voluntary group, census data show that involuntary participants still experienced by far the greatest improvements in neighborhood conditions compared with voluntary participants. That these involuntary participants actually *reported* fewer benefits from these moves on a number of dimensions, compared with voluntary families, is a serious wake-up call for advocates of involuntary deconcentration.

On the other hand, the displacement of families from the project site in 1998 and 1999 was accompanied by a prolonged political fight, and took place in the midst of an affordable-housing crisis. The notoriety of the case may have heightened families' awareness of and resentment toward their plight, and could have led to either a more critical evaluation of their new environments or a more romantic assessment of their old neighborhood. Furthermore, *Hollman* displaced a large population of recent Southeast Asian immigrants, more than half of whom did not want to leave their north side homes. Multivariate analysis demonstrated in many cases that in this population, and among older families, relocation was a less-beneficial experience. In this scenario, then, the relative lack of deconcentration benefits among displaced families is less surprising.

Demolition and decommissioning of large concentrations of public and publicly subsidized housing might be justified by subsequent improvements in these communities. It could be that reducing concentrations of poverty helps to reintroduce private capital investment in such communities. Coupled, then, with renewed public-sector attention, these neighborhoods might become revitalized, and problems of crime, delinquency, and joblessness might be reduced. Whether this, in fact, is the case is a matter for other studies (and is the subject of ongoing HUD evaluations of the HOPE VI program). The evidence presented here, however, suggests that the other justification for such action—that displaced and relocated families will experience benefits from the process—is problematic.

NOTES

1. It should be noted that there were many among the displaced families that were quite willing to move out of the north side projects. We still put these families among the involuntary group because it is not their state of mind we are examining in this chapter, but their program status. The chief objective of the analysis is to determine whether these two methods of deconcentrating the poor have implications for the experiences of the families involved.

2. The information reported in this chapter comes from several sources. Interviews were conducted with relocation counselors during 1998 and 1999 to gather information on their practices and on the relocation process in general. In addition, the relocation files of MPHA were examined for each family relocated from the north side projects. The file provides basic demographic information on the families as well as information on preferences and ultimate relocation outcomes. In all, the displacement experience of over 400 families was examined. Finally, we conducted interviews with families that were involuntarily displaced from the north side and families that volunteered to be deconcentrated, using either the mobility certificates or moving into replacement housing. Interviews were also conducted with participants in the city's regular Section 8 program and a sample of public housing residents who remained in concentrated neighborhoods within Minneapolis. Interviews with more than 600 families in the four groups (voluntary, involuntary, regular Section 8, and stay-in-place public housing) were conducted. A total of 618 interviews were completed between June 1999 and February 2000. The completed sample includes 195 displaced households, 32 residents of replacement housing, 18 families that used the special mobility certificates, 200 regular Section 8 participants, and 173 stay-at-home public housing households. For more information on the survey process, see Minnesota Center for Survey Research (2000).

3. There is some evidence that displaced families were cognizant of their abilities to compete (or not) in the local housing market. Families with the highest incomes among the displaced and that felt more able to compete in the market stated preferences that reflected their relatively greater market power; they wanted to become homeowners. On the other hand, unemployed households were significantly more likely to prefer public housing or Section 8, and long-term public housing residents—families that had not experienced the private housing market in many years—were also likely to express a preference for public housing over the other two options.

4. Seventy-eight percent of Southeast Asian families preferred to stay in the central cities. Among elderly households, 85 percent wished to stay in the city. Eighty-two percent of large families (5 or more people) also preferred the central cities.

5. In the Twin Cities metropolitan area, of course, the "central city" can mean either Minneapolis or Saint Paul. In this case, it almost exclusively refers to Minneapolis. Very few families considered Saint Paul as a relocation option.

6. Seven percent of relocated families moved without housing assistance and moved into private rental housing. Southeast Asian families were most likely to purchase a home (25 percent compared with 4 percent of blacks and 6 percent of white families), while African Americans were more likely to use the Section 8 program (43.4 percent, compared with 30.5 percent of Southeast Asians and 35.3 percent of whites). The larger the household size, the greater the odds that a family ended up in public housing, and first-round relocatees were significantly less likely than later relocatees to go to other public housing. Finally, predictably enough, those expressing a preference for public housing were more likely than others to get into public housing. Families that ended up in Section 8 housing typically were smaller households, and first-round relocatees. White families were slightly less likely than African-American families to become Section 8 participants.

7. Once again, the term "central city" refers primarily to Minneapolis in this case. Only 2.3 percent of families moved to Saint Paul. In a small number of cases making up about 1 percent, destinations outside of the inner-ring suburbs meant a community outside of the entire metropolitan area.

8. A locational match occurred if a family actually moved to one of the communities they indicated as a preference. This analysis was done with grouped categories such as "northern inner-ring suburb." Thus, if a family indicated a desire to relocate to north suburban Brooklyn Park and ended up in Brooklyn Center, Robbinsdale, or New Hope (also northern inner-ring suburbs), this, too, was coded as a locational match because the family had voiced a preference for a northern inner-ring suburb and had indeed located to such a suburb (though not necessarily the same one). This is clearly a generous definition of locational match and should lead to a high rate of matching among relocatees. Another factor that should increase the rate of locational matching as measured here is the fact that relocatees had the opportunity to identify more than one locational preference. If their actual outcome matched any of the preferences they stated, then a locational match is said to have occurred. On the whole, then, we should anticipate a high rate of locational matching to have occurred among relocatees.

9. We do this by calculating several socioeconomic neighborhood characteristics of the "average" relocatee family. In addition, we determine whether the new homes occupied by relocatees are located in minority- or poverty-concentrated neighborhoods. The *Hollman* consent decree was designed to facilitate the deconcentration of public housing residents, but displaced families were allowed to relocate to any neighborhood they wanted, providing that comparable housing could be found. Thus, we examine the extent to which displaced families were able to relocate out of minority- or poverty-concentrated areas. For the purposes of the consent decree, and therefore this analysis, minority concentration is defined as a census tract more than 28.7 percent minority, and poverty concentration is a tract more than 33.5 percent below the poverty level (or 31.7 percent or more for census tracts in Saint Paul and 12.2 percent or more for suburban areas of the region).

10. In the north side neighborhood from which families were relocated, 75 percent of the households had incomes of less than $15,000 in 1990, compared with one-third (33.2 percent) of residents in the average relocation neighborhood. The median income of the average relocation neighborhood was more than three times that of the north

side neighborhoods ($23,863 compared with $7,810). Although 60.5 percent of the north side residents received public assistance, only 17.1 percent of the residents of the average relocation neighborhood did so. The average relocatee came from a neighborhood with 79.7 percent of the children and 72.8 percent of the entire population below the poverty level, and moved into a neighborhood in which 35.3 percent of the children and 25.1 percent of the entire population lived in poverty. See table A.1 in the appendix for a full breakdown.

11. Those relocating to the central cities inhabited neighborhoods that, on average, had much higher levels of the "distress" indicators (low education, income, and employment status, and high poverty) compared with those relocating to non–central city areas. The average central-city relocation neighborhood was 29.3 percent non-white (over the court's definition of minority concentrated), 36 percent very low income, 18.8 percent on public assistance, and 27.6 percent below the poverty level. These numbers are in all but one case more than three times the corresponding figures for the average inner-ring suburban relocation neighborhood, and more than four times greater than the average non–inner ring, non–central city relocation destination. The central-city relocation neighborhoods also have, on average, much higher levels of female-headed households, unemployed residents, low-rent units, and low-value homes than the relocation neighborhoods outside of the central cities. The median household income of the city relocation neighborhoods is less than two-thirds that of the average inner-ring suburban destination of relocatees, and just over one-half that of the outlying suburban destinations. See table A.2 in the appendix.

12. Based on logistic regression. The dependent variable for the analysis is whether or not the relocation neighborhood is non-concentrated.

13. Thirty-seven percent of those who stayed within the central cities moved to neighborhoods that were both minority- and poverty-concentrated compared with none of those who moved out of the central cities. Fifteen percent of those who moved within the central cities moved to neighborhoods that were minority-concentrated, compared with none of those who moved out of the central cities. On the other hand, only 45 percent of those who moved within the central cities relocated to a neighborhood that was not concentrated by minority or poverty, compared with 75 percent of those who moved to the inner ring, and 100 percent of those who moved beyond the inner ring.

14. The City of Minneapolis between 1980 and 1990 saw an overall increase in poverty of 5 percentage points. The increase for Hennepin County was less than 2 percentage points, and it was 1.3 percentage points for the region. The average increase in poverty for the neighborhoods to which relocatees moved was more than 7 percentage points. In fact, 29.5 percent of the relocatees moved to neighborhoods that experienced more than a 10 percentage point increase in the proportion of families below the poverty level during the 1980s. The increase in minority population for the city during the 1980s was 8.3 percent overall. The same increase for the county was 3.7 percent, and for the region as a whole, 2.3 percent. The neighborhoods to which relocatees moved, however, experienced on the average a 12.8 percentage point increase in minority residents during the same time period. One-third of relocatees moved to neighborhoods that had gained between 10 and 20 percent minority residents during the previous decade, and another 23 percent moved to neighborhoods that saw an increase of more than 20 percentage points in minority residents during the 1980s.

15. The current neighborhoods have slightly more very low income families on average (37.9 percent to 34.0 percent), lower median incomes ($21,481 to $23,076), more families receiving public assistance (20.8 percent to 18.4 percent), more children in poverty (40.9 percent to 36.3 percent), and a higher overall poverty rate (29.3 percent to 26.2 percent) than did the relocation neighborhoods of families that moved (all t-statistics significant at $p < .05$). The current neighborhoods of families that have subsequently moved are also characterized by lower-cost housing, having a larger percentage of low-rent units (22.3 percent to 18.7 percent) and lower median house values ($59,197 to $62,247) compared with the initial relocation neighborhoods (see table A.3 in the appendix).

The propensity to move again is also related to where, and in what type of housing the relocated families resettled. Thirty-seven percent of the relocatees in Section 8 housing, and 39 percent of the relocatees who moved into the private market without subsidies, have moved again, compared with 21 percent of the homeowners and 23 percent of those who relocated to public housing. Finally, 41 percent of those who moved to the inner-ring suburbs have moved again, compared with 28 percent of those who moved within the central cities and 29 percent of those who moved beyond the inner-ring suburbs. This pattern is largely accounted for by the fact that 8 of 10 families that initially moved to the western inner-ring suburbs moved again. In fact, six of the seven families that moved to a single apartment complex moved again within the time frame of this study.

16. These neighborhoods to which the movers have ultimately located are adding minority and poor residents at rates that are higher than the initial relocation neighborhoods. More than one-third of the movers (34.4 percent) have ultimately located in a neighborhood in which the poor population grew by more than 10 percent during the 1980s, while 19.2 percent moved to neighborhoods with no change or a reduction in the poverty rates during those years. Sixty percent of movers are now in neighborhoods in which the minority population grew by more than 10 percentage points during the 1980s.

One-third (or 18) of the movers actually relocated to non-concentrated neighborhoods and then subsequently moved back into neighborhoods that were either poverty- or minority-concentrated, or both. Seven families made the opposite move, from a relocation neighborhood that was concentrated to a subsequent neighborhood that was not concentrated. On balance, therefore, mover-families are slightly more likely to be reconcentrated than the entire population of displacees.

17. None of the families displaced from the north side site participated in the SMP. Though displaced families were given Section 8 subsidies in many cases, they were not limited in the choice of the new neighborhood, thus the subsidies (though they came from the pool of Section 8 certificates and vouchers that HUD had committed to the city for SMP) were used as regular Section 8 assistance, and are not considered part of the SMP. In the case of the replacement-housing units, very few of them were up and operating by the time the displacement of north side families occurred. Thus Minneapolis occupants of the replacement housing have come primarily from the MPHA waiting list and from those living in Minneapolis public housing in other concentrated neighborhoods. See table A.4 in the appendix for the demographic characteristics of SMP participants.

18. Participation in SMP is defined as expressing an interest in the program and making an attempt to lease up a unit using a Special Mobility certificate. When families entered the program and utilized the mobility counseling services, an information file was created for them. Counselors recorded their location preferences and a series of demographic

characteristics. These files provide the basis for the following analysis and represent all of the program participants through March 2002. To the mobility counseling database, we have added census data to reflect the neighborhood characteristics of the families' original neighborhood (the one in which they lived when they entered the program) and their destination neighborhood (the one to which they moved as a result of the program). In the analyses to follow, these are also called the "pre- and post-move" neighborhoods.

19. The average age of heads of households among SMP participants was 37 years, compared with 44 years for displaced families. The average household size for SMP families was 3.76, compared with 4.1 for displaced families. Forty percent of the SMP participants were employed at the time they entered the program, compared with just 22 percent of the displaced families. The average monthly income of participant households was $1,090 at the time they entered the program, compared with $932 for displaced families.

20. Employed participants were less likely than others to prefer a central-city destination and more likely to prefer a move to a developing suburban area. The highest-income group was somewhat more likely to prefer a location outside of the inner ring of suburbs compared with the lower-income groups. More than 60 percent of the preferences stated by Southeast Asian families and more than 70 percent of the preferences of the "other" racial groups (American Indians and Hispanics) were for central-city locations. This compares with less than one-half of the preferences of white and black participants. Single parents were more likely to prefer a Minneapolis destination than were non-single parents.

21. The data show that one-third of African-American participants were able to lease up units in the program, slightly more than the program-wide lease-up rate of 28.1 percent. Southeast Asian immigrants, however, had a greater than 50 percent lease-up rate, far superior to all other groups in the program.

22. Close to 40 percent of single-parent households successfully leased up a unit, also exceeding the program rate. Interestingly, larger households had higher lease-up rates than smaller households had; over 40 percent of large households succeeded compared with only 25 percent of the smallest households. The average household size for families that successfully leased up an apartment is 4.08 compared with 3.59 for unsuccessful families. Interestingly, having a job or a higher income seems not to be associated with program success. Only 27 percent of families that were employed leased up units, essentially matching the overall program rate. Successful lease-up rates differed insignificantly across income levels. Having an automobile increased the chances of success in the program only slightly; 34.4 percent of automobile owners leased up.

23. Families that stated a preference for a central-city location were slightly more likely to meet their preference than families that stated a preference for the suburbs (65 percent vs. 51 percent). Southeast Asian families, for example, moved to their preferred community 90.9 percent of the time. Larger families also matched their preferences more frequently than did smaller families (68.8 percent vs. 50 percent). Having an automobile did not increase one's chances of ending up in the community of one's preference, nor did being employed. In fact, only 40 percent of employed families met their location preference.

24. The average SMP participant used to live in a neighborhood in which 44.1 percent of the residents were very low income, 23.6 percent were on public assistance, 56.9 percent of the children lived below the poverty level, and 39 percent of the entire population was poor. The average relocated SMP family lived in a neighborhood in which only 22.3 percent of the residents were very low income, only 8.5 percent were on public assistance, and

only 18.7 percent of the children and 12.1 percent of the population lived below the poverty level. These are sizable changes that show a significant reduction in the poverty of program participants' neighborhoods. The median household income of participants' neighborhoods increased from $18,206 to $30,611. The percentage of neighbors who were homeowners doubled from 31.5 percent to 62.3 percent. The only two characteristics for which there was not a sizable and statistically significant change was in the percentage of the population with a college degree (28 percent for both origin and destination neighborhoods), and median home value (in the low- to mid-$70,000 range in both neighborhoods). SMP applicants, on average, moved from neighborhoods in which 53.2 percent of the residents were white to neighborhoods in which whites made up 86.1 percent of residents. See table A.5 in the appendix.

25. See table A.6 in the appendix.

26. See table A.7 in the appendix for more information on the differences between the replacement-housing neighborhoods and the original north side site. Table A.8 in the appendix shows slight differences in the neighborhood profiles of city and suburban replacement units. Though most of the differences are statistically significant, they are not large in most cases. City neighborhoods that contain replacement units are 88.6 percent white; suburban replacement housing neighborhoods are 95.7 percent white. There are differences in income, with suburban replacement neighborhoods averaging $11,000 more in median household income than the city neighborhoods.

27. There are more homeowners on average in the scattered-site neighborhoods, and a slightly higher percentage of large units (three or more bedrooms). The housing stock in the scattered-site neighborhoods is also somewhat more likely to be old (built before 1939). See table A.9 in the appendix.

28. According to interviews with a sample of families, just 32 percent of voluntary participants looked only in the central cities, while 68 percent looked in the region's suburbs. Voluntary mobility participants were also more likely to look outside the inner-ring suburbs for their housing (40 percent compared with only 9 percent of the involuntary group). Furthermore, the voluntary group reported that their choice of neighborhoods was guided by the positive attributes of those neighborhoods (such as safety, or the quality of the house or the community) 58 percent of the time. The families displaced from the north side mentioned these positive neighborhood attributes only 34 percent of the time, essentially the same rate at which the Section 8 and the public housing comparison groups mentioned them (37 percent and 34 percent, respectively). Displaced families and the two comparison group members were much more likely to say that they chose their current neighborhood because it was what they could afford, or it was familiar to them, or that they had no choice. Southeast Asian, African-American, and Native American respondents were significantly more likely than white respondents to report difficulties in the housing search process.

29. This is based on the neighborhood characteristics of the survey respondents.

30. The characteristics of the *Hollman* settlement allow, for the first time, an examination of both voluntary and involuntary methods in the same housing market, at the same time. We are able to determine both whether deconcentration improved the living conditions of families (what could be called a *program effect*) and whether the impacts of voluntary mobility are different from those experienced by involuntarily deconcentrated families (a *method effect*). Typical research designs compare families' relocation experiences

with their self-reported situations prior to relocation, or alternatively, with the experiences of a control group of similarly situated families. For *Hollman* families, we are able to employ both methods of analysis.

31. A total of 618 interviews were completed. Respondents included 195 displaced households, 32 residents of replacement housing, 18 families that have used the special mobility certificates, 200 regular Section 8 participants, and 173 stay-at-home public housing households. The interviews were completed in 1999 when very few of the replacement units were operational and very few of the SMP vouchers were in use, accounting for the relatively small number of voluntary mobility families.

There are important differences in the demographic characteristics of the survey groups, reflecting the different compositions of these groups generally. Households that volunteered for mobility were significantly younger on average (mid-30s compared with early 40s) than members of the other groups and reported significantly higher incomes (by $221 to $324 per month) than other respondents. On both of these items, displaced families differed from the voluntary group but not from the control groups. Displaced households were typically larger than the control group families, though not statistically different from the voluntary group. Displaced households were also much more likely to be Southeast Asian (57 percent) than the other groups (for which Southeast Asians accounted for no more than 26 percent in any single group) and had relatively fewer African Americans and European Americans than the other groups. Displaced households were also significantly more likely to lack a high school education and to have spent more than five years on public assistance than were members of the other three groups. The sample subgroups differed in the length of time they had been at their current addresses. As expected, the Hollman families reported a much shorter period of residence at their current addresses (just under two years) than did the control groups (just under four years for the Section 8 group, and five and one-half years for the stay-at-home public housing group).

32. The test statistic for the bivariate analysis comparing the five survey groups is the Mann-Whitney U, which tests for difference in rankings across two independent samples. The pre- to post-move analysis tests for differences within a single population. Thus, the test statistic used is the Wilcoxin Signed Rank test. See tables A.10 and A.11 in the appendix. Multivariate tests were done using regression and controlling for the demographic characteristics of the five survey groups and the length of time respondents had been living in their new homes. The results reported in this part of the chapter refer to the findings of the multivariate analyses.

33. Respondents were asked if their children have friends in the neighborhood and whether their children play with others in the neighborhood. The bivariate analysis shows greater levels of social activity among the voluntary group children than among respondents who were displaced from the north side. When controlling for group differences, the statistical difference between voluntary and involuntary groups remains only for the item "plays with others in the neighborhood." The pre- to post-move analysis supports this conclusion. The multivariate analysis also shows that Southeast Asian respondents consistently reported significantly less social interaction for their children.

34. African Americans were more likely to receive help moving in compared with the other racial groups, while Southeast Asian respondents were significantly less likely to receive help from neighbors. There are no differences across racial categories in reported mistreatment from neighbors. This does not mean, however, that the mistreatment was not

related to race. Thirty-two percent of those who gave a reason for their mistreatment at the hands of their new neighbors mentioned race. This did not vary by the location of the family. Southeast Asian respondents were much more likely to mention race as the reason for troubles with neighbors than were African Americans (43 percent to 17 percent).

35. Two-thirds of the voluntary group (66 percent) reported having made new friends in their neighborhoods, compared with only 43 percent of the involuntarily displaced families. In this respect, the voluntarily mobile are similar to the Section 8 comparison group, in which 63 percent of respondents reported new friends in the neighborhood. The public housing comparison group is in the middle, not statistically different from the voluntary or the involuntary group.

36. See tables A.12 and A.13 in the appendix.

37. The involuntary group is less involved in community activities than are the voluntary movers, and significantly less involved than the two comparison groups as well. One-third of displaced respondents reported being involved in community activities, compared with one-half of the voluntary group respondents, 54 percent of the Section 8 group, and 53 percent of the public housing group. Both treatment groups report less volunteerism in their current neighborhoods compared with the Section 8 and public housing groups.

When compared with their previous place of residence, the involuntarily displaced reported a significant decline in community activity and volunteerism, while the voluntary group members reported no change. The displaced respondents report that prior to moving, 44 percent were involved in community activities. After relocating, that figure went down to 33 percent. Likewise with volunteering, 27 percent reported doing so prior to moving, but only 12 percent reported volunteering in their new communities. See tables A.14 and A.15 in the appendix.

38. At the same time, both voluntary and involuntary *Hollman* families reported more interracial relationships than did members of the Section 8 comparison group (with no difference between the *Hollman* families and the public housing comparison group). Both the involuntary and voluntary mobility groups had significantly fewer same-race friends compared with the Section 8 group (54 and 45 percent, respectively). Interestingly, the Section 8 comparison group reported, on average, the highest percentage of same-race friends (73 percent of the new friends made by this group were of the same race), higher even than the public housing comparison group.

When asked how satisfied they were with the racial makeup of their current neighborhoods, *Hollman* families did not differ from the control groups, and the displaced group members actually reported greater satisfaction post-move than they had prior to moving. Furthermore, when asked whether racial intolerance was a problem in their neighborhoods, the displaced group reported it to be less of a problem in their new neighborhoods, and they reported it to be less of a problem compared with both control groups. There were no effects, either across groups or across time for the voluntary group.

39. The two voluntary groups have been aggregated in the analysis thus far, but for the indicators of social isolation, there are important distinctions. Unfortunately, these subgroups are too small to permit further analysis and do not allow a multivariate analysis controlling for group differences. As a result, these findings must be treated as preliminary.

40. Tables A.16 and A.17 in the appendix list the specific neighborhood characteristics rated by the survey respondents. Controlling for demographic differences across the

groups, consistent and positive program effects for both treatment groups occur only for the grocery store and parks items. The voluntary group experienced a negative program effect for satisfaction with bus service. The analysis also indicates methods effects for satisfaction with bus service and proximity to place of worship. In both cases, the voluntary group registered less satisfaction than displaced families. These findings are consistent with the fact that voluntary group members are more geographically scattered than are the displaced households, due to the restriction that they relocate to non-concentrated neighborhoods.

41. This latter finding can be explained by the fact that all of the displaced families came from public housing where their rents were limited to 30 percent of their incomes and utilities were included. After displacement, most families had moved out of public housing and had been faced with either a down payment or rent deposit, and were typically paying additionally for their utilities. There seem to be no program effects related to the size of the unit, and contradictory effects related to cost. See table A.18 in the appendix.

Another interesting pattern is the relatively low satisfaction of regular Section 8 households with the quality and condition of their units relative to all of the other groups, treatment and control. The data here suggest that either these units do not compare favorably on quality and condition with public housing, replacement housing, and even the housing to which displaced families relocate, or that Section 8 participants had higher expectations for the quality of their units that are not being met.

42. Table A.18 shows the voluntary group reported higher levels of satisfaction than did the displaced group for overall housing satisfaction and for cost of housing. For example, though the percentage of those in both groups satisfied with their housing and the cost of their housing is high (above 75 percent in all cases), it is slightly higher among the voluntary group members. Table A.19 in the appendix shows even more evidence in this regard. While both treatment groups show positive change on satisfaction with their homes in general and the quality of their homes, the magnitude of the change is much greater for the voluntary group. In addition, the voluntary group shows significantly greater satisfaction with the size of their homes from pre- to post-move, while the displaced group shows no difference. Finally, the voluntary group is more satisfied with the cost of their housing post-move while the displaced group is actually significantly less satisfied than they had been.

These findings are reinforced by the multivariate analysis. The treatment group as a whole is more satisfied than the control group in general housing satisfaction and in housing quality when all demographic variables are introduced. But variable effects are shown for the two treatment groups on housing cost and quality. The analysis shows greater pre- to post-move changes for the voluntary group on all four housing satisfaction measures.

43. For example, only 13 percent of the displaced group and 18 percent of the voluntary group reported that drug use is a problem in their neighborhoods, compared with 47 percent of the Section 8 group and 33 percent of the public housing respondents. For example, 39 percent of the displaced group rated graffiti a problem in their old neighborhoods, compared with just 9 percent in their new neighborhoods. The percentage of voluntary group respondents who rated graffiti as a problem dropped from 32 percent pre-move to just 4 percent after the move. See tables A.20 and A.21 in the appendix.

44. Seventy-eight percent of the displaced group and 90 percent of the voluntary group reported feeling safe in their current neighborhood, compared with just 64 percent of the Section 8 group and 63 percent of the public housing group (see table A.22 in the appendix). *Hollman* families were more satisfied with the level of safety in their neighborhoods than were the comparison groups; 74 percent of the displaced group and 88 percent of the voluntary group were satisfied, compared with just 57 percent of the Section 8 and the public housing groups. Finally, *Hollman* families reported that their children felt safer in their new neighborhoods. There is also slight evidence of method effects, as the voluntary group members reported slightly higher perceptions of safety than did the involuntary group members on two items. There were no differences across any of the groups on perceptions of how safe children felt at school (though the percentages were uniformly high across the groups).

The pre- to post-move comparison reinforces the notion that the move made by *Hollman* families resulted in a greater sense of safety (see table A.23 in the appendix). The voluntary group members reported a greater sense of safety on three items compared with their previous place of residence. The percentage of voluntary group members who felt safe in their neighborhoods rose from 54 to 90 percent, the percentage who reported that their children felt safe in the neighborhood rose from 46 to 87 percent after the move. The involuntary group reported feeling safer and being more satisfied with the safety of their neighborhood, but no change occurred relative to the sense of safety among their children.

45. Twenty-two percent of the Section 8 group and 16 percent of the public housing group reported being the direct victims of one of the crimes listed, compared with only 8 percent of the involuntary group and 6 percent of the voluntary group. Similarly, 36 percent of the Section 8 group and 35 percent of the public housing group reported being exposed to the crimes listed either directly or through a neighbor, compared with only 16 percent of the involuntary group and 9 percent of the voluntary group. The pre- to post-move changes showed greater reduction in crime victimization and exposure among the involuntary group, though the voluntary group also showed improvement on some items. Interestingly, the only pre- to post-move improvements among the voluntary group members were related to their neighbors' victimization, not their own. See tables A.24 and A.25 in the appendix.

46. See Briggs (1998) and Wilson (1996).

47. Though this concern is real, it should be pointed out that the very high concentration of minorities and poverty on the north side site in Minneapolis has no match in the entire metropolitan area.

48. As slow as it has been in Minneapolis, it has been even slower elsewhere. See Popkin, Galster, et al. (2000).

49. These findings are consistent with others reported for the MTO program and among households deconcentrated in Yonkers. See Briggs (1997) and HUD (1999).

9

e Limits of Deconcentration

ty is beginning to be seen as a panacea.
—James E. Rosenbaum, 1995

lly a more suppressive move that governments can take in this society,
here we can live. Would any other people in this Country even be
ubjects for such policies? And, would any other People not raise holy
ought that they should be shunted around from area to area, in the
ing white fear that whites will flee an area?
—Excerpt from a letter to the NAACP,
in *Housing Desegregation and Federal Policy*, 1986

c housing for 100 years. This is not just about these residents. Why
sidents dictate how everybody's going to live for the next 100 years?
lic Housing Executive Director Joseph Schuldiner, responding to
residents' opposition to the demolition of their homes, 1999

verty is never easy, being poor in a community of con-
ed poverty heaps additional burdens upon people.
communities often receive inferior public services, and therefore
are home to, for example, the most troubled and poorest-performing
public schools. Furthermore, these communities are often remote from
areas enjoying the most robust job creation and expansion, making it
physically difficult for the poor to access new jobs. Such communities
limit the type of "bridging" social capital that residents need to improve
their situations (Briggs 1998). Some experts even argue that these communities foster an oppositional culture that values and rewards "antisocial" behaviors and substitutes a set of behavioral norms different

from those held in American society at large.[1] These norms, while perhaps adaptive to the extreme conditions existing in neighborhoods of concentrated poverty, only serve to further isolate those who adopt them from society as a whole.

While concentrated poverty devastates families, it is similarly destructive for the wider communities in which poor neighborhoods are located.[2] Municipal governments face dwindling tax revenues as the private sector withdraws and property values decline. Service costs, however, increase with the growth of a population more dependent on public and social services. The Detroit Scenario, which has so worried people in the Twin Cities, typifies cities virtually abandoned by the middle class, and plagued by vast areas of underutilized land, a decaying infrastructure, and a highly segregated and impoverished population. Surrounding these cities, meanwhile, are white, middle-class, and affluent suburbs free of the social, fiscal, and infrastructural problems so characteristic of central cities.

Previous studies of deconcentration efforts have typically focused narrowly on the changing conditions reported by families that have been moved out of concentrated poverty and into middle-class and suburban communities. This kind of research is necessary to determine the direct programmatic effects of deconcentration efforts, and the record of voluntary deconcentration reflected in such studies is, in fact, impressive. Evidence suggests that deconcentration, indeed, is achieved (at least when one looks at the relocation of participant households and not at the neighborhoods left behind) and that life conditions and participants' perceptions of those conditions improve (Rosenbaum and Harris 2001; Rubinowitz and Rosenbaum 2001). The record is so pleasing, in fact, that Rosenbaum (1995) suggests that mobility programs have become a panacea for those policymakers, advocates, and urban policy analysts looking to solve urban poverty problems. The record on involuntary deconcentration is not nearly as extensive, but does tend to indicate the potential for both individual benefits[3] and community benefits.[4] Most of the existing research on both voluntary and involuntary deconcentration is quite limited, however, in what it can tell us more broadly about deconcentration as public policy. The Minneapolis case study presented in these pages sets deconcentration within a broader context—the context of regional politics associated with poverty and affordable housing. That broader context provides the opportunity for a more complete view of deconcentration.

Deconcentrating Poverty by Dispersing Subsidized Housing

Despite the positive research results associated with Gautreaux and MTO, there are several reasons to suggest that mobility programs will fall far short of making a significant impact on the problem of concentrated poverty. In fact, more than simply not solving the problem, it is quite possible that an approach limited to the dispersal of subsidized housing will not even make the problem better.

Limits of Tenant-Based Assistance

Voluntary and involuntary dispersal efforts rely heavily on tenant-based housing assistance. Ultimately, the potential for tenant-based assistance to deconcentrate the poor rests upon a series of shaky propositions about the availability of units, their attractiveness to low-income families, and property managers' willingness to accept such households. Though studies show that tenant-based assistance provides families with more locational choice than do project-based programs, recent experiences in housing markets across the country also show how difficult this form of housing subsidy can be to use (Popkin, Buron, et al. 2000). In the first few years of the Section 8 program, for example, less than half (45 percent) of the households that qualified were able to find satisfactory housing with their certificates. By the mid-1980s, that share increased to 60 percent (65 percent for vouchers). By the mid-1990s, the success rate for large cities nationally was up to 80 percent, though there was considerable variability across cities.[5] Mobility programs, however, achieved significantly lower lease-up rates. The Gautreaux program, designed to move African-American families into Chicago-area neighborhoods with few minorities, was able to achieve a lease-up rate in the low 20 percent range (HUD 1999; Popkin, Buron, et al. 2000). That is, for every four or five families that tried, only one actually found an apartment for which it could use the Section 8 subsidy. MTO achieved a 47 percent lease-up rate across its five program sites, an improvement over Gautreaux, but still with a failure rate in excess of one in two (HUD 1999). In Minneapolis, more than 700 special mobility vouchers and certificates were made available to help families escape concentrated poverty in 1995. In more than six years of trying, however, the city was able to successfully launch only 79 families.

Mobility programs are hindered by a lack of units at or below fair market rents (FMRs). In some communities, the lack of suitable stock renders the approach futile. Very tight rental markets in New York City, Dallas, Omaha, Hartford, Chicago, and Minneapolis have compromised dispersal efforts in those cities.[6] In suburban Baltimore, for example, only 15 percent of the dwellings have rents that meet program limits (Ladd and Ludwig 1997). In suburban Minneapolis, less than 10 percent of rental units qualify for and accept Section 8 subsidies (HOME Line 2000). One of the original criticisms of the Section 8 program, of course, was that it does not address housing shortages, but instead assumes a slack market. In reality, a slack market for low-cost rental housing in non-concentrated suburban America rarely exists.

Participants of mobility programs are doubly restricted in their housing search compared with conventional Section 8 participants. Like all Section 8 participants, mobility program participants are restricted to apartments that lease at or below the HUD-established FMR level. Furthermore, these participants are restricted to units located only in certain neighborhoods—neighborhoods that meet the program's criteria for low poverty or low racial concentration. Therefore, FMRs may not be high enough to allow participants access to many suburban markets (Tegeler, Hanley, and Liben 1995), and additional restrictions make it difficult for participants to successfully use their subsidies at all.

Private landlords are not required to accept Section 8 applicants, so mobility programs must generate voluntary participation from building owners and operators. Recruitment of new landlords or new units in middle-income areas is critical to the smooth and effective operation of mobility programs. The Gautreaux program in Chicago, implemented by a nonprofit organization with considerable experience in affordable-housing issues in the city's suburbs, was still hampered by the difficulties of attracting large numbers of new landlords. Chicago-area landlords harbored negative attitudes toward the Section 8 program and its participants and therefore exhibited limited willingness to participate in the program (Rubinowitz 1992; Rubinowitz and Rosenbaum 2001). In some cases, too much visibility in such a program can lead to neighborhood opposition, which, in turn, might negatively affect landlord reactions.

In addition to the limitations inherent to subsidies, dispersal efforts also are constrained by the difficulties low-income residents face in negotiating housing markets. Neighborhood amenities, including service endowments, public transportation facilities, and access to medical care and social services, strongly influence the poor's mobility decisions. Many low-income families use public transportation and social services, none of which are readily available in outlying neighborhoods. Communities without shopping and service facilities within walking distance of residences will not work for many low-income families.

Dispersal also depends upon a range of individual barriers and preferences, including health, household makeup, and motivational and self-sufficiency issues. A family's makeup may force members to rely on nearby friends and family for child care. Health issues may diminish families' ability to move away from established social networks as well. Finally, individual motivational levels also strongly impact a family's ability to move to outlying neighborhoods.

The assumption that poor families *want* to move to outlying areas is also questionable. Many mobility participants fear discrimination in the housing search and harassment in new communities. Some are reluctant to participate in the programs because of perceived financial barriers, while others are reluctant to move away from familiar areas. In Omaha, for example, "many residents were so unwilling to make desegregative moves that they waited until the 120-day restricted period was lifted and they could use their Section 8 certificate or voucher in an impacted area" (Popkin, Galster, et al. 2000, 76). In New Haven, members of the plaintiff class did not want to move to the suburbs, away from friends and support networks (Urban Institute 2000). In some cities, housing authorities struggle to allocate all the mobility certificates they have. Even those who move out may turn around and move back to impacted neighborhoods at a later date, a possibility that prompts many observers to suggest that long-term support is necessary for those who relocate.[7] Reluctance to participate in mobility programs is by no means universal, however. Chicago's Gautreaux program regularly generated thousands more applicants than it could accommodate.

On top of the barriers to mobility already mentioned must still be placed another set—the poverty and, typically, the race of Section 8 users. Section 8 families are "inexperienced housing consumers who typically seek housing in the context of a discriminatory dual housing market" (Polikoff 1995, 22). White households are more successful in using Section 8 allowances outside of poor and minority neighborhoods than are black households (HUD 1995). Minority households, on the other hand, spend more time looking for housing, look in fewer neighborhoods, and search in neighborhoods with less physical and socioeconomic distance from their current homes than do white families of similar incomes (Polikoff 1995).

Furthermore, virtually every analysis of housing discrimination undertaken over the past 20 years shows that discrimination continues to pervade housing markets in all regions (Yinger 1998). Combined with continued discrimination in suburban areas (Bendick, Jackson, and Reinoso 1994; Stoll 1999; Turner 1998), these market distortions prevent low-income and minority populations from dispersing throughout metropolitan areas, even if they want to. Section 8, by itself, simply does not eliminate the barriers to mobility that exist for very low income families. The evidence shows that even though Section 8 housing allowances allow assisted households a greater geographic spread than do project-based subsidies, the dispersal of Section 8 households is no greater than the dispersal of poor households in general (Cronin and Rasmussen 1981; Polikoff 1995; Stucker 1986).

Creaming

Voluntary dispersal efforts have a "creaming" effect. By their nature, such programs apply to only a subset of the poor in concentrated poverty. This subset, on the whole, is likely to be more motivated, more functional, and have broader life experiences and abilities—in short, have greater levels of human capital—than those who do not volunteer. Of course, some highly motivated and very functional families decide they want to remain in their communities—for a variety of reasons. But very few less-motivated or dysfunctional families participate in voluntary deconcentration programs.

Beyond this self-selection, mobility programs also often employ a formal screening process. Gautreaux officials, for example, carefully screened applicants and even made home visits to evaluate potential participants' housekeeping habits. This screening was carried out to ensure the success of the families in their new environments and to protect the image of the program. According to Rosenbaum and Miller (1997), screening in mobility programs does not have to be highly selective, but it is essential to "reassure" third-party participants, such as landlords and neighbors, that the program's participants have the resources and abilities to meet the program's demands.

The low lease-up rates (of 50 percent or less) for mobility programs also differentiate ultimate program participants from others. It is likely that those who are successful are systematically different from those who are not, though no research has been completed that would even answer that question.

In Minneapolis, voluntary participants were different from the involuntary and comparison groups on a number of dimensions. They were younger, more likely to be employed, and had higher incomes. The experience of scattered-site programs suggests that the residents of these units were also systematically different from the overall public housing population. In at least three such programs that have been studied, participants were shown to be different from the overall profile of public housing residents. For example, when compared with residents of traditional public housing, scattered-site residents in Cincinnati tended to have higher incomes and were more likely to be employed (Varady and Preiser 1998). Scattered-site residents in Yonkers, New York, were significantly different from other public housing residents; they were more racially diverse and economically independent (Galster and Zobel 1998). This situation resulted from both the PHA's tendency to "reward" working families with scattered-site housing and the ability of families with more resources to work the PHA system to their advantage (Varady and Preiser 1998). These, of course, are just the measurable demographic differences between dispersal participants and the rest of the public housing population. Unmeasured differences include life experience, motivation, or other characteristics that may differentiate the two groups.

In the end, there is little wonder about the demonstrated successes of mobility programs, particularly when the participants are carefully selected from the eligible pool of subsidized households, and success is measured only among those few who actually lease a unit. Mobility programs have not been the answer, however, for those residents who do not want to leave their neighborhoods, do not meet program standards, or are unable to find an appropriate unit and a willing landlord.

Scale

Creaming is part of a larger movement evident in dispersal strategies to self-limit their scope. Mobility programs like MTO and Gautreaux face a paradox—they must remain small to remain politically viable, but smallness ensures that they will never adequately address the problem of concentrated poverty. Gautreaux, for example, operated below the radar of neighbors and officials in receiving communities. One of the noted benefits of mobility approaches over unit-based deconcentration (such as scattered-site or fair-share housing) is that locating a single family in a receiving community does not require a hearing before a planning commission and/or city council approval, as do unit-based programs. In effect, mobility can be a stealth program of deconcentration, a program that can be snuck by unsuspecting and potentially resistant neighbors and officials in receiving communities.

Advocates for mobility programs point out that only about 1.8 million poor families live in extreme poverty areas in the United States, and facilitating the movement of at least one-third of them in metropolitan areas across the country would not be an impossible task, at least not technically (Polikoff 1995). Such movement would be impossible, however, if we are (a) restricted to publicly subsidized families only, and (b) constrained to sneak all of them into the suburbs without their new neighbors noticing. In fact, it is clear that a significant expansion of mobility would be necessary to approach the scale needed to affect patterns of concentrated poverty in the United States. However, the difficulty of using tenant-based assistance in non-impacted neighborhoods, landlords' reluctance to participate in mobility programs, and the creaming and self-selection inherent in the programs all work to limit mobility's viability as a solution to concentrated poverty. Gautreaux, the largest mobility program in the country, moved 5,000 families in 20 years. Yet the City of Chicago alone has close to three million residents, 41,000 units of public housing, and, in 1990, more than 205,000 poor people living in concentrated poverty. Mobility programs in the United States, to date, have served less than 15,000 households (Polikoff 1995). Even mobility advocates such as Rubinowitz (1992) argue that programs like Gautreaux can, at best, play only a modest role in dealing with concentrated poverty in central-city areas.

The Limits of Unit-Based Dispersal Approaches

Voluntary deconcentration that relies on project-based assistance is just as likely to be of limited scope, but for different reasons. Most suburban communities have a built-up unmet demand for more affordable housing. Suburban housing agencies typically have lengthy waiting lists of families qualified for whatever subsidized or low- and moderate-income housing might be built. Myron Orfield's attempt in the early to mid-1990s to create a mandatory fair-share program for the Minneapolis–Saint Paul region, perhaps the most well-known regionalist proposal of the past decade (vetoed three times straight by the governor), could have fully operated for more than 25 years before it produced enough units to meet the year-one demand for low- and moderate-income housing in the region's inner-ring suburbs. It would have taken an additional 25 years to meet the year-one demand in the region's developing suburbs (Hsieh 1994). That is, Orfield's program could have produced housing units for 50 years before a single inner-city family would necessarily have been deconcentrated to a suburban housing unit.

Most suburban agencies prefer to serve families on their own waiting lists before facilitating the relocation of inner-city families. Suburban jurisdictions frequently use residency requirements to minimize the degree of central city out-migration that occurs as a result of these programs. These residency requirements are especially significant in metropolitan areas already suffering from a serious lack of affordable housing in the suburbs. The Minneapolis deconcentration lawsuit resulted in the creation of 144 replacement-housing units in suburban parts of the region between 1996 and 2000. Even though 70 percent of them were set aside for Minneapolis residents, only 57 percent are now actually occupied by Minneapolis families (Brandt 2001). One suburban county declined to participate in the replacement-housing program because, by the terms of the consent decree, it could not reserve all its units for suburban families. In another suburban county, suburban families occupied 46 of the first 50 replacement units built.

The country's largest fair-share program, in New Jersey, allows communities to fulfill up to half their low-cost housing obligation by paying other localities to build the necessary housing (Field, Gilbert, and Wheeler 1997). In practice, poorer communities, with greater percentages of people of color, have received payment in exchange for taking a portion of whiter, more affluent communities' housing obligations. Among the 54 deals reached in New Jersey between 1987 and 1996, all but one involved the transfer of affordable-housing obligations from wealthier to poorer communities. The average sending community had a population that was 2 percent African American, while the average receiving community was 27 percent African American. Suburban areas in New Jersey can fulfill the rest of their obligation by providing low-cost housing for the elderly and imposing residency preferences that allow them to direct the units to families already residing in the community.

Finally, of the units that are built in suburban areas, most are occupied by white families already living in the suburbs. In fact, the amount of city-to-suburb dispersal among lower-income and minority households through the Mt. Laurel program has been minuscule. Of more than 2,600 households in Mt. Laurel housing, only 6.8 percent were families that moved from the city to the suburbs (Wish and Eisdorfer 1997). Less than 2 percent were African Americans who moved from the city to the suburbs. When the movement of African Americans from the suburbs back into the city is taken into account, the net rate of African-American dispersal is less than 1 percent. Thus, fair-share programs, though justifiable on other conditions, show little potential for achieving central-city mobility.

The Limits of Involuntary Dispersal

Involuntary dispersal is even less effective in actually deconcentrating the poor. Because people who are displaced are given full choice in relocating, many move into other parts of the neighborhood from which they have been displaced. The typical displaced family, as was seen in Minneapolis, simply does not move very far away.[8] As a result, new neighborhood conditions are not as good as those found with voluntary deconcentration efforts. As of June 1998, 79 percent of families relocated out of Chicago public housing lived in census tracts that were 90 percent or more black, and 94 percent lived in tracts in which the average income was $15,000 or less (Rumbler 1998). Another study found that only 6 percent of displaced families moved to tracts that were less than 10 percent of their own race (Rubenstein 1988). Displaced families, the studies show, are followers of racial change rather than pioneers. Unlike the pattern for voluntary mobility programs, counseling assistance does not have much impact in helping to disperse families involuntarily displaced (Varady and Walker 2000). In Minneapolis, fully half the displaced families did not even manage to relocate to a non-concentrated neighborhood. Families involuntarily deconcentrated also do not report the same magnitude of improvement in their living conditions as do participants in voluntary programs.

Promises of relocation assistance and preference for replacement housing do not always materialize. Public authorities easily manipulate rules governing relocation and replacement housing—to the detriment of the low-income families the rules are meant to assist. In Atlanta, for example, most residents of the city's first HOPE VI project did not receive relocation assistance (Keating 2000). Many very low income families find that they do not qualify or meet the screening criteria for replacement housing built on the site of their old neighborhoods (Popkin, Buron, et al. 2000). These are the very same families that confront the greatest challenges using Section 8 subsidies in the rental market.

Political Limitations

In addition to the inherent programmatic limitations of deconcentration efforts, political opposition also works to restrict their scope and effectiveness. The political fragility of mobility programs, for example, is well illustrated by what happened to MTO in Baltimore in 1995. Local politicians were easily able to whip up an intense political reaction to the program, appealing to racial fears and images of low-income, inner-city blacks invading stable suburban communities. The controversy ultimately ended the MTO program, limiting expenditures (and therefore the program's scope) to the amounts already authorized by Congress. The prospect of more suburban resistance to such "social engineering" by HUD was more than members of Congress were willing to endure. In Dallas, suburban homeowners successfully sued to stop the development of scattered-site public housing being built pursuant to the *Walker v. HUD* desegregation suit. Scattered-site units in Hartford, Connecticut, were targets of arson.

These cases, as well as the events in Minneapolis, indicate that the very arguments for deconcentration provide the basis for opposition in the region's outlying areas. The reasoning seems straightforward enough. Deconcentration advocates in effect say to the suburbs, "'Too many poor people are a serious problem for us, so it is necessary for you to take some." This sets dispersal efforts in the worst possible political context by emphasizing the pathologies of concentrated poverty as the basis for what is, in essence, a question of fair housing. In the end, deconcentration provides little hope for generating regional cooperation. The federal government's first generation of dispersal efforts, based on racial desegregation, had better political footing than deconcentration of poverty. Dispersal programs undertaken in the late 1960s and early 1970s could be justified on the basis of fairness and equal opportunity, and as a means of reversing decades of illegal discrimination. Even these high-minded ideals could not, in the end, overcome the entrenched social divisions of that era. Twenty-five years later, however, the justifications used for dispersal are significantly less compelling. Suburban residents and their elected officials might be excused if they conclude that they are being asked to accept central-city pathologies into their own communities.

Deconcentration has also produced political opposition from *within* poor communities themselves. The opposition can take different forms. First, there are those who defend the communities that public officials are trying to break up through displacement and redevelopment. Ample evidence from a number of cities indicates that participants often object to the loss of their homes, and that many residents prefer not to move from their units (Vale 1997). The Chicago Cabrini-Green HOPE VI project generated significant resident opposition, and was among the most acrimonious HOPE VI projects in the nation—this, in one of America's most notoriously dangerous public housing projects. Many of the residents of Cabrini-Green, though noting the deficiencies of the project, "often [thought] of their part of Chicago as a good place to live" (Bennett and Reed 1999, 201).

To some, deconcentration is seen as a means of diluting minority political strength by draining off resources, attention, commitment, and people from the black community (Rubinowitz 1992). Forced dispersal programs, furthermore, "imply a view of valid community as white over black and solidifies an already entrenched racial hierarchy" (Rubinowitz 1992; Tein 1992). At the very least, mobility programs may imply that suburban areas are preferable, compared with cities. In Minneapolis, some leaders of the north side community invoked this argument in opposition to the public housing demolition. As one member of the "*Hollman* 14" said about the decree, "Folks of color have never had a problem living with folks of color. Somebody outside the community decided that" (Diaz 1999g).

Alternatively, there are those who consider involuntary displacement of poor families an inappropriate use of public power, and resettlement too disruptive of low-income families. Even if residents agree that their current neighborhoods are not good places to live, involuntary displacement and forced relocation via tenant-based assistance are likely to generate opposition. Residents of Chicago's other notorious public housing project, the Robert Taylor Homes, were reluctant to be moved into Section 8 units. A residents' survey showed that two-thirds opposed demolition and the conversion of subsidies to tenant-based Section 8 assistance.[9] The difficulties of making Section 8 work for very low income families caught up in hot real estate markets make housing allowances a poor substitute for public housing, and many public housing families know that.

Scenes of African Americans picketing the HOPE VI demolition of their homes are reminiscent of the Urban Renewal program and highway construction that together displaced an estimated 3.8 million people between 1956 and 1972 (Fainstein and Fainstein 1986, 49). In such a context, deconcentration is simply part of a history of forced migrations for people of color and the poor, and represents a coercive use of state authority not imposed on other populations.

The Communities Left Behind

A paradoxical element inherent to deconcentration strategies, as embodied by mobility or unit-based dispersal programs, is that they are typically not about improving the conditions in neighborhoods with concentrated poverty (with the exception of HOPE VI, an involuntary approach). Gautreaux is not designed to improve the poor neighborhoods within Chicago, nor is MTO being judged by whether it improves conditions in the central neighborhoods of the five cities where it operates. Fair-share and scattered-site housing programs do not address conditions in such neighborhoods either.

Proponents rarely argue that dispersal will reduce the intensity of poverty in central neighborhoods, thus making them more attractive to private investment and even the return of a middle class. Such a return of investment might, in fact, produce some positive neighborhood effects for those left behind. There is little evidence, however, that voluntary dispersal programs achieve these results. Indeed, the possibilities seem so remote that proponents do not even mention them, and the official studies of Gautreaux and MTO do not investigate them. Deconcentration, instead, has typically meant that a limited number of participants have been provided "access to higher-quality municipal services. Meanwhile, most low-income African-American families remain concentrated in segregated areas of the city" (Wilen and Stasell 2000, 140).

Rather than expecting dispersal programs to improve conditions in neighborhoods of concentrated poverty, it is more reasonable to expect that voluntary dispersal, in fact, may worsen these conditions. If voluntary dispersal efforts "cream," and they do, then those left behind are, on the whole, even more disadvantaged as a group than they were prior to dispersal. Dispersal in all likelihood intensifies the concentration of disadvantage in the communities left behind. This situation will also, if anything, intensify the individual and community-level problems associated with concentrated poverty.

Involuntary deconcentration efforts, such as HOPE VI, will have different impacts on communities of concentrated poverty. HOPE VI has produced very striking improvements in micro-neighborhoods across the country. Previously decrepit and dangerous public housing projects have been transformed into attractive and viable developments, with a greater mixture of uses and a larger assortment of incomes among residents. These programs have clearly improved the public housing projects themselves. Four things, however, have not yet been determined about HOPE VI transformations. First, it is unclear whether these changes are sustainable over a longer period of time (Nyden 1998). Second, the likelihood that such mixed-income communities offer true benefits to the lower-income families residing there is uncertain (Keating 2000; Popkin, Buron, et al. 2000; Schwartz and Tajbakhsh 1997). Third, it is unclear whether the new micro-neighborhoods will have positive spillover effects on the surrounding communities (Schwartz and Tajbakhsh 1997). Fourth, there are as yet no follow-up studies tracking the effects of displacement on public housing families.

The ongoing HUD evaluation of HOPE VI will attempt to document the extent of more widespread neighborhood revitalization as a result of public housing redevelopment. If such positive spillover occurs, the program's potential for deconcentrating poverty is magnified significantly. On the other hand, if the program is too successful at generating positive spillover benefits, it may result in neighborhood gentrification, displacement, and transformation. Successful dispersal policy, as distinguished from gentrification policy, must strike a balance between a scale of change so small that it fails to generate reductions in social pathologies, on the one hand, and so large that it results in total gentrification and dislocation of the poor, on the other.

Is a Concerted Effort to "Deconcentrate Poverty" Counterproductive?

Deconcentration and the "New Community Development"

Concerns over concentrated poverty rarely deal with actual causes. Instead, concentrated poverty has become the chief evil of urban politics over the past decades because of its effects, including high drug use, crime rates, school delinquency, out-of-wedlock childbirth, and so on. As these behaviors of the central-city poor are described on the evening news, decried by political pundits, and identified by politicians as the country's single greatest domestic challenge, the politics of urban poverty in America begin to slide away from dealing with root causes to dealing with symptoms instead. Among neighborhood activists, the shift in perspective is from identifying the external systems that produce neighborhood poverty to focusing on the damaging behaviors of some of those residing in poverty neighborhoods. The great urban neighborhood struggle of the 1970s was against redlining by lenders and insurers, and what was perceived as the slow and unwarranted strangulation of urban communities by these outside institutions. In the 1980s, neighborhood activists responded to the disinvestment of non-local capital and the decentralization of economic functions away from central-city neighborhoods. The concentration-of-poverty paradigm, however, forced current neighborhood activists to turn inward: There are simply too many poor people.

It was but a short step for many from recognizing that too many poor people were a problem for their neighborhoods to concluding that the poor themselves were the problem. Such a conclusion was only reinforced by the moral panic about crack cocaine and inner-city gang activity that emerged in the late 1980s, roughly the same time that concentrated poverty was being recognized as a social issue. As criminal justice efforts across the country briefly hijacked the community development movement, neighborhood improvement was defined as protection from "those people," and long-term stabilization was equated with their removal. It was in such an environment that "Weed and Seed," a program that in operation focused on criminal justice projects, could become the country's main urban revitalization program. In this setting, legislators across the country called for tougher sentencing guidelines, including the so-called "three-strikes-and-you're-out" provision to deal with repeat offenders. So it was no accident that even this policy was adapted for the inner-city poor in 1997 when the federal government introduced a "one-strike-and-you're-out" policy for public housing residents. This policy, and various "drug-free zones" that impose tougher sentencing in certain neighborhoods, ensure that people living in concentrated poverty routinely receive harsher penalties than other citizens for the same crimes, and sometimes even for crimes they themselves did not commit.[10]

Such a discourse complements a neoconservative view of urban policy that emphasizes the "failure" of community development, the culpability of government programs to reduce poverty (which purportedly end up creating greater dependency among the poor), and, ultimately, the shiftlessness of the urban poor.[11] While more reactionary observers in the 1980s and 1990s claimed inherent intellectual inferiority among the poor, and counseled a triage approach (Herrnstein and Murray 1996), liberal observers were writing and talking about the culture of incivility, the oppositional culture of urban ghettos, and the phenomenal failure of community development efforts.[12] The concentration-of-poverty paradigm joined, at least superficially, these elements of the right and the left, concluding that place-based efforts have failed, and the concentration of dysfunctional families is the problem to be addressed. That the agreement between the left and the right was only superficial might matter to academic observers, but it matters little at the level of neighborhood politics. The prescriptions are pretty much the same: Reduce efforts to improve the lives of poor people in place, and encourage (or force) their relocation.

The Race to the Bottom

City officials and neighborhoods across the central cities and into the first-ring suburbs of the Twin Cities region accepted the concentration-of-poverty argument. As the paradigm gained wider currency, urban neighborhood groups and city and suburban officials began to look for ways to reduce their poverty concentrations. What they settled on was, at the least, a newfound reluctance to produce more subsidized housing, and at a greater extreme, the resolve to demolish some of the existing affordable housing.

When accepted as a political strategy, deconcentration justifies the redirection of community development efforts away from the declining housing stock of poor neighborhoods and/or away from poorer residents. In Minneapolis, deconcentration meant shifting housing rehabilitation resources away from rental housing and toward homeownership subsidies. It meant shifting priorities out of the central neighborhoods and toward outlying areas. To deconcentration advocates, subsidized multifamily housing was one of the factors that "anchored" the poor to the central cities' core neighborhoods. This thinking, of course, reversed the existing formula for successful community development. Previously, community development advocates had considered subsidized multi-family housing rehabilitation as a means of improving run-down properties that already existed in the neighborhood—properties that in most cases were poorly managed, were the location typically of neighborhood problems, and were not assets to their communities. Subsidized rehabilitation, in fact, resulted in the physical improvement of the building and, typically, in better property management. In the concentration-of-poverty paradigm, however, multifamily rehabilitation does not produce such benefits to low-income communities; it only works to further concentrate poor families. Attempts by public agencies to redirect building subsidies out of concentrated neighborhoods are, in practice, a form of self-imposed redlining of low-income neighborhoods, with the potential for worsening building and housing conditions.

Deconcentration justifies the opinion put forth by many neighborhood groups in core Twin Cities urban areas that they "have done their fair share" of affordable housing—in fact, more than their fair share. Even first-ring suburbs have bought into the argument, and decided that they, too, need to deconcentrate poverty within their boundaries by eliminating the poor's housing options. The new community development strategy resulting from adoption of the deconcentration paradigm is about reducing services for lower-income families and attracting more middle-income homebuyers. This approach has been widely embraced, even in communities where an overwhelming majority of the residents are tenants and the housing stock rental.

The deconcentration argument undeniably introduced a more regional perspective to many involved in community development. However, acceptance of that regional perspective was greatest in those communities (central neighborhoods) that had been most active in providing affordable housing, with a resulting negative impact. The idea of deconcentration convinced community leaders that many of their problems were not of their own making, that their neighborhoods were part of a regional system of communities, and that other areas were thriving at their expense. These central areas, therefore, resolved to do less, and urge, encourage, and wait for other areas to do more. The difficulty, however, was that the developing suburbs—areas that had the least amount of affordable housing and had benefited most from the system— were still no more willing to accept low-cost housing than they had been before.

In fact, the concentration-of-poverty argument provided the basis for the suburbs' continued opposition to affordable housing. They were convinced—by media accounts of violence in central-city neighborhoods, by reports of the decline in city schools, and by the very words used by the deconcentration advocates—that too much poverty was bad for a community. This viewpoint quite nicely reinforced what suburban residents had always felt about low-cost housing. What the concept of deconcentration wrought in Minneapolis and Saint Paul was a version of the "race to the bottom." Activists and officials in virtually every community wanted to limit their exposure to the poor by limiting low-cost housing.

Dispersal—An Overly Narrow Response to Concentrated Poverty

In theory, a range of potential policy responses address the problem of concentrated poverty. The concentration of assisted housing is only one factor shown to have contributed to the problem. Focusing on where the poor live may, in fact, not even be a fruitful avenue for deconcentration efforts. Recent research has shown, for example, that the spatial redistribution of the nonpoor and their tendency to further segregate themselves from lower-income households increase neighborhood poverty rates.[13] A more comprehensive policy to address urban poverty, therefore, would extend beyond the relocation of assisted households to address zoning and other regulatory barriers erected by exclusive and exclusionary communities.[14] Such an approach would impact the distribution of non-assisted housing units and the resulting income profile of developing areas. Poverty policy would then be expanded beyond the narrow confines of subsidized housing. Assisted housing is, in any case, a very small segment of any given housing market—a segment that has not grown in the recent past nor is likely to in the near future. To truly address poverty in American urban areas, we must be willing to be more directive about the spatial distribution of the nonpoor and non-assisted housing.

Similarly, policy responses could be tied to other factors that have been argued to contribute to socioeconomic segregation, including racial discrimination in housing and employment, local governmental fragmentation, the "inelasticity" of central cities, and the fiscal incentive structure of local government. Systematic public and private disinvestment from central cities in favor of outlying and smaller metropolitan areas has accelerated the movement of economic opportunities out of central areas. The phenomenon of concentrated poverty is highly variable from one place to another; consequently, the problem demands a multifaceted response to address a range of processes. Bollens (1997), for example, suggests a series of policies that go beyond the mobility approach. These efforts would include limiting suburban sprawl (though the relationship between sprawl and segregation is debated[15]), encouraging a jobs/housing balance, targeting transportation and redevelopment activities to encourage brownfield development, requiring regional impact analyses for development, and promoting regional revenue sharing.

Various public policies at different levels of government facilitate growing economic disparities and the resultant geographic bifurcation of the American urban landscape. As Dreier, Mollenkopf, and Swanstrom (2001) argue, federal policies have consistently favored investment in suburban areas over central cities, and encouraged fragmentation and competition among cities within metropolitan areas.[16] Local policies—from racial zoning and land use restrictions to the system of local public financing in metropolitan areas—also have contributed to concentrations of wealth and poverty in America's urban areas. These authors and others suggest a range of policies aimed at opening housing markets, tax-base sharing, and targeting federal incentives to encourage more equitable metropolitan growth patterns (Dreier, Mollenkopf, and Swanstrom 2001; Orfield 1997; Rusk 1999).

Serving the interests of disadvantaged central neighborhoods also requires a sustained effort at improving neighborhood conditions for the people who live there. Traditional community development efforts to improve the physical stock of inner-city housing, to locate and provide essential services for people who need them, and to enhance community networks and strengthen community institutions must be a part of the effort. Targeted, comprehensive community-building initiatives that harness the efforts of a range of public, private, and nonprofit actors to redirect the poorest central-city neighborhoods can, as Rusk argues, have greater impact as part of a more comprehensive approach to economic disparities.

A broader approach to urban poverty should include a program of voluntary mobility that enables families to voluntarily move out of central neighborhoods and into other communities. Though some of these actions are appropriately undertaken by local governments, they are, in many cases, better set within the activities of regional or statewide bodies. The federal government could easily play a role in encouraging and supporting all of them. A combination of these approaches improves upon the antipoverty strategy by affecting more than just the small portion of the housing market that is government subsidized.

Not the least important to a more effective regional strategy for reducing geographic disparities is abandonment of "deconcentration" as the political rationale. As the Twin Cities case shows, the discourse surrounding deconcentration gives rise to a politics that is not conducive to regional cooperation, not supportive of low-income populations, and unlikely, in any event, to achieve its stated goals. In the Twin Cities case, regional progress on low-income housing development in the suburbs went forward only when "deconcentration" receded from the public discourse and other rationales for spreading affordable housing replaced it.

A responsible antipoverty policy should not lead with the demolition of low-cost housing and the forced relocation of the poor. This nation's history with the urban renewal program suggests that without complementary actions to reduce exclusionary barriers and incentives that foster and facilitate growing socioeconomic disparities—and the geographic expression of those disparities—the scattering of poor people, in itself, accomplishes little.

NOTES

1. See, for example, Wilson (1987).

2. See Orfield (1997) and Rusk (1999).

3. See Varady and Walker (2000).

4. See, for example, Vale (1997).

5. See, for example, Weicher (1990). The lease-up rate for Section 8 actually decreased somewhat over the last half of the 1990s, dropping to 69 percent, according to a recent HUD study. See Finkel and Buron (2001).

6. For information on New York City, Dallas, and Omaha, see Popkin, Galster, et al. (2000). For Hartford, see Donovan (1994). For Chicago, see Bennett and Reed (1999) and Popkin, Buron, et al. (2000).

7. See, for example, Popkin, Galster, et al. (2000) and Turner (1998).

8. See Varady and Walker (2000) for evidence on four other cities.

9. This survey was done in response to the Chicago Housing Authority's contention that they had two surveys showing overwhelming support for Section 8. See Rogal (1999).

10. The "one strike" provisions in public housing, for example, can result in the eviction of an entire household if anyone in that household is associated with drug activity.

11. For representative examples of this thought, see Banfield (1970); Mead (1986); and Murray (1984).

12. See the arguments in Orfield (1997) and Rusk (1999) on the failure of community development. See also Lemann (1994) on this point.

13. Holloway et al. (1998, 546–47) found that "the neighborhood distribution of poor Blacks and Whites worked to reduce neighborhood poverty exposure." The community studied by these authors was Columbus, Ohio.

14. Such an approach is advocated by Anthony Downs (2001).

15. See Downs (1999) and Pendall (2001).

16. Dreier, Mollenkopf, and Swanstrom argue that these effects have been both direct and indirect. Even policies such as highway construction, defense spending, and housing policy that are not explicitly intended to have urban impacts have, in fact, favored suburban development. More explicit urban policies such as urban renewal and public housing have more directly contributed to socio-spatial segregation.

Appendix

Table A.1. Neighborhood Profiles in the Twin Cities Area, by Location

Neighborhood characteristic	North side project site	Relocation neighborhood	Significance	City of Minneapolis	County	Region
Race/ethnicity						
White (%)	5.8	64.5	***	78.4	89.3	92.1
Black (%)	45.6	23.2	***	13.0	5.8	3.6
Asian (%)	47.2	6.4	***	4.3	2.9	2.6
Education						
College graduates (%)	5.3	25.3	***	30.3	31.6	27.1
Income						
Very low income[a] (%)	75.1	33.2	***	29.6	18.1	16.6
With income (%)	40.9	75.2	***	79.2	84.2	85.5
Receiving public assistance (%)	60.5	17.1	***	10.5	6.1	5.5
Children in poverty (%)	79.7	35.3	***	30.6	13.5	11.2
Population in poverty (%)	72.8	25.1	***	18.5	9.2	8.1
Median household income ($)	7,810	23,863	***	25,324	35,659	36,565

Household status						
Female-headed households (%)	29.1	13.7	***	26.3	16.3	14.4
Employment						
Labor force employed (%)	34.7	69.3	***	69.1	73.6	74.3
Housing						
Homeowners (%)	3.8	51.0	***	49.7	63.4	68.7
Housing units built before 1939 (%)	14.1	46.4	***	53.2	24.0	20.5
Housing units with 3+ bedrooms (%)	14.5	40.4	***	35.1	48.8	54.0
Low-rent housing units[b] (%)	79.9	19.3	***	20.4	13.6	13.8
Low-value homes[c] (%)	100	73.3	***	63.6	35.9	39.0
Median home value ($)	49,326	63,852	***	71,500	89,700	87,400

Source: 1990 Census.

Notes: $N = 426$. The test for statistical significance applies to the "north side project site" and "relocation neighborhood" columns. Data are from the 1990 census because the 2000 census did not contain data for the north side project site, which was entirely demolished by the time of the 2000 census.

[a] Income less than $15,000.

[b] Rents below $300.

[c] Values below $75,000.

$* p < .05$, $** p < .01$, $*** p < .001$.

Table A.2. Relocation Neighborhood Profiles in the Twin Cities Area, by Community and Housing Type

Neighborhood characteristic	Type of community			Type of housing		
	Central cities	Inner-ring suburbs	Other	Home-ownership	Public housing	Section 8 housing
Race/ethnicity						
Non-white (%)	29.3***	9.3	5.6	75.8**	62.6	62.1***
Education						
College graduates	24.1***	32.2	40.0	21.2**	27.4	24.7***
Income						
Very low income[a] (%)	36.0***	13.4	10.4	24.4***	35.0	34.1**
Receiving public assistance (%)	18.8***	5.7	4.1	12.1**	18.1	17.8***
In poverty (%)	27.6***	7.7	5.4	15.9**	26.9	26.3**
Median household income ($)	22,017***	36,158	41,913	29,200***	23,085	22,726***

Household status						
Female-headed households (%)	14.8***	8.3	5.8	11.4	14.1	14.1*
Employment						
Labor force employed (%)	67.4***	82.3	84.0	72.6**	68.1	69.8
Housing						
Homeowners (%)	49.7**	61.2	64.0	68.7***	50.1	45.5***
Low-rent housing units[b] (%)	21.3***	3.7	7.1	12.7**	22.5	17.4*
Low-value homes[c] (%)	79.0***	38.1	20.7	75.1	73.8	71.2
Median home value ($)	60,499***	83,405	113,200	64,161	67,095	60,441
n	373	44	9	66	172	145

Source: Author's calculations from 1990 census data and Minneapolis Public Housing Authority relocation files.

Note: The t-test compares the means for central cities with those of the inner-ring suburbs, and the means for home ownership and Section 8 housing with public housing.

[a]Income less than $15,000.
[b]Rents below $300.
[c]Values below $75,000.
*$p < .10$, **$p < .05$, ***$p < .01$.

Table A.3. Profiles of Original and Relocation Neighborhoods in the Twin Cities Area (for Relocatees Who Have Moved More Than Once)

Neighborhood characteristic	Initial relocation neighborhood	Current neighborhood	Significance
Race/ethnicity			
White (%)	63.3	60.4	—
Black (%)	23.8	24.0	—
Asian (%)	7.0	9.3	**
Education			
High school graduates (%)	29.1	30.3	**
College graduates (%)	25.4	30.3	***
Income			
Very low income[a] (%)	34.0	37.9	***
With income (%)	75.3	72.4	***
Receiving public assistance (%)	18.4	20.8	**
Children in poverty (%)	36.3	40.9	**
Population in poverty (%)	26.2	29.3	**
Median household income ($)	23,076	21,481	**
Household status			
Female-headed households (%)	15.0	15.4	—
Employment			
Labor force employed (%)	68.7	66.6	—
Housing			
Homeowners (%)	45.9	45.4	—
Housing units built before 1939 (%)	43.6	47.3	—
Housing units with 3+ bedrooms (%)	37.6	36.5	—
Low-rent housing units[b] (%)	18.7	22.3	**
Low-value homes[c] (%)	73.2	77.3	—
Median home value ($)	62,247	59,197	**

Source: Author's calculations from 1990 census data and Minneapolis Public Housing Authority relocation files.

Note: N = 180.

[a] Income less than $15,000.

[b] Rents below $300.

[c] Values below $75,000.

*p < .10, **p < .05, ***p < .01.

Table A.4. Demographics of Special Mobility Program (SMP) Participants in the Twin Cities Area

Characteristic	Number of participants
Race/ethnicity ($n = 225$)	
African American	165 (73.3)
American Indian	12 (5.3)
Hispanic	2 (0.9)
Southeast Asian	33 (14.7)
White	11 (4.9)
Other	2 (0.9)
Single-parent household ($n = 223$)	183 (80.6)
Average age of head of household ($n = 275$)	37.09
Average household size ($n = 230$)	3.76
1–2 people	71 (31.3)
3–4 people	96 (42.3)
5 or more people	60 (26.4)
Average number of children under age 18 ($n = 227$)	2.45
0	25 (11.0)
1–2	115 (50.7)
3–4	60 (26.4)
5 or more	27 (11.8)
Employed ($n = 215$)	85 (39.5)
Has automobile ($n = 204$)	90 (44.1)
Monthly income status ($n = 206$)	
Average monthly income ($)	1,090
< $750	66 (32.0)
$750–$1,500	92 (44.7)
> $1,500	48 (23.3)

Source: Author's calculations from Minneapolis Public Housing Authority files on SMP participants.

Notes: $N = 285$. The figures in parentheses represent the percentage of those individuals for whom the relevant information is available.

Table A.5. Neighborhood Profiles for Special Mobility Program (SMP) Participants in the Twin Cities Area, by Location

Neighborhood characteristic	Pre-move neighborhood	Post-move neighborhood	Significance	Metropolitan area
Race/ethnicity				
White (%)	53.2	86.1	***	92.1
Black (%)	27.9	8.0	***	3.6
Education				
College graduates (%)	28.2	28.4	—	27.1
Income				
Very low income[a] (%)	44.1	22.3	***	16.6
Receiving public assistance (%)	23.6	8.5	***	5.5
Children in poverty (%)	56.9	18.7	***	11.2
Population in poverty (%)	39.0	12.1	***	8.1
Median household income ($)	18,206	30,611	***	36,565
Household status				
Female-headed households (%)	16.5	8.1	***	14.4
Employment				
Labor force employed (%)	68.1	76.3	***	74.3
Housing				
Homeowners (%)	31.5	62.3	***	68.7
Housing units built before 1939 (%)	50.8	32.6	***	20.5
Housing units with 3+ bedrooms	31.0	44.7	***	54.0
Low-rent housing units[b] (%)	23.8	10.2	***	13.8
Low-value homes[c] (%)	73.1	57.7	**	39.0
Median home value ($)	70,885	75,408	—	87,400

Source: Author's calculations from 1990 census data and Minneapolis Public Housing Authority files on SMP participants.

Notes: N = 73. The test for statistical significance applies to "pre-move neighborhood" and "post-move neighborhood" columns.

[a] Income less than $15,000.

[b] Rents below $300.

[c] Values below $75,000.

*p < .05, **p < .01, ***p < .001.

Table A.6. Post-Move Neighborhood Profiles for Special Mobility Program (SMP) Participants in the Twin Cities Area, by Community Type

Neighborhood characteristic	Central city	Inner-ring suburb	Developing suburb
Race/ethnicity			
White (%)	80.8	91.6	95.1
Black (%)	11.7	4.2	1.4
Education			
College graduates (%)	23.7	31.4	40.2
Income			
Very low income[a] (%)	28.4	18.1	8.5
Receiving public assistance (%)	11.1	6.6	2.9
Children in poverty (%)	24.5	16.1	4.8
Population in poverty (%)	16.0	9.3	3.9
Median household income ($)	26,031	17,392	41,436
Household status			
Female-headed households (%)	9.0	8.2	5.2
Employment			
Labor force employed (%)	71.9	79.7	86.3
Housing			
Homeowners (%)	61.1	58.5	69.1
Housing units built before 1939 (%)	53.5	5.2	1.6
Housing units with 3+ bedrooms (%)	41.6	44.6	53.8
Low-rent housing units[b] (%)	13.8	5.7	4.0
Low-value homes[c] (%)	79.5	33.6	19.0
Median home value ($)	64,053	83,582	100,607
n	45	17	14

Source: Author's calculations from 1990 census data and Minneapolis Public Housing Authority files on SMP participants.

Note: All of the differences in means in this table are statistically significant ($p < .05$), except the figures for "female-headed households."

[a] Income less than $15,000.
[b] Rents below $300.
[c] Values below $75,000.

*Table A.7. Profile of the Average Replacement Unit Neighborhood
Compared with Other Neighborhoods in the Twin Cities Area*

Neighborhood characteristic	Replacement unit neighborhood	North side project site	Metropolitan area
Race/ethnicity			
White (%)	94.2	5.8	92.1
Black (%)	1.9	45.6	3.6
Education			
College graduates (%)	35.6	5.3	27.1
Income			
Very low income[a] (%)	12.6	75.1	16.6
Receiving public assistance (%)	3.9	60.5	5.5
Children in poverty (%)	8.2	79.7	11.2
Population in poverty (%)	5.6	72.8	8.1
Median household income ($)	40,290	7,810	36,565
Household status			
Female-headed households (%)	5.6	29.1	14.4
Employment			
Labor force employed (%)	81.1	34.7	74.3
Housing			
Homeowners (%)	75.7	3.8	68.7
Housing units built before 1939 (%)	17.8	14.1	20.5
Housing units with 3+ bedrooms (%)	58.8	14.5	54.0
Low-rent housing units[b] (%)	8.7	79.9	13.8
Low-value homes[c] (%)	32.7	100	39.0
Median home value ($)	91,290	49,326	87,400

Source: Author's calculations from 1990 census data and Minneapolis Public Housing Authority replacement housing data.

Notes: N = 429. All the differences in means between the "replacement unit neighborhood" and "north side project site" columns are statistically significant (*p* < .05).

[a] Income less than $15,000.
[b] Rents below $300.
[c] Values below $75,000.

Table A.8. Profiles of Minneapolis and Suburban Replacement Unit Neighborhoods in the Twin Cities Area

Neighborhood characteristic	Minneapolis replacement unit neighborhoods	Suburban replacement unit neighborhoods	Significance
Race/ethnicity			
White (%)	88.6	95.7	***
Black (%)	5.1	1.0	***
Education			
College graduates (%)	36.1	35.4	—
Income			
Very low income[a] (%)	19.8	10.6	***
Receiving public assistance (%)	6.2	3.2	***
Children in poverty (%)	12.9	6.9	***
Population in poverty (%)	8.8	4.7	***
Median household income ($)	31,892	42,646	***
Household status			
Female-headed households (%)	6.1	5.4	*
Employment			
Labor force employed (%)	76.5	82.4	***
Housing			
Homeowners (%)	68.0	77.8	***
Housing units built before 1939 (%)	59.2	6.2	***
Housing units with 3+ bedrooms (%)	46.1	62.4	***
Low-rent housing units[b]	6.1	9.5	**
Low-value homes[c]	59.7	25.1	***
Median home value ($)	73,190	96,369	***

Source: Author's calculations from 1990 census data and Minneapolis Public Housing Authority replacement housing data.

Note: N = 429.

[a] Income less than $15,000.

[b] Rents below $300.

[c] Values below $75,000.

$*p < .05, **p < .01, ***p < .001.$

Table A.9. Profiles of Scattered-Site and Project-Based Replacement Unit Neighborhoods in the Twin Cities Area

Neighborhood characteristic	Scattered-site neighborhoods	Project-based neighborhoods	Significance
Race/ethnicity			
White (%)	94.3	93.8	—
Black (%)	1.9	2.0	—
Education			
College graduates (%)	14.8	12.4	***
Income			
Very low income[a] (%)	11.5	14.9	***
Receiving public assistance (%)	3.5	4.6	***
Children in poverty (%)	6.9	11.0	***
Population in poverty (%)	5.1	6.7	**
Median household income ($)	41,446	37,927	**
Household status			
Female-headed households (%)	5.2	6.3	***
Employment			
Labor force employed (%)	82.3	78.8	***
Housing			
Homeowners (%)	78.1	70.8	***
Housing units built before 1939 (%)	20.0	13.2	**
Housing units with 3+ bedrooms (%)	60.8	55.1	**
Low-rent housing units[b] (%)	8.0	10.3	*
Low-value homes[c] (%)	32.3	33.5	—
Median home value ($)	92,128	89,578	—

Source: Author's calculations from 1990 census data and Minneapolis Public Housing Authority replacement housing data.

Note: N = 429.

[a] Income less than $15,000.

[b] Rents below $300.

[c] Values below $75,000.

p < .05, **p* < .01, ***p* < .001.

Table A.10. Reported Experiences among Children of Hollman Families and Comparison Group Members in the Twin Cities Area

"My child . . ."	(a) Displaced	(b) Voluntary	(c) a–b p value	(d) Section 8	(e) a–d p value	(f) b–d p value	(g) Public housing	(h) a–g p value	(i) b–g p value
Likes school	84	78	—	78	—	—	83	—	—
Does well in school	76	87	—	81	—	—	72	—	—
Receives attention from teacher	82	85	*	70	—	—	79	—	*
Has friends in the neighborhood	53	73	***	66	—	—	53	—	**
Plays with others in the neighborhood	49	77	***	68	***	—	51	—	**
n	158	48	—	143	—	—	148		

Source: Author's calculations from survey results.

Notes: Figures in the cells indicate the percentage of respondents who agreed with each statement. Shaded cells indicate a negative program effect (i.e., a statistically significant relationship that is opposite the direction posited by the program hypothesis). Columns (c), (e), (f), (h), and (i) report the statistical differences between the figures in the two specified columns.

*$p < .05$, **$p < .01$, ***$p < .001$, based on Mann-Whitney U test.

Table A.11. Reported Experiences among Children of Hollman Families in the Twin Cities Area, Pre- and Post-Move

"My child . . ."	Displaced			Voluntary		
	Pre-move	Post-move	p value	Pre-move	Post-move	p value
Likes school	89	84	—	87	78	—
Does well in school	85	76	—	87	87	—
Receives attention from teacher	88	82	*	74	85	—
Has friends in the neighborhood	74	53	***	67	73	—
Plays with others in the neighborhood	76	49	***	71	77	—
n		158			48	

Source: Author's calculations from survey results.

Notes: Survey answers were coded from 1 (strongly agree) to 5 (strongly disagree). Figures in the cells indicate the percentage of respondents who "agreed" or "strongly agreed" with each statement. Shaded cells indicate a negative program effect (i.e., a statistically significant relationship that is opposite the direction posited by the program hypothesis).

$*p < .05$, $**p < .01$, $***p < .001$, based on Wilcoxin Signed Rank test.

Table A.12. *Reported Neighboring Behaviors among Hollman Families and Comparison Group Members in the Twin Cities Area*

"In your neighborhood in the past six months, how often did you . . ."	(a) Displaced	(b) Voluntary	(c) a–b p value	(d) Section 8	(e) a–d p value	(f) b–d p value	(g) Public housing	(h) a–g p value	(i) b–g p value
Say hello to your neighbors?	52	68	*	74	***	—	67	***	—
Talk with your neighbors for more than 10 minutes?	27	44	*	43	***	—	37	*	—
Borrow things from your neighbors?	2	6	—	1	—	—	1	—	—
Use your neighbor's telephone?	3	8	—	4	*	—	1	—	—
Have lunch or dinner with your neighbors?	3	0	—	2	—	—	2	—	—
Borrow your neighbor's car?	1	0	—	0	—	—	0	—	—
Watch your neighbor's child or have him or her watch yours?	5	10	—	7	*	—	7	—	—
n	195	50	—	199	—	—	173	—	—

Source: Author's calculations from survey results.

Notes: Survey answers were coded from 1 (daily) to 6 (never). Figures in cells indicate the percentage of respondents who reported engaging in the behaviors at least four to five times per week. Columns (c), (e), (f), (h), and (i) report the statistical differences between the figures in the two specified columns. Shaded cells indicate a negative program effect (i.e., a statistically significant relationship that is opposite the direction posited by the program hypothesis).

$*p < .05$, $**p < .01$, $***p < .001$, based on Mann-Whitney U test.

Table A.13. *Reported Neighboring Behaviors among* Hollman *Families in the Twin Cities Area, Pre- and Post-Move*

"In your neighborhood in the past six months, how often did you . . ."	Displaced			Voluntary		
	Pre-move	Post-move	p value	Pre-move	Post-move	p value
Say hello to your neighbors?	71	52	***	80	68	—
Talk with your neighbors?	52	27	***	60	44	**
Borrow things from your neighbors?	6	3	*	6	6	—
Use your neighbor's telephone?	5	3	***	2	8	—
Have lunch or dinner with your neighbors?	3	3	**	2	0	—
Borrow your neighbor's car?	0	1	—	2	0	—
Watch your neighbor's child or have him or her watch yours?	11	5	**	6	10	—
n		195			50	

Source: Author's calculations from survey results.

Notes: Survey answers were coded from 1 (daily) to 6 (never). Figures in cells indicate the percentage of respondents who reported engaging in the behaviors at least four or five times per week. Shaded cells indicate a relationship opposite the expectations of the program hypothesis.

*p < .05, **p < .01, ***p < .001, based on Wilcoxin Signed Rank test.

Table A.14. *Reported Community Activities among Hollman Families and Comparison Group Members in the Twin Cities Area*

"In this neighborhood, have you or your children been . . ."	(a) Displaced	(b) Voluntary	(c) a–b p value	(d) Section 8	(e) a–d p value	(f) b–d p value	(g) Public housing	(h) a–g p value	(i) b–g p value
Involved in community activities?	33	50	*	54	***	—	53	***	—
A volunteer for any organization?	12	10	—	26	***	*	28	***	*
n	195	50	—	200	—	—	173	—	—

Source: Author's calculations from survey results.

Notes: Figures in cells indicate the percentage of respondents answering "yes." Columns (c), (e), (f), (h), and (i) report the statistical differences between the figures in the two specified columns. Shaded cells indicate a negative program effect (i.e., a statistically significant relationship that is opposite the direction posited by the program hypothesis).

$* p < .05$, $** p < .01$, $*** p < .001$, based on χ^2.

Table A.15. *Reported Community Activities of Hollman Families in the Twin Cities Area, Pre- and Post-Move*

"Is this neighborhood, have you or your children been . . ."	Displaced			Voluntary		
	Pre-move	Post-move	p value	Pre-move	Post-move	p value
Involved in community activities?	44	33	*	52	50	—
A volunteer for any organization?	27	12	**	22	10	—
n		195			50	

Source: Author's calculations from survey results.

Notes: Figures in cells indicate the percentage of respondents answering "yes." Shaded cells indicate a negative program effect (i.e., a statistically significant relationship that is opposite the direction posited by the program hypothesis).

$*p < .05$, $**p < .01$, $***p < .001$, based on χ^2.

Table A.16. *Neighborhood Satisfaction as Rated by Hollman Families and Comparison Group Members in the Twin Cities Area*

"How satisfied are you with . . ."	(a) Displaced	(b) Voluntary	(c) a–b p value	(d) Section 8	(e) a–d p value	(f) b–d p value	(g) Public housing	(h) a–g p value	(i) b–g p value
Bus service in the neighborhood?	75	64	—	86	***	***	77	*	—
Schools in the neighborhood?	77	77	—	60	**	*	72	—	—
Proximity to a place of worship?	56	49	—	57	—	—	49	—	—
Proximity to friends?	58	72	—	60	—	—	59	—	—
Proximity to health care?	76	65	—	80	*	—	81	*	—
Child care in the neighborhood?	44	63	—	40	—	—	48	—	—
Grocery stores in the neighborhood?	86	84	—	69	***	**	62	***	***
Parks and playgrounds in the neighborhood?	76	88	—	70	—	*	66	*	*
n	195	50	—	199	—	—	173	—	—

Source: Author's calculations from survey results.

Notes: Figures in cells indicate the percentage of respondents answering "somewhat satisfied" or "very satisfied." Columns (c), (e), (f), (h), and (i) report the statistical differences between the figures in the two specified columns. Shaded cells indicate a negative program effect (i.e., a statistically significant relationship that is opposite the direction posited by the program hypothesis).

*p < .05, **p < .01, ***p < .001, based on Mann-Whitney U test.

Table A.17. *Neighborhood Satisfaction as Rated by* Hollman *Families in the Twin Cities Area, Pre- and Post-Move*

"How satisfied are you with . . ."	Displaced			Voluntary		
	Pre-move	*Post-move*	*p value*	*Pre-move*	*Post-move*	*p value*
Bus service in the neighborhood?	81	75	★	85	64	★
Schools in the neighborhood?	81	77	—	79	77	—
Proximity to a place of worship?	57	56	—	66	49	—
Proximity to friends?	76	58	★★★	76	72	—
Proximity to health care?	85	76	★	82	65	—
Child care in the neighborhood?	47	44	—	62	63	—
Grocery stores in the neighborhood?	81	86	★	72	84	—
Parks and playgrounds?	74	76	—	59	88	★★
n	195			50		

Source: Author's calculations from survey results.

Notes: Figures in cells indicate the percentage of respondents answering "somewhat satisfied" or "very satisfied." Shaded cells indicate a negative program effect (i.e., a statistically significant relationship that is opposite the direction posited by the program hypothesis).

★ $p < .05$, ★★ $p < .01$, ★★★ $p < .001$, based on Wilcoxin Signed Rank test.

Table A.18. *Housing Satisfaction as Rated by Hollman Families and Comparison Group Members in the Twin Cities Area*

"How satisfied are you with . . ."	(a) Displaced	(b) Voluntary	(c) a–b p value	(d) Section 8	(e) a–d p value	(f) b–d p value	(g) Public housing	(h) a–g p value	(i) b–g p value
Your home in general?	80	84	*	66	**	**	73	—	*
The size of your home?	80	78	—	74	—	—	80	***	—
The cost of your home?	75	86	*	70	***	*	87	—	—
The quality of your home?	78	84	—	60	***	***	77	—	—
n	195	50	—	199	—	—	173	—	—

Source: Author's calculations from survey results.

Notes: Figures in cells indicate the percentage of respondents answering "somewhat satisfied" or "very satisfied." Columns (c), (e), (f), (h), and (i) report the statistical differences between the figures in the two specified columns. Shaded cells indicate a negative program effect (i.e., a statistically significant relationship that is opposite the direction posited by the program hypothesis).

*$p < .05$, **$p < .01$, ***$p < .001$, based on Mann-Whitney U test.

Table A.19. Housing Satisfaction as Rated by Hollman Families in the Twin Cities Area, Pre- and Post-Move

"How satisfied are you with . . ."	Displaced			Voluntary		
	Pre-move	Post-move	p value	Pre-move	Post-move	p value
Your home in general?	72	80	*	46	84	***
The size of your home?	77	80	—	64	78	*
The cost of your home?	88	75	***	62	86	**
The quality of your home?	72	78	*	48	84	***
n	195			50		

Source: Author's calculations from survey results.

Notes: Figures in cells indicate the percentage of respondents answering "somewhat satisfied" or "very satisfied." Shaded cells indicate a negative program effect (i.e., a statistically significant relationship that is opposite the direction posited by the program hypothesis).

$*p < .05$, $**p < .01$, $***p < .001$, based on Wilcoxin Signed Rank test.

Table A.20. *Severity of Neighborhood Problems as Rated by Hollman Families and Comparison Group Members in the Twin Cities Area*

"In your neighborhood, how much of a problem is (are) . . ."	(a) Displaced	(b) Voluntary	(c) a–b p value	(d) Section 8	(e) a–d p value	(f) b–d p value	(g) Public housing	(h) a–g p value	(i) b–g p value
Graffiti?	9	4	—	17	***	***	11	**	**
Public drinking?	19	12	—	39	***	***	29	**	*
Drug use?	13	18	—	47	***	***	33	***	**
Abandoned buildings?	9	12	—	27	***	**	16	*	*
n	195	50	—	199	—	—	173	—	—

Source: Author's calculations from survey results.

Notes: Figures in cells indicate the percentage of respondents answering "moderate problem" or "major problem." Columns (c), (e), (f), (h), and (i) report the statistical differences between the figures in the two specified columns.

*$p < .05$, **$p < .01$, ***$p < .001$, based on Mann-Whitney U test.

Table A.21. *Severity of Neighborhood Problems as Rated by Hollman Families in the Twin Cities Area, Pre- and Post-Move*

"How much of a problem is (are) . . ."	Displaced			Voluntary		
	Pre-move	Post-move	p value	Pre-move	Post-move	p value
Graffiti?	39	9	***	32	4	***
Public drinking?	48	19	***	50	12	***
Drug use?	44	13	***	51	18	***
Abandoned buildings?	31	9	***	34	12	**
n		195			50	

Source: Author's calculations from survey results.

Note: Figures in cells indicate the percentage of respondents answering "moderate problem" or "major problem."

*p < .05, **p < .01, ***p < .001, based on Wilcoxin Signed Rank test.

Table A.22. Perceptions of Safety among Hollman Families and Comparison Group Members in the Twin Cities Area

	(a)	(b)	(c)	(d)	(e)	(f)	(g)	(h)	(i)
			a–b		a–d	b–d	Public	a–g	b–g
	Displaced	Voluntary	p value	Section 8	p value	p value	housing	p value	p value
Respondents who feel safe in current neighborhood (%)	78	90	—	64	***	***	63	***	***
Respondents who are satisfied with the safety of their current neighborhood (%)	74	88	*	57	***	***	57	***	***
Respondents who report their children feel safe in their current neighborhood (%)	69	87	*	59	*	***	55	**	***
Respondents who report their children feel safe in school (%)	90	87	—	79	—	—	81	—	—
n	195	50	—	199	—	—	173	—	—

Source: Author's calculations from survey results.
Note: Columns (c), (e), (f), (h), and (i) report the statistical differences between the figures in the two specified columns.
*p < .05, **p < .01, ***p < .001, based on Mann–Whitney U test.

Table A.23. *Perceptions of Safety among Hollman Families in the Twin Cities Area, Pre- and Post-Move*

	Displaced			Voluntary		
	Pre-move	Post-move	p value	Pre-move	Post-move	p value
Respondents who feel safe in their current neighborhood (%)	63	78	***	54	90	***
Respondents who are satisfied with the safety of their current neighborhood (%)	59	74	**	44	88	***
Respondents who report their children feel safe in their current neighborhood (%)	65	69	—	46	87	***
Respondents who report their children feel safe in school (%)	89	90	—	87	87	—
n		195			50	

Source: Author's calculations from survey results.

*p < .05, **p < .01, ***p < .001, based on Wilcoxin Signed Rank test.

Table A.24. *Reported Exposure to Crime and Victimization among Hollman Families and Comparison Group Members in The Twin Cities*

"In the past six months . . ."	(a) Displaced	(b) Voluntary	(c) a–b p value	(d) Section 8	(e) a–d p value	(f) b–d p value	(g) Public housing	(h) a–g p value	(i) b–g p value
1. Has your home been broken into?	4	2	—	10	*	—	9	—	—
2. Have you been robbed or attacked?	1	0	—	4	—	—	2	—	—
3. Have your children been robbed or attacked?	3	4	—	10	*	—	5	—	—
4. Has a neighbor's home been broken into?	7	6	—	20	***	*	20	***	*
5. Have your neighbors been robbed or attacked?	5	0	—	6	—	—	10	—	—
VICTIM (1–3)	8	9	—	22	***	*	16	*	—
EXPOSURE (1–5)	16	6	—	36	***	**	35	***	**
n	195	50	—	199	—	—	173	—	—

Source: Author's calculations from survey results.

Note: Columns (c), (e), (f), (h), and (i) report the statistical differences between the figures in the two specified columns.

$*p < .05, **p < .01, ***p < .001$, based on χ^2.

Table A.25. *Reported Exposure to Crime and Victimization among Hollman Families in the Twin Cities Area, Pre- and Post-Move*

	Displaced			Voluntary		
	Pre-move	Post-move	p value	Pre-move	Post-move	p value
1. Home broken into	13	4	**	14	2	—
2. Been robbed or attacked	7	1	**	6	0	—
3. Children robbed or attacked	7	3	—	6	4	**
4. Neighbor's home broken into	27	7	***	32	6	**
5. Neighbors robbed or attacked	16	5	**	23	0	**
VICTIM (1–2)	20	8	**	17	6	—
EXPOSURE (1–5)	35	16	**	36	9	**

Source: Author's calculations from survey results.

$*p < .05, **p < .01, ***p < .001$, based on χ^2.

References

Aaronson, Daniel. 1997. "Sibling Estimates of Neighborhood Effects." In *Neighborhood Poverty, Volume 2: Policy Implications in Studying Neighborhoods,* edited by Jeanne Brooks-Gunn, Greg J. Duncan, and J. Lawrence Aber (80–93). New York: Russell Sage Foundation Press.

Abramsky, Sasha. 1998. "Yonkers Race Trap." *City Limits* 23(September/October): 24–29.

Alex-Assensoh, Yvette. 1995. "Myths about Race and the Underclass." *Urban Affairs Review* 31(1): 3–19.

———. 1997. "Race, Concentrated Poverty, Social Isolation, and Political Behavior." *Urban Affairs Review* 33(2): 209–27.

American Friends Service Committee. 1994. "Outcry Stalls Access to Housing in Baltimore Suburbs." *The NIMBY Report,* Number 10. September/October.

Anderson, Elijah. 1990. *Streetwise: Race, Class, and Change in an Urban Community.* Chicago: University of Chicago Press.

———. 1991. "Neighborhood Effects on Teenage Pregnancy." In *The Urban Underclass,* edited by Christopher Jencks and Paul E. Peterson (375–98). Washington, D.C.: Brookings Institution.

Anderson, G. R., Jr. 2001. "Ted's Excellent Adventure." *City Pages,* 23 May. http://www.citypages.com/databank/22/1068/article9567. (Accessed April 18, 2002.)

Anglin, Roland. 1994. "Searching for Justice: Court-Inspired Housing Policy as a Mechanism for Social and Economic Mobility." *Urban Affairs Quarterly* 29(3): 432–53.

Awada, Pat. 2001. "Communities Should Decide." *Saint Paul Pioneer Press,* 25 June, 9A.

Babb, Carol E., Louis G. Pol, and Rebecca F. Guy. 1984. "The Impact of Federally Assisted Housing on Single-Family Housing Sales: 1970–1980." *Mid-South Business Journal* (July): 13–17.

Baird, Jeffrey C. 1980. "The Effects of Federally Subsidized Low-Income Housing on Residential Property Values in Suburban Neighborhoods." Northern Virginia Board of Realtors Research Study. December.

Baker, Ann. 1993. "Homelessness Growing Rapidly." *St. Paul Pioneer Press,* 17 November, 1C.

Baker, Ann, and Dan Browning. 1996. "Raze or Renovate: West Side Residents Struggle over Concord Square." *St. Paul Pioneer Press,* 25 September, 1B.

Banfield, Edward. 1970. *The Unheavenly City.* Boston: Little, Brown and Company.

Baron, Dan. 1990. "Communities Push 'Reinvestment' of Drug Assets." *Neighborhood Works* 13(3): 1.

Barton, Stephen E. 1998. "Social Housing versus Housing Allowances: Choosing Between Two Forms of Housing Subsidy at the Local Level." *Journal of the American Planning Association* 62(1): 108–19.

Bast, Peter. 1999. "Section 8 Certificates/Vouchers Successful Leasing Study." Presented to the Hollman Implementation Group, October 7.

Bauerlein, Monika. 1996. "Hollman Lurches On." *City Pages,* 3 April, 6.

Bauman, John F. 1987. Public Housing, Race, and Renewal: Urban Planning in Philadelphia, 1920–1974. Philadelphia: Temple University Press.

Belkin, Lisa. 1999. *Show Me a Hero.* Boston: Little, Brown and Company.

Bendick, Marc, Jr., Charles W. Jackson, and Victor A. Reinoso. 1994. "Measuring Employment Discrimination Through Controlled Experiments." *Review of Black Political Economy* 23: 25–48.

Bennett, Larry. 1998. "Do We Really Wish to Live in a Communitarian City?: Communitarian Thinking and the Redevelopment of Chicago's Cabrini-Green Public Housing Complex." *Journal of Urban Affairs* 20(2): 99–116.

———. 1999. "Restructuring the Neighborhood: Public Housing Rehabilitation and Neighborhood Dynamics in Chicago." Paper presented at the Annual Meeting of the Urban Affairs Association, Louisville, Ky., April.

Bennett, Larry, and Adolph Reed Jr. 1999. "The New Face of Urban Renewal: The Near North Redevelopment Initiative and the Cabrini-Green Neighborhood." In *Without Justice for All: The New Liberalism and Our Retreat from Racial Equality,* edited by Adolph Reed Jr. (175–211). Boulder, Colo.: Westview Press.

Berg, Steve. 1993. "Must Suburbs Be Abolished to Save Cities?" *Minneapolis Star Tribune,* 11 July, A1.

Bickford, Adam, and Douglas S. Massey. 1991. "Segregation in the Second Ghetto: Racial and Ethnic Segregation in American Public Housing, 1977." *Social Forces* 69(4): 1011–36.

Bier, Thomas E., and Ivan Maric. 1994. "IRS Homeseller Provision and Urban Decline." *Journal of Urban Affairs* 16(2): 141–45.

"Body Count." 1995. *City Pages,* 5 July, 3.

Bollens, Scott A. 1997. "Concentrated Poverty and Metropolitan Equity Strategies." *Stanford Law and Policy Review* 8(2): 11–23.

Brandt, Steve. 1995. "Plans Would Invest in Green Spaces." *Minneapolis Star Tribune,* 18 July, B5.

———. 1996. "At High-Rises, Many Face High Anxieties." *Minneapolis Star Tribune,* 1 December, B1.

———. 1997. "Moderate Housing Is Axed from Plan." *Minneapolis Star Tribune,* 13 December, A1.

———. 1998. "Redevelopment Reimagines Minneapolis' North Side." *Minneapolis Star Tribune,* 30 November, A1.

————. 1999a. "Core Cities Boom, Outer Suburbs Lag in Home Price Gains." *Minneapolis Star Tribune,* 7 March. http://www.startribune.com/stOnLin. (Accessed April 23, 2001.)

————. 1999b. "Hollman Demolition Resumes This Morning." *Minneapolis Star Tribune,* 26 October, B1.

————. 1999c. "Judge OKs Demolition of Housing Projects in Minneapolis." *Minneapolis Star Tribune,* 1 October, B1.

————. 1999d. "Minneapolis Rejects Last-Minute Offer to Settle with NAACP." *Minneapolis Star Tribune,* 28 September, B1.

————. 1999e. "Residents Question Possible Northside Developers." *Minneapolis Star Tribune,* 7 March, B1.

————. 1999f. "A Symbol of Public Housing Loses the Roof over Her Head." *Minneapolis Star Tribune,* 4 May, B1.

————. 2001. "Housing Settlement Misses Its Mark." *Minneapolis Star Tribune,* 4 February, A1.

Brandt, Steve, and Norman Draper. 1995. "House the Poor, Sure; the Fight Is over Where." *Minneapolis Star Tribune,* 5 June, A4.

Brauer, David. 1995. "Interview: Sharon Sayles Belton, Minneapolis Mayoral Candidate." *Twin Cities Reader,* 27 October, 17.

Briggs, Xavier de Souza. 1997. "Moving Up versus Moving Out: Neighborhood Effects in Housing Mobility Programs." *Housing Policy Debate* 8(1): 195–234.

————. 1998. "Brown Kids in White Suburbs: Housing Mobility and the Many Faces of Social Capital." *Housing Policy Debate* 9(1): 177–221.

Briggs, Xavier de Souza, Joe Darden, and Angela Aidala. 1999. "In the Wake of Desegregation: Early Impacts of Scattered-Site Public Housing on Neighborhoods in Yonkers, New York." *Journal of the American Planning Association* 65: 27–49.

Broede, Jim. 1996. "Low-Income Housing Plan Hits Opposition." *St. Paul Pioneer Press,* 1 September, 1B.

Brooks-Gunn, Jeanne, Greg J. Duncan, Pamela Kato Klebanov, and Naomi Sealand. 1993. "Do Neighborhoods Influence Child and Adolescent Development?" *American Journal of Sociology* 99(2): 353–95.

Brophy, Paul C., and Rhonda N. Smith. 1997. "Mixed-Income Housing: Factors for Success." *Cityscape* 3(2): 3–32.

Brunswick, Mark. 1999. "Sides Set Up for Hotly Disputed Minneapolis NAACP Election." *Minneapolis Star Tribune,* 2 January. http://webserv5.startribune.com:80. . .Story:65756759. (Accessed February 26, 1999.)

Buchta, Jim. 1998. "Rental Market Still Tight, with Low Vacancies and Rising Rents." *Minneapolis Star Tribune,* 22 August. http://www.startribune.com/stories/417/35905.html. (Accessed March 23, 2002.)

————. 2001. "Shortage of Workers Sometimes Tied to Housing." *Minneapolis Star Tribune,* 26 March. http://www.startribune.com/stOnLin. (Accessed April 23, 2001.)

Buchta, Jim, and Neal Gendler. 1998. "The Strong Housing Market Continues." *Minneapolis Star Tribune,* 3 January. http://www.startribune.com/stories/417/11431.html. (Accessed March 22, 2002.)

Buerger, Michael E. 1994. "A Tale of Two Targets: Limitations of Community Anticrime Actions." *Crime and Delinquency* 40(3): 411–36.

Builders Association of the Twin Cities, in cooperation with the Center for Energy and Environment. 2000. *Fees, Infrastructure Costs, and Density.* Roseville, Minn.: Builders Association of the Twin Cities.

Bullard, Robert D. 1990. *Dumping in Dixie: Race, Class, and Environmental Quality.* Boulder, Colo.: Westview Press.

Bullard, Robert D., and Charles Lee. 1994. "Racism and American Apartheid." In *Residential Apartheid: The American Legacy,* edited by Robert D. Bullard, J. Eugene Grigsby III, and Charles Lee (1–16). Los Angeles: University of California Press.

Burby, Raymond J., and William M. Rohe. 1989. "Deconcentration of Public Housing: Effects on Residents' Satisfaction with Their Living Environments and Their Fear of Crime." *Urban Affairs Quarterly* 25(1): 117–41.

Burchell, Robert W., David Listokin, and Arlene Pashman. 1994. Regional Housing Opportunities for Lower-Income Households: A Resource Guide to Affordable Housing and Regional Mobility Strategies. Washington, D.C.: U.S. Department of Housing and Urban Development.

Byrum, Oliver E. 1992. *Old Problems in New Times: Urban Strategies for the 1990s.* Chicago: American Planning Association.

Calmore, John O. 1980. "Fair Housing v. Fair Housing: The Problems with Providing Increased Housing Opportunities through Spatial Deconcentration." *Clearinghouse Review* 14 (May).

Carter, William H., Michael H. Schill, and Susan M. Wachter. 1998. "Polarization, Public Housing and Racial Minorities in U.S. Cities." *Urban Studies* 35(10): 1889–911.

Case, Anne, and Lawrence Katz. 1991. "The Company You Keep: The Effects of Family and Neighborhood on Disadvantaged Youth." NBER Working Paper 3705. Cambridge, Mass.: National Bureau of Economic Research.

Cassano, Dennis. 1994. "Rezoning to Build Low-Income Housing Voted Down in Eagan." *Minneapolis Star Tribune,* 9 December, B1.

Chambliss, William J. 1994. "Policing the Ghetto Underclass: The Politics of Law and Law Enforcement." *Social Problems* 41(2): 177–94.

Chandler, Mittie O. 1990. "Dispersed Public Housing: Does It Make Any Difference?" Paper presented at the Urban Affairs Association meeting, Charlotte, N.C., April 18–21.

Chapin, Stuart F. 1938. "The Effects of Slum Clearance and Rehousing on Family and Community Relationships in Minneapolis." *American Journal of Sociology* 43(5): 744–63.

Cisneros, Henry G. 1995. *Regionalism: The New Geography of Opportunity.* Washington, D.C.: U.S. Department of Housing and Urban Development.

Citizen's League. 1994. *Why We Should Build Inclusive Communities: The Case for a Regional Housing Policy in the Twin Cities Metropolitan Area.* Final Report of the Committee on Housing Policy and Metropolitan Development. Minneapolis: Citizen's League.

Clawson, Linda. 1996. "Police Academy Discussed for Citizens." *Milwaukee Journal Sentinel,* 18 January, 3.

Cohn, Samuel, and Mark Fossett. 1998. "The Other Reason Job Suburbanization Hurts Blacks." *Urban Affairs Review* 34(1): 94–125.

Community Action for Suburban Hennepin. 1995. "Diminished Choices: The Shrinking Market for Section 8 in Suburban Hennepin County." Hopkins, Minn.: Community Action for Suburban Hennepin.

Cooke, Thomas J. 1999. "Geographic Context and Concentrated Urban Poverty within the United States." *Urban Geography* 20(6): 552–66.

Corcoran, Mary, Roger H. Gordon, Deborah Laren, and Gary Solon. 1989. "Effects of Family and Community Background on Men's Economic Status." NBER Working Paper 2896. Cambridge, Mass.: National Bureau of Economic Research.

Coulton, Claudia J. 1996. "Effects of Neighborhoods on Families and Children: Implications for Services." In *Children and Their Families in Big Cities: Strategies for Service Reform,* edited by Alfred J. Kahn and Sheila B. Kamerman (87–120). New York: Columbia University School of Social Work, Cross-National Studies Program.

Craig, Lois. 1972. "The Dayton Area's 'Fair Share' Housing Plan Enters the Implementation Phase." *City* (January/February): 50–56.

Crane, Jonathan. 1991. "The Epidemic Theory of Ghettos and Neighborhood Effects on Dropping Out and Teenage Childbearing." *American Journal of Sociology* 96(5): 1226–59.

Cronin, Francis J., and David W. Rasmussen. 1981. "Mobility." In *Housing Vouchers for the Poor: Lessons from a National Experiment,* edited by Raymond J. Struyk and Marc Bendick Jr. (107–28). Washington, D.C.: Urban Institute Press.

Cummings, Paul M., with John D. Landis. 1993. *Relationships between Affordable Housing Developments and Neighboring Property Values.* Working Paper 599. Berkeley: Institute of Urban and Regional Development, University of California at Berkeley.

Danielson, Michael N. 1976. *The Politics of Exclusion.* New York: Columbia University Press.

Danziger, Sheldon, and Peter Gottschalk. 1987. "Earnings Inequality, the Spatial Concentration of Poverty, and the Underclass." *American Economic Review* 77(2): 211–15.

Datcher, Linda. 1982 "Effects of Community and Family Background on Achievement." *Review of Economics and Statistics* 64(1): 32–41.

DeSalvo, Joseph S. 1974. "Neighborhood Upgrading Effects of Middle-Income Housing Projects in New York City." *Journal of Urban Economics* 1(3): 269–77.

Desena, Judith. 1994. "Local Gatekeeping Practices and Residential Segregation." *Sociological Inquiry* 64 (Summer): 307–21.

Diaz, Kevin. 1993. "A New Kind of Street Fighting: In Fight on Blight, Does Might Make Right?" *Minneapolis Star Tribune,* 26 December, A1.

———. 1995. "$100 Million Coming from HUD." *Minneapolis Star Tribune,* 14 January, A1.

———. 1997. "Few Steps Taken to Resolve Enormous Housing Crunch." *Minneapolis Star Tribune,* 26 August, B1.

———. 1999a. "$300,000 City Plan Would Reopen Housing Projects." *Minneapolis Star Tribune,* 27 July, B1.

———. 1999b. "Glenwood Public Housing Demolitions Postponed Once Again." *Minneapolis Star Tribune,* 18 August, B1.

———. 1999c. "Hollman Panel Calls for Bigger Affordable Housing Guarantee." *Minneapolis Star Tribune,* 10 July, B1.

———. 1999d. "Minneapolis Ratifies NAACP Deal on Demolishing Projects." *Minneapolis Star Tribune,* 18 September, B1.

———. 1999e. "NAACP Compromises with City on Hollman Demolitions." *Minneapolis Star Tribune,* 3 September, B1.

———. 1999f. "NAACP Rejects Public Housing Compromise." *Minneapolis Star Tribune,* 21 September, B1.

———. 1999g. "Once-Heralded Deal to Demolish Projects Now Faces Criticism." *Minneapolis Star Tribune,* 15 August, B1.

———. 1999h. "Sayles Belton Pledges to Speed Housing Plan." *Minneapolis Star Tribune,* 19 June, A1.

———. 1999i. "With Demolition at a Halt, Dialogue Planned." *Minneapolis Star Tribune,* 10 June, B1.

Donovan, Shaun. 1994. "Moving to the Suburbs: Section 8 Mobility and Portability in Hartford." Working Paper W94-3. Cambridge, Mass.: Joint Center for Housing Studies.

Donnelly, Patrick G., and Charles E. Kimble. 1997. "Community Organizing, Environmental Change, and Neighborhood Crime." *Crime & Delinquency* 43(4): 493–511.

Downs, Anthony. 1973. *Opening Up the Suburbs: An Urban Strategy for America.* New Haven, Conn.: Yale University Press.

———. 1999. "Some Realities about Sprawl and Urban Decline." *Housing Policy Debate* 10(4): 955–74.

———. 2001. *Housing Policies in the New Millennium.* http://www.brookings.edu/ urban/speeches/housingpolicy.htm. (Accessed November 4, 2001.)

Draper, Norman. 1993. "Twin Cities' Core Has Worst Poverty Rate for Minorities." *Minneapolis Star Tribune,* 13 December, A1.

Dreier, Peter, John Mollenkopf, and Todd Swanstrom. 2001. *Place Matters: Metropolitics for the Twenty-First Century.* Lawrence: University Press of Kansas.

Duncan, Greg J. 1994. "Families and Neighbors as Sources of Disadvantage in the Schooling Decisions of White and Black Adolescents." *American Journal of Education* 103(1): 20–53.

Duncan, Greg J., Jeanne Brooks-Gunn, and Pamela Klebanov. 1994. "Economic Deprivation and Early Childhood Development." *Child Development* 65(2): 296–318.

Economic Research Corporation. 1994. *Downtown Minneapolis Housing Study.* Prepared for the Minneapolis Community Development Agency.

Egan, Timothy. 1996. "Police Surveillance of Streets Turns to Video Cameras and Listening Devices." *The New York Times,* 7 February, A8.

Elam, Jon. 1993. "Too-High Rental Percentage Causes Lack of City Stability." *Minneapolis Star Tribune,* 19 July, A9.

Ellen, Ingrid Gould, and Margery Austin Turner. 1997. "Does Neighborhood Matter? Assessing Recent Evidence." *Housing Policy Debate* 8(4): 833–66.

Ellwood, David T. 1988. *Poor Support.* New York: Basic Books.

Epp, Gayle. 1996. "Emerging Strategies for Revitalizing Public Housing Communities." *Housing Policy Debate* 7(3): 563–88.

Fainstein, Susan, and Norman Fainstein, eds. 1986. *Restructuring the City: The Political Economy of Urban Development.* New York: Longman.

Family Housing Fund. 2000. "Working Doesn't Always Pay for a Home." Minneapolis: Family Housing Fund.

Field, Patrick, Jennifer Gilbert, and Michael Wheeler. 1997. "Trading the Poor: Intermunicipal Housing Negotiation in New Jersey." *Harvard Negotiation Law Review* 2(1): 1–33.

Finkel, Meryl, and Larry Buron. 2001. *Study on Section 8 Voucher Success Rates, Volume 1: Quantitative Study of Success Rates in Metropolitan Areas.* Washington, D.C.: U.S. Department of Housing and Urban Development.

Freeman, Lance. 2001. *The Impact of Assisted Housing on Concentrated Poverty.* Washington, D.C.: Fannie Mae Foundation.

Freeman, Lance, and Hilary Botein. 2002. "Subsidized Housing and Neighborhood Impacts: A Theoretical Discussion and Review of the Evidence." *Journal of Planning Literature* 16(3): 359–78.

Frieden, Bernard J. 1985. "Housing Allowances: An Experiment That Worked." In *Federal Housing Policy and Programs: Past to Present,* edited by J. Paul Mitchell (365–82). New Brunswick, N.J.: Center for Urban Policy Research.

Friedman, Joseph, and Daniel H. Weinberg. 1983. "History and Overview." In *The Great Housing Experiment,* edited by Joseph Friedman and Daniel H. Weinberg (11–22). Urban Affairs Annual Reviews, vol. 24. Beverly Hills: Sage Publications.

Furst, Randy. 1996a. "Sharing the Wealth or Cutting Ties?" *Minneapolis Star Tribune,* 12 July, B3.

———. 1996b. "Southeast Asians Protest Housing Demolition." *Minneapolis Star Tribune,* 30 May, B3.

———. 1997. "Hmong Ask Judge to Reopen Housing Settlement." *Minneapolis Star Tribune,* 19 July, A3.

———. 1999. "Dozens Decry Public-Housing Relocation in Protest Outside Minneapolis Agency." *Minneapolis Star Tribune,* 10 April, B6.

Furstenberg, Frank F., Jr. 1993. "How Families Manage Risk and Opportunity in Dangerous Neighborhoods." In *Sociology and the Public Agenda,* edited by William Julius Wilson (231–58). Newbury Park, Calif.: Sage Publications.

Fyfe, Nicholas, and Jon Bannister. 1994. "The Eyes on the Street: Closed Circuit Television Surveillance in Public Spaces." Paper presented at the annual conference of the American Association of Geographers, Chicago.

Galster, George C. 1990. "Federal Fair Housing Policy: The Great Misapprehension." In *Building Foundations: Housing and Federal Policy,* edited by Denise DiPasquale and Langley C. Keyes (137–56). Philadelphia: University of Pennsylvania Press.

Galster, George C., and Heather Keeney. 1993. "Subsidized Housing and Racial Change in Yonkers, New York." *Journal of the American Planning Association* 59(2): 172–81.

Galster, George C., and Anne Zobel. 1998. "Will Dispersed Housing Programmes Reduce Social Problems in the U.S.?" *Housing Studies* 13(5): 605–22.

Galster, George C., Roberto G. Quercia, and Alvaro Cortes. 2000. "Identifying Neighborhood Thresholds: An Empirical Exploration." *Housing Policy Debate* 11(3): 701–32.

Galster, George C., Anna M. Santiago, Robin E. Smith, and Peter A. Tatian. 1999. *Assessing Property Value Impacts of Dispersed Housing Subsidy Programs.* Washington, D.C.: U.S. Department of Housing and Urban Development.

GAO. *See* U.S. General Accounting Office.

Gardner, Bill. 1994. "Eagan Rejection of Low-Income Homes Criticized." *St. Paul Pioneer Press,* 10 December, 1C.

Garofalo, James, and Maureen McLeod. 1989. "Structure and Operations of Neighborhood Watch Programs in the United States." *Crime and Delinquency* 35(3): 326–44.

Gendler, Neal. 2000a. "Home Buyers Not up in ARMs over Rising Interest Rates." *Minneapolis Star Tribune,* 3 June. http://www.startribune.com/stOnLin. (Accessed September 13, 2000.)

———. 2000b. "Housing Demand Keeps Rental Tight, Boosts Home Building." *Minneapolis Star Tribune,* 15 July. http://www.startribune.com/stOnLin. (Accessed September 13, 2000.)

Gillaspy, Tom. 1993. *Affordable Housing Study—Analysis of the 1990 Census PUMS Data.* Memorandum to the Minnesota Planning Staff to the Governor's Blue Ribbon Task Force on Metropolitan Housing. September 2.

Goering, John M., ed. 1986. *Housing Desegregation and Federal Policy.* Chapel Hill: University of North Carolina Press.

Goering, John M., Ali Kamely, and Todd Richardson. 1997. "Recent Research on Racial Segregation and Poverty Concentration in Public Housing in the United States." *Urban Affairs Review* 32(5): 723–45.

Goering, John M., H. Stebbins, and M. Siewart. 1995. *Promoting Housing Choice in HUD's Rental Assistance Programs.* Washington, D.C.: Office of Policy Development and Research, Department of Housing and Urban Development.

Goetz, Edward G. 1996. "The US War on Drugs as Urban Policy." *International Journal of Urban and Regional Research* 20(3): 539–49.

———. 2000. "Fair Share or Status Quo? The Twin Cities Livable Communities Act." *Journal of Planning Education and Research* 20(1): 37–51.

———. 2002a. *Hollman Report No. 6: The Experiences of Hollman Families.* Minneapolis: Center for Urban and Regional Affairs, University of Minnesota.

———. 2002b. *Hollman Report No. 7: Relocation Assistance.* Minneapolis: Center for Urban and Regional Affairs, University of Minnesota.

Goetz, Edward G., and Mara Sidney. 1994a. *Government Support for Nonprofit Housing in the Twin Cities.* Research report, Housing Program, University of Minnesota.

———. 1994b. "Revenge of the Property Owners: Community Development and the Politics of Property." *Journal of Urban Affairs* 16(4): 319–34.

———. 1997. "Local Policy Subsystems and Issue Definition: An Analysis of Community Development Policy Change." *Urban Affairs Review* 32(4): 490–512.

Goetz, Edward G., Karen Chapple, and Barbara Lukermann. 2002a. *The Affordable Housing Legacy of the Minnesota Land Use Planning Act.* Minneapolis: Center for Urban and Regional Affairs, University of Minnesota.

———. 2002b. "Implementing the Fair Share Housing Provisions of the Minnesota Land Use Planning Act." Unpublished manuscript, Hubert H. Humphrey Institute of Public Affairs, University of Minnesota, Minneapolis.

Goetz, Edward G., Hin Kin Lam, and Anne Heitlinger. 1996. *There Goes the Neighborhood? The Impact of Subsidized Multi-Family Housing on Urban Neighborhoods.* Minneapolis: Center for Urban and Regional Affairs, University of Minnesota.

Goldstein, Ira, and William L. Yancey. 1986. "Public Housing Projects, Blacks, and Public Policy: The Historical Ecology of Public Housing in Philadelphia." In *Housing Desegregation and Federal Policy,* edited by John M. Goering (262–89). Chapel Hill: University of North Carolina Press.

Goode, Erich, and Nachman Ben-Yehuda. 1994. *Moral Panics: The Social Construction of Deviance.* Cambridge, Mass.: Blackwell Publishers.

Gordon, Diana R. 1994. The Return of the Dangerous Classes: Drug Prohibition and Policy Politics. New York: W. W. Norton & Co.

Gray, Robert, and Steven Tursky. 1986. "Location and Racial/Ethnic Occupancy Patterns for HUD-Subsidized Family Housing in Ten Metropolitan Areas." In *Housing Desegregation and Federal Policy,* edited by John M. Goering (235–52). Chapel Hill: University of North Carolina Press.

Hanratty, Maria, Sara McLanahan, and Elizabeth Pettit. 1997. "The Impact of the Los Angeles Moving to Opportunity Program on Residential Mobility: Neighborhood Characteristics and Early Child and Parent Outcomes." Presented at the U.S. Department of Housing and Urban Development's Moving to Opportunity Research Conference, Washington, D.C., November 20–21.

Hartje, Sandra Chris. 1998. *The Impact of State Lead Policy on Affordable Rental Housing in Minneapolis and Saint Paul, Minnesota, from 1991 to 1995.* Doctoral thesis, University of Minnesota, Saint Paul.

Hartman, Chester W. 1995. "Shelterforce Interview: Roberta Achtenberg." *Shelterforce* (January/February): 7.

Hartman, Chester W., and Gregg Carr. 1969. "Housing Authorities Reconsidered." *Journal of the American Institute of Planners* 35(1): 10 21.

Hartung, John M., and Jeffrey R. Henig. 1997. "Housing Vouchers and Certificates as a Vehicle for Deconcentrating the Poor: Evidence from the Washington, D.C., Metropolitan Area." *Urban Affairs Review* 32(3): 403–19.

Haveman, Robert H., and Barbara L. Wolfe. 1994. *Succeeding Generations: On the Effects of Investments in Children.* New York: Russell Sage Foundation Press.

Hawkins, Beth. 1999. "Let's Break a Deal." *City Pages,* 6 October, 8.

Herrnstein, Richard J., and Charles Murray. 1996. *The Bell Curve: Intelligence and Class in American Life.* New York: Free Press.

Hirsch, Arnold R. 1996. *Making the Second Ghetto: Race and Housing in Chicago, 1940–1960,* 2d ed. New York: Cambridge University Press.

Hogan, James. 1996. *Scattered-Site Housing: Characteristics and Consequences.* Washington, D.C.: U.S. Department of Housing and Urban Development.

Hogan, James, and Dorothy L. Lengyel. 1985. "Experiences with Scattered-Site Housing." *Urban Resources* 2 (winter): 9–14.

Hollman/North Minneapolis Human Development Coalition. 1998. "Minutes of September 2, 1998, Meeting." Hollman/North Minneapolis Human Development Coalition.

Holloway, Steven R., Deborah Bryan, Robert Chabot, Donna M. Robers, and James Rulli. 1998. "Exploring the Effects of Public Housing on the Concentration of Poverty in Columbus, Ohio." *Urban Affairs Review* 33(6): 767–89.

———. 1999. "Race, Scale, and the Concentration of Poverty in Columbus, Ohio, 1980 to 1990." *Urban Geography* 20(6): 534–51.

HOME Line. 2000. *Vouchers to Nowhere.* Minneapolis: HOME Line.

Hopfensperger, Jean. 2000. "Study: Affordable Housing Problem Hits Moderate-Income Earners." *Minneapolis Star Tribune,* 12 July, A1.

Hotakainen, R. 1990. "Housing Called Casualty of Drug War." *Minneapolis Star Tribune,* 19 April, B1.

Hsieh, Ren-Her. 1994. "Fair Share Housing as a Mechanism for Seeking Metropolitan Stability and Deconcentrating Poverty." Master's Thesis, Humphrey Institute of Public Affairs, University of Minnesota.

HUD. See U.S. Department of Housing and Urban Development.

Hughes, Mark A. 1989. "Misspeaking Truth to Power: A Geographical Perspective on the 'Underclass' Fallacy." *Economic Geography* 65: 187–207.

Ihlandfeldt, Keith R., and David L. Sjoquist. 1998. "The Spatial Mismatch Hypothesis: A Review of Recent Studies and Their Implications for Welfare Reform." *Housing Policy Debate* 9(4): 849–92.

Innovative Housing Institute. 1998. *The House Next Door.* http://www.inhousing.org/house1.htm. (Accessed October 23, 1998.)

Inskip, Leonard. 1996. "Southeast Asian Council Helping Hmong Prepare for Life after Sumner-Olson." *Minneapolis Star Tribune,* 27 February, A11.

Institute on Race and Poverty. 1996. *Examining the Relationship between Housing, Education, and Persistent Segregation.* Minneapolis: Institute on Race and Poverty.

Jackson, Kenneth T. 1985. *Crabgrass Frontier: The Suburbanization of the United States.* New York: Oxford University Press.

Jargowsky, Paul A. 1996. *Poverty and Place: Ghettos, Barrios, and the American City.* New York: Russell Sage Foundation.

Jargowsky, Paul A., and Mary Jo Bane. 1991. "Ghetto Poverty in the United States, 1970–1980." In *The Urban Underclass,* edited by Christopher Jencks and Paul E. Peterson (235–73). Washington, D.C.: Brookings Institution.

Jencks, Christopher, and Susan E. Mayer. 1990. "The Social Consequences of Growing Up in a Poor Neighborhood." In *Inner-City Poverty in America,* edited by Laurence Lynn Jr. and Michael G. H. McGeary (111–86). Washington, D.C.: National Academy Press.

Johnson, Michael P., Helen F. Ladd, and Jens Ludwig. 2002. "The Benefits and Costs of Residential Mobility Programmes for the Poor." *Housing Studies* 17(1): 125–38.

Johnson, William C. 1998. *Growth Management in the Twin Cities Region: The Politics and Performance of the Metropolitan Council.* Minneapolis: Center for Urban and Regional Affairs, University of Minnesota.

Jordan, Anne. 1993. "Walls That Unite." *Governing* (October): 32–35.

Judd, Dennis. 1999. "Symbolic Politics and Urban Policies: Why African-Americans Got So Little from the Democrats." In *Without Justice for All: The New Liberalism and Our Retreat from Racial Equality,* edited by Adolph Reed Jr. (123–50). Boulder, Colo.: Westview Press.

Kain, John. 1968. "Housing Segregation, Negro Unemployment, and Metropolitan Decentralization." *Quarterly Journal of Economics* 82 (May): 175–97.

Kasarda, John D. 1989. "Urban Industrial Transition and the Urban Underclass." *Annals of the American Academy of Political and Social Sciences* 501: 26–47.

———. 1990. "Structural Factors Affecting the Location and Timing of Urban Underclass Growth." *Urban Geography* 11(3): 234–64.

Kaszuba, Mike. 1996. "Lines Are Drawn over Affordable Housing." *Minneapolis Star Tribune,* 14 July, B1.

———. 1998a. "As Key Vote Nears on Apartments, Suburbs Poised to 'Tear 'Em All Down.'" *Minneapolis Star Tribune,* 22 February, B1.

———. 1998b. "Brooklyn Park's Deal to Raze Apartments Raises Eyebrows." *Minneapolis Star Tribune,* 27 May, A1.

———. 1998c. "Owner Halts Plan to Raze Apartments." *Minneapolis Star Tribune,* 13 August, B1.

Katz, Lawrence F., Jeffrey R. Kling, and Jeffrey B. Liebman. 2001. "Moving to Opportunity in Boston: Early Results of a Randomized Mobility Experiment." *Quarterly Journal of Economics* 116(2): 607–54.

Kaufman, Julie E., and James E. Rosenbaum. 1992. "The Education and Employment of Low-Income Black Youth in White Suburbs." *Educational Evaluation and Policy Analysis* 14(3): 229–40.

Keating, Larry. 2000. "Redeveloping Public Housing: Relearning Urban Renewal's Immutable Lessons." *Journal of the American Planning Association* 66(4): 384–97.

Keating, W. Dennis. 1994. *The Suburban Racial Dilemma: Housing and Neighborhoods.* Philadelphia: Temple University Press.

Keith, Nathaniel S. 1973. *Politics and the Housing Crisis since 1930.* New York: Universe Books.

Kleit, Rachel Garshick. 2001a. "Neighborhood Relations in Scattered-Site and Clustered Public Housing." *Journal of Urban Affairs* 23(3–4): 409–30.

———. 2001b. "The Role of Neighborhood Social Networks in Scattered-Site Public Housing Residents' Search for Jobs." *Housing Policy Debate* 12(3): 541–74.

Ladd, Helen F., and Jens Ludwig. 1997. "Federal Housing Assistance, Residential Relocation, and Education Opportunities: Evidence from Baltimore." *AEA Papers and Proceedings: State and Local Public Policy* 87(2): 272–77.

Lane, Jeremy. 1999. "Legal Aid Funds Explained." *Minnesota Spokesman-Recorder,* 25–31 March, 4C.

Lang, Robert E., and Steven P. Hornburg. 1998. "What Is Social Capital and Why Is It Important to Public Policy?" *Housing Policy Debate* 9(1): 1–16.

Laszewski, Charles. 1998. "Residents Battle to Keep Apartments." *St. Paul Pioneer Press,* 17 February, 1C.

League of Women Voters of Minneapolis. 1992. *Affordable Housing: Does Zoning Make a Difference?* Minneapolis: League of Women Voters of Minneapolis.

Lee, Chang-Moo, Dennis P. Culhane, and Susan M. Wachter. 1999. "The Differential Impacts of Federally Assisted Housing Programs on Nearby Property Values: A Philadelphia Case Study." *Housing Policy Debate* 10(1): 75–94.

Leger, Mireille L., and Stephen D. Kennedy. 1990. *Final Report of the Freestanding Housing Voucher Demonstration.* Cambridge, Mass.: Abt Associates.

Leitner, Helga. 1990. "Cities in Pursuit of Economic Growth: The Local State as Entrepreneur." *Political Geography Quarterly* 9(2): 146–70.

Lemann, Nicholas. 1991. "Chasing the Dream: Deep South, Dark Ghetto, Middle-Class Enclaves." *New Perspective Quarterly* 8(3): 30–35.

———. 1994. "The Myth of Community Development." *The New York Times Magazine,* 29 January, 27.

Leyden, Peter. 1992 "Disparity in Income Widened in 1980s." *Minneapolis Star Tribune,* 26 July, A1.

Listokin, David. 1976. *Fair Share Housing Allocation.* New Brunswick, N.J.: Center for Urban Policy Research.

Lowry, Ira. 1983. *Experimenting with Housing Allowances.* Cambridge, Mass.: Oelgeschlager, Gunn and Hain.

Luce, Thomas F., Jr., Barbara L. Lukermann, and Herbert Mohring. 1994. *Regional Sewer System Rate Structure Study.* Saint Paul: Metropolitan Council.

Ludwig, Jens, Greg J. Duncan, and Paul Hirschfield. 2001. "Urban Poverty and Juvenile Crime: Evidence from a Randomized Housing-Mobility Experiment." *Quarterly Journal of Economics* 116(2): 655–80.

Ludwig, Jens, Greg J. Duncan, and Joshua C. Pinkston. 2000. *Neighborhood Effects on Economic Self-Sufficiency: Evidence from a Randomized Housing-Mobility Experiment.* Northwestern University/University of Chicago Joint Center for Poverty Research Working Paper 159. Evanston, Ill.: Northwestern University.

Ludwig, Jens, Helen F. Ladd, and Greg J. Duncan. 2001. "The Effects of Urban Poverty on Educational Outcomes: Evidence from a Randomized Experiment." In *Brookings-Wharton Papers on Urban Affairs,* vol. 2, edited by William G. Gale and Janet Rothenberg Pack (147–88). Washington, D.C.: Brookings Institution Press.

Lukermann, Barbara L., Thomas F. Luce Jr., and Herbert Mohring. 1995. "Public Policies That Hurt the Urban Core." *CURA Reporter* 25(1): 1–7.

Lukermann, Barbara L., Douglas Snyder, and Thomas F. Luce Jr. 1994. *Examination of Factors Controlling the Location of Commercial and Industrial Development within the Metropolitan Area.* Saint Paul: Metropolitan Council.

Lynch, Sarah. 2001. "Suburban Resistance: 1993–2001." Unpublished paper, Hubert H. Humphrey Institute of Public Affairs, University of Minnesota, Minneapolis.

Lyons, Robert, and Scott Loveridge. 1993. *An Hedonic Estimation of the Effect of Federally Subsidized Housing on Nearby Residential Property Values.* Staff paper series P93-6. Saint Paul: Department of Agricultural and Applied Economics, University of Minnesota.

Mack, Linda. 1995. "What Makes a House a Home?" *Minneapolis Star Tribune,* 27 February, 1B.

Malaby, Elizabeth G. D., and Barbara L. Lukermann. 1996. "Given Choice: The Effects of Portability in Section 8 Rental Housing Assistance." *CURA Reporter* 26(2): 12–15.

Martin, Judith A., and Antony Goddard. 1989. *Past Choices/Present Landscapes: The Impact of Urban Renewal on the Twin Cities.* Minneapolis: Center for Urban and Regional Affairs, University of Minnesota.

Massey, Douglas S., and Nancy A. Denton. 1993. *American Apartheid: Segregation and the Making of the Underclass.* Cambridge, Mass.: Harvard University Press.

Massey, Douglas S., and Mitchell Eggers. 1990. "The Ecology of Inequality: Minorities and the Concentration of Poverty, 1970–1980." *American Journal of Sociology* 95(5): 1153–88.

Massey, Douglas S., and Shawn M. Kanaiaupuni. 1993. "Public Housing and the Concentration of Poverty." *Social Science Quarterly* 74(1): 109–22.

Massey, Douglas S., Andrew B. Gross, and Mitchell L. Eggers. 1991. "Segregation, the Concentration of Poverty, and the Life Chances of Individuals." *Social Science Research* 20: 397–420.

Maurer, Mark. 1992. "Young Black Men and the Criminal Justice System: A Growing National Problem." Washington, D.C.: The Sentencing Project.

McClure, Kirk. 1998. "Housing Vouchers versus Housing Production: Assessing Long-Term Costs." *Housing Policy Debate* 9(2): 355–71.

McDonnell, Judith. 1997. "The Role of 'Race' in the Likelihood of City Participation in the United States Public and Section 8 Existing Housing Programmes." *Housing Studies* 12(2): 231–45.

Mead, Lawrence M. 1986. *Beyond Entitlement: The Social Obligations of Citizenship.* New York: Free Press.

Meddis, Sam Vincent. 1993. "Is the Drug War Racist? Disparities Suggest the Answer Is Yes." *USA Today,* 23 July, 1A.

Metropolitan Council. 1985. *Managing Growth in the Twin Cities Metropolitan Area: A Response to Land Use Issues Raised by the Legislative Auditor.* Saint Paul: Metropolitan Council.

———. 1992. *Trouble at the Core: The Twin Cities Under Stress.* Saint Paul: Metropolitan Council.

———. 1994. *Keeping the Twin Cities Vital.* Saint Paul: Metropolitan Council.

Meyer, Stephen G. 2000. *As Long As They Don't Move Next Door: Segregation and Racial Conflict in American Neighborhoods.* Lanham, Md.: Rowman and Littlefield Publishers.

Meyerson, Martin, and Edward C. Banfield. 1955. *Politics, Planning and the Public Interest.* Glencoe, Ill.: Free Press.

Mincy, Ronald. B. 1988. "Industrial Restructuring, Dynamic Events and the Racial Composition of Concentrated Poverty." Paper prepared for planning meeting of the Social Science Research Council on Industrial Restructuring, Local Political Economies, and Communities and Neighborhoods. New York, September.

Minneapolis, City of. 1998. "Request for Proposals for a Lead Developer to Assist in the Creation of a Mixed-Use, Mixed-Income, High-Amenity Community on the Near Northside of Minneapolis." Minneapolis: Near Northside Implementation Committee.

Minneapolis Affordable Housing Task Force. 1999. *Minneapolis Affordable Housing Task Force Report.* Submitted to Minneapolis Mayor Sharon Sayles Belton and the Minneapolis City Council, July 15.

Minneapolis Public Housing Authority. 1997. "Sumner Field Focus Group 4/8/96 Meeting Minutes." In *Action Plan for Redevelopment of the Sumner Field, Glenwood, Lyndale and Olson Public Housing Developments and Adjacent Land in Minneapolis,* vol. 2. Minneapolis: Minneapolis Public Housing Authority, December 31.

Minneapolis Star Tribune. 1999. "Editorial: Affordable Housing—Seeing beyond the Hollman Decree." *Minneapolis Star Tribune,* 22 August, A24.

———. 2002. "Editorial: Nellie Stone Johnson, A Life Devoted to Public Service." *Minneapolis Star Tribune,* 4 April.

Minnesota Center for Survey Research. 2000. *Neighborhood and Housing Survey 1999: Results and Technical Report.* Minneapolis: Minnesota Center for Survey Research.

Minnesota Spokesman-Recorder. 1998. "Introducing Hollman Forum 1999." *Minnesota Spokesman-Recorder,* 24–30 December, 1A, 10A.

———. 1999a. "Hollman Protesters Arrested." *Minnesota Spokesman-Recorder,* 21 June, 1A.

———. 1999b. "Hollman: What It's All About." *Minnesota Spokesman-Recorder,* 7–13 January, 1A.

———. 1999c. "Lucille's Kitchen Cooks Hollman." *Minnesota Spokesman-Recorder,* 25 February–3 March, 1.

Moberg, David. 1995. "No Vacancy!" *Shelterforce* (January/February): 11–13.

Mohring, Herbert, and David Anderson. 1994. *Congestion Pricing for the Twin Cities Metropolitan Area.* Saint Paul: Metropolitan Council.

Morrison, Blake. 1995. "Projects' Residents Finally See Escape from Roaches, Bullets." *St. Paul Pioneer Press*, 18 January, 1A.

Murray, Charles. 1984. *Losing Ground: American Social Policy, 1950–1980.* New York: Basic Books.

National Housing Law Project. 2002. *False HOPE: A Critical Assessment of the HOPE VI Public Housing Redevelopment Program.* Oakland, Calif.: National Housing Law Project.

Newberg, Sam. 2001. "Moving Minnesota: The Twin Cities Face a Regionwide Crisis: The Lack of Affordable Housing." *Planning* 67(12): 28–31.

Newman, Sandra J., and Ann B. Schnare. 1997. " '. . . And a Suitable Living Environment': The Failure of Housing Programs to Deliver on Neighborhood Quality." *Housing Policy Debate* 8(4): 703–41.

Nickel, Denise R. 1995. "The Progressive City? Urban Redevelopment in Minneapolis." *Urban Affairs Review* 30(3): 355–77.

Norris, Donald F., and James X. Bembry. 1998. "Moving to Opportunity in Baltimore: Neighborhood Choice and Neighborhood Satisfaction." Paper presented at the 1998 annual meeting of the Urban Affairs Association, Fort Worth, Texas, April 21–25.

Nourse, Hough O. 1963. "The Effect of Public Housing on Property Values in St. Louis." *Land Economics* 39(4): 443–41.

Nyden, Philip. 1998. "Comment on James E. Rosenbaum, Linda K. Stroh, and Cathy A. Flynn's 'Lake Parc Place: A Study of Mixed-Income Housing.' " *Housing Policy Debate* 9(4): 741–48.

Office of the Legislative Auditor, State of Minnesota. 2001. *Affordable Housing.* Saint Paul: Office of the Legislative Auditor, State of Minnesota.

Orfield, Myron. 1997. *Metropolitics: A Regional Agenda for Community and Stability.* Washington, D.C.: Brookings Institution Press.

Oseid, Tammy J., and Amy Sherman. 2001. "Council Puts Off Vote on Housing." *St. Paul Pioneer Press*, 18 September, 1C.

Owens, Mitchell. 1994. "Saving Neighborhoods One Gate at a Time." *New York Times*, 25 August, C1.

Pendall, Rolf. 2000. "Why Voucher and Certificate Users Live in Distressed Neighborhoods." *Housing Policy Debate* 11(4): 881–910.

———. 2001. "Exploring Connections Between Density, Sprawl, and Segregation by Race and Income in U.S. Metropolitan Areas, 1980–1990." Paper presented at the Annual Meeting of the Association of Collegiate Schools of Planning, Cleveland, Ohio, November 2–5.

Pitcoff, Winton. 1993. "CARE, NRP Change Little after Merger." *The Surveyor*, March, 2.

Polikoff, Alexander, ed. 1995. *Housing Mobility: Promise or Illusion?* Washington, D.C.: The Urban Institute.

Popkin, Susan J., Larry F. Buron, Diane K. Levy, and Mary K. Cunningham. 2000. "The Gautreaux Legacy: What Might Mixed-Income and Dispersal Strategies Mean for the Poorest Public Housing Tenants?" *Housing Policy Debate* 11(4): 911–42.

Popkin, Susan J., George Galster, Kenneth Temkin, Carla Herbig, Diane K. Levy, and Elise Richer. 2000. *Baseline Assessment of Public Housing Desegregation Cases: Cross-*

Site Report, vol. 1. Washington, D.C.: U.S. Department of Housing and Urban Development.

Pope, Annette A. 1995. *Section 8 Certificates and Vouchers: Where Are They Going?* Washington, D.C.: Metropolitan Washington Council of Governments.

Quinlan, Michael. 1996. "Policing Program Sidelined by Budget." *Louisville Courier-Journal*, 9 February, 1A.

Rabiega, William A., Ta-Win Lin, and Linda M. Robinson. 1984. "The Property Value Impacts of Public Housing Projects in Low- and Moderate-Density Residential Neighborhoods." *Land Economics* 60(2): 174–79.

Rabin, Yale. 1987. "The Roots of Segregation in the Eighties: The Role of Local Government Actions." In *Divided Neighborhoods: Changing Patterns of Racial Segregation*, edited by Gary Tobin (208–26). Newbury Park, Calif.: Sage Publications.

Rasmussen, David W. 1980. "The Urban Impacts of the Section 8 Existing Housing Assistance Program." In *The Urban Impacts of Federal Policies*, edited by Norman J. Glickman (243–63). Baltimore: Johns Hopkins University Press.

Reeves, Jimmie L., and Richard Campbell. 1994. *Cracked Coverage: Television News, the Anti-Cocaine Crusade, and the Reagan Legacy.* Durham, N.C.: Duke University Press.

Ricketts, Errol R., and Isabel V. Sawhill. 1988. "Defining and Measuring the Underclass." *Journal of Policy Analysis and Management* 7: 316–25.

Rogal, Brian J. 1999. "Tayloring Plans—Section 8 Questioned: Survey Casts Doubt on CHA Plans." *Chicago Reporter* (June). http://www.chicagoreporter.com/1999/06-99/0699cha.htm. (Accessed June 21, 1999.)

Rosenbaum, Emily, and Laura E. Harris. 2001. "Residential Mobility and Opportunities: Early Impacts of the Moving to Opportunity Demonstration Program in Chicago." *Housing Policy Debate* 12(2): 321–46.

Rosenbaum, James E. 1991. "Black Pioneers—Do Their Moves to the Suburbs Increase Economic Opportunity for Mothers and Children?" *Housing Policy Debate* 2(4): 1179–213.

———. 1995. "Changing the Geography of Opportunity by Expanding Residential Choice: Lessons from the Gautreaux Program." *Housing Policy Debate* 6(1): 231–70.

Rosenbaum, James E., and Patricia Meaden. 1992. "Harassment and Acceptance of Low-Income Black Youth in White Suburban Schools." Evanston, Ill.: Center for Urban Affairs and Policy Research.

Rosenbaum, James E., and Shazia Rafiullah Miller. 1997. "Can Residential Mobility Programs Be Preferred Providers of Tenants?" *Poverty Research News.* http://www.lcpr.org/spring97/articles3.html. (Accessed March 2, 1999.)

Rosenbaum, James E., and Susan J. Popkin. 1990. *Economic and Social Impacts of Housing Integration: A Report to the Charles Stewart Mott Foundation.* Evanston, Ill.: Center for Urban Affairs and Policy Research.

———. 1991. "Employment and Earnings of Low-Income Blacks Who Move to Middle-Class Suburbs." In *The Urban Underclass*, edited by Christopher Jencks and Paul E. Peterson (342–56). Washington, D.C.: Brookings Institution.

Rosenbaum, James E., Marilyn J. Kulieke, and Leonard S. Rubinowitz. 1987. "Low-Income Black Children in White Suburban Schools: A Study of School and Student Responses." *Journal of Negro Education* 56(1): 35–43.

————. 1988. "White Suburban Schools' Responses to Low-Income Black Children: Source of Successes and Problems." *The Urban Review* 20(1): 28–41.

Rosenbaum, James E., Linda K. Stroh, and Cathy A. Flynn. 1998. "Lake Parc Place: A Study of Mixed-Income Housing." *Housing Policy Debate* 9(4): 703–40.

Rossi, Peter H., and Robert A. Dentler. 1961. *The Politics of Urban Renewal: The Chicago Findings.* New York: Free Press of Glencoe.

Rubenstein, James M. 1988. "Relocation of Families for Public Improvement Projects: Lessons from Baltimore." *Journal of the American Planning Association* (spring): 185–96.

Rubinowitz, Leonard S. 1992. "Metropolitan Public Housing Desegregation Remedies: Chicago's Privatization Program." *Northern Illinois University Law Review* 12(3): 590–669.

Rubinowitz, Leonard S., and James E. Rosenbaum. 2001. *Crossing the Class and Color Lines: From Public Housing to White Suburbia.* Chicago: University of Chicago Press.

Rumbler, Bill. 1998. "Despite Section 8 Vouchers, Segregation Perpetuates." *Chicago Sun Times,* 6 December.

Rusk, David. 1993. *Cities without Suburbs.* Washington, D.C.: Woodrow Wilson Center Press.

————. 1999. *Inside Game/Outside Game: Winning Strategies for Saving Urban America.* Washington, D.C.: Brookings Institution Press.

St. Anthony, Neal. 2001. "On Business: Business' Top Issues Change." *Minneapolis Star Tribune,* 3 April. http://www.startribune.com/stOnLin. (Accessed April 23, 2001.)

Salama, Jerry J. 1999. "The Redevelopment of Distressed Public Housing: Early Results from HOPE VI Projects in Atlanta, Chicago, and San Antonio." *Housing Policy Debate* 10(1): 95–142.

Sampson, Robert J. 1999. "What 'Community' Supplies." In *Urban Problems and Community Development,* edited by Ronald R. Ferguson and William T. Dickens (241–92). Washington, D.C.: Brookings Institution Press.

Sampson, Robert J., and Stephen W. Raudenbusch. 1999. "Systematic Social Observation of Public Spaces: A New Look at Disorder in Urban Neighborhoods." *American Journal of Sociology* 105(3): 603–51.

Santiago, Anna M., George C. Galster, and Peter Tatian. 2001. "Assessing the Property Value Impacts of the Dispersed Housing Subsidy Program in Denver." *Journal of Policy Analysis and Management* 20(1): 65–88.

Saunders, Linda, and Michael J. Woodford. 1979. *The Effect of a Federally Assisted Housing Project on Property Values.* Jefferson County, Colo.: Colorado State University Extension Service.

Sayles Belton, Sharon. 2002. "Leadership." Public presentation at Hubert H. Humphrey Institute of Public Affairs, Minneapolis, Minn., April 23.

Schafer, Robert. 1972. "The Effect of BMIR Housing on Property Values." *Land Economics* 48(3): 282–86.

Schill, Michael H. 1991. "Deconcentrating the Inner City Poor." *Chicago-Kent Law Review* 67: 795–853.

————. 1997. "Chicago's Mixed-Income New Communities Strategy: The Future Face of Public Housing?" In *Affordable Housing and Urban Redevelopment in the United*

States, edited by Willem van Vliet (135–57). Urban Affairs Annual Reviews, vol. 46. Thousand Oaks, Calif.: Sage Publications.

Schill, Michael H., and Samantha Friedman. 1999. "The Fair Housing Amendments Act of 1988: The First Decade." *Cityscape: A Journal of Policy Development and Research* 4(3): 57–78.

Schill, Michael H., and Susan M. Wachter. 1995. "The Spatial Bias of Federal Housing Law and Policy: Concentrated Poverty in Urban America." *University of Pennsylvania Law Review* 143: 1284–349.

Schwartz, Alex, and Norman Glickman. 1992. *Rebuilding Downtown: A Case Study of Minneapolis.* New Brunswick, N.J.: Center for Urban Policy Research.

Schwartz, Alex, and Kian Tajbakhsh. 1997. "Mixed-Income Housing: Unanswered Questions." *Cityscape: A Journal of Policy Development and Research* 3(2): 71–92.

Seals, Leola. 1998. "Hollman, Uncut." *Minnesota Spokesman-Recorder,* 14–20 January, 1A.

Sedway, Lynn, and Associates. 1983. *Impact of Affordable Housing on Property Values.* Report prepared for the Ecumenical Association for Housing.

Semer, Milton P., Julian H. Zimmerman, Ashley Foard, and John M. Frantz. 1976. *Housing in the Seventies: Working Papers,* vol. 1. National Housing Policy Review. Washington, D.C.: U.S. Government Printing Office.

Sherman, Amy. 2001a. "Housing Advocates Seek Apology from Mayor." *St. Paul Pioneer Press,* 15 August, 2B.

———. 2001b. "Housing Backers Get Message Out Front." *St. Paul Pioneer Press,* 16 October, 2B.

———. 2001c. "Task Force May Take Stand on Housing." *St. Paul Pioneer Press,* 13 October, 2B.

Skogan, Wesley G. 1990. *Disorder and Decline: Crime and the Spiral of Decay in American Neighborhoods.* New York: Free Press.

Spence, L. H. 1993. "Rethinking the Social Role of Public Housing." *Housing Policy Debate* 4(3): 355–68.

Stoll, Michael A. 1999. "Spatial Mismatch, Discrimination, and Male Youth Employment in the Washington, D.C., Area: Implications for Residential Mobility Policies." *Journal of Policy Analysis and Management* 18(1): 77–98.

Struyk, Raymond J. 1991. "Preservation Policies in Perspective." *Housing Policy Debate* 2(2): 383–411.

Stucker, Jennifer L. 1986. "Race and Residential Mobility: The Effects of Housing Assistance Programs on Household Behavior." In *Housing Desegregation and Federal Policy,* edited by John M. Goering (253–61). Chapel Hill: University of North Carolina Press.

Taeuber, Karl, and Alma Taeuber. 1965. *Negroes in Cities: Residential Segregation and Neighborhood Change.* Chicago: Aldine Publishing.

Tegeler, Philip D., Michael L. Hanley, and Judith Liben. 1995. "Transforming Section 8: Using Federal Housing Subsidies to Promote Individual Housing Choice and Desegregation." *Harvard Civil Rights-Civil Liberties Law Review* 30: 451–86.

Tein, Michael R. 1992. "The Devaluation of Nonwhite Community in Remedies for Public Housing Discrimination." *University of Pennsylvania Law Review* 140: 1463–503.

Thompson, Timothy. 1996. "Promoting Mobility and Equal Opportunity: *Hollman v. Cisneros." Journal of Affordable Housing* 5(3): 237–60.

Tonrys, Michael. 1995. *Malign Neglect: Race, Crime and Punishment in America.* New York: Oxford University Press.

Turner, Margery Austin. 1998. "Moving Out of Poverty: Expanding Mobility and Choice through Tenant-Based Housing Assistance." *Housing Policy Debate* 9(2): 373–94.

United Way of Minneapolis Area. 1995. *The Face of the Twin Cities: Another Look.* Minneapolis: United Way.

Urban Coalition. 1994. *Housing Segregation in the Twin Cities.* Saint Paul: The Urban Coalition.

———. 1997. *Relocation and New Housing Study of Sumner Field Public Housing Residents in 1996: Report to the Legal Aid Society of Minneapolis.* Saint Paul: The Urban Coalition.

Urban Institute. 2000. *Baseline Assessment of Public Housing Desegregation Cases: Case Studies,* volume 2. Washington, D.C.: U.S. Department of Housing and Urban Development.

U.S. Department of Housing and Urban Development. 1995. *Tenant-Based Housing Assistance Works.* Issue Brief No. 2: 1–5. Washington, D.C.: Office of Policy Development and Research, U.S. Department of Housing and Urban Development.

———. 1996. *Expanding Housing Choices for HUD-Assisted Families: First Biennial Report to Congress—Moving to Opportunity for Fair Housing and Urban Development.* Washington, D.C.: Office of Policy Development and Research. April.

———. 1998. *Case Studies of Vouchered-Out Assisted Properties.* Washington, D.C.: U.S. Department of Housing and Urban Development.

———. 1999. *Moving to Opportunity for Fair Housing Demonstration Program: Current Status and Initial Findings.* Washington, D.C.: U.S. Department of Housing and Urban Development.

U.S. General Accounting Office. 1995. *Public Housing: Converting to Housing Certificates Raises Major Questions about Cost.* Washington, D.C.: U.S. General Accounting Office.

———. 1997. *HOPE VI Demonstration.* Washington, D.C.: U.S. General Accounting Office.

Vale, Lawrence J. 1997. "The Revitalization of Boston's Commonwealth Public Housing Development." In *Affordable Housing and Urban Redevelopment in the United States,* edited by Willem van Vliet (100–34). Thousand Oaks, Calif.: Sage Publications.

Vang, Tong Xai, Chou Sue Noua, May Vue, Mee Vang, Ka Khang, Cher Xeng Yang, Yia Thao, and Phia Moua. 1999. "Northside Redevelopment Called Secret War." *Minnesota Spokesman-Recorder,* 25–31 March, 5C.

Varady, David P., and Wolfgang F. E. Preiser. 1998. "Scattered-Site Public Housing and Housing Satisfaction." *Journal of the American Planning Association* 64(2): 189–207.

Varady, David P., and Carole C. Walker. 2000. "Vouchering Out Distressed Subsidized Developments: Does Moving Lead to Improvements in Housing and Neighborhood Conditions?" *Housing Policy Debate* 11(1): 115–162.

Vogel, Jennifer. 1993a. "Bad New Tenant." *City Pages,* 16 June, 10.

————. 1993b. "Neighbors with Attitude: Cops, Fear, and 'Neighborhood Revitalization.' " *City Pages,* 5 May, 9.

von Sternberg, Bob. 1994. "Study Finds Concentrations of Poverty in Metro Area." *Minneapolis Star Tribune,* 21 January, B1.

Wacquant, Loic J. D., and William Julius Wilson. 1989. "The Cost of Racial and Class Exclusion in the Inner City." *Annals of the American Academy of Political and Social Sciences* 501 (January): 8–25.

Walsh, Edward. 1993. "Guns in Public Housing Force Showdown of Rights vs. Needs." *Minneapolis Star Tribune,* 26 December, A8.

Walsh, James. 1998. "Crime-Reduction Strategy Should End, NAACP Says." *Minneapolis Star Tribune,* 26 September, B1.

Warren, Elizabeth. 1986. "The Dispersal of Subsidized Housing in Chicago: An Index for Comparisons." *Urban Affairs Quarterly* 21(4): 484–500.

————. 1987. "Measuring the Dispersal of Subsidized Housing in Three Cities." *Journal of Urban Affairs* 8(1): 19–34.

Warren, Elizabeth, Robert M. Aduddell, and Raymond Tatalovich. 1983. *The Impact of Subsidized Housing on Property Values: A Two Pronged Analysis of Chicago and Cook County Suburbs.* Urban Insight Series No. 13. Chicago: Center for Urban Policy, Loyola University of Chicago.

Wascoe, Dan, Jr. 1998. "Minneapolis Loses Tax Base to Metro Property-Tax Pool." *Minneapolis Star Tribune,* 16 February, B3.

Washington, Wayne, and Duchesne Paul Drew. 1995. "Home Is Where the Hardship Is." *Minneapolis Star Tribune,* 26 January, A1.

Watson, Thomas. 2000. "Nothing Changed/Everything Changed: Reflections on the Northside Neighbors for Justice and the Affordable Housing Movement in Minneapolis." Unpublished paper.

Weicher, John C. 1990. "The Voucher/Production Debate." In *Building Foundations: Housing and Federal Policy,* edited by Denise DiPasquale and Langley C. Keyes (263–92). Philadelphia: University of Pennsylvania Press.

Weintraub, Adam. 1996. "Police Program for Middle School." *Cincinnati Enquirer,* 10 February, B7.

Weisman, Jonathan. 1996. "True Impact of GOP Congress Reaches Well beyond Bills." *Congressional Quarterly* 54(36): 2515–20.

Weiss, Marc A. 1985. "The Origins and Legacy of Urban Renewal." In *Federal Housing Policy and Programs: Past and Present,* edited by J. Paul Mitchell (253–76). New Brunswick, N.J.: Center for Urban Policy Research.

Wells, Amy Stuart, and Robert L. Crain. 1994. "Perpetuation Theory and the Long-Term Effects of School Desegregation." *Review of Educational Research* 64(4): 531–55.

Wilen, William P., and Wendy L. Stasell. 2000. "*Gautreaux* and Chicago's Public Housing Crisis: The Conflict between Achieving Integration and Providing Decent Housing for Very Low-Income African Americans." *Clearinghouse Review* 34(3–4): 117–45.

Williams, Kale. 1998. "Fair Housing for Everybody—Including the Poor." *The Fair Housing Report* (winter): 15–16.

Wilson, William Julius. 1987. *The Truly Disadvantaged: The Inner City, the Underclass, and Public Policy.* Chicago: University of Chicago Press.

————. 1996. *When Work Disappears.* New York: Knopf.

Wish, Naomi Bailin, and Stephen Eisdorfer. 1997. "The Impact of Mount Laurel Initiatives: An Analysis of the Characteristics of Applicants and Occupants." *Seton Hall Law Review* 27: 1268–337.

Wright, Pat. 1998. "The Privatization of Public Housing Leads to Affordable Housing Crisis." *PRAGmatics* 1(2): 3, 13.

Yinger, John. 1998. "Housing Discrimination Is Still Worth Worrying About." *Housing Policy Debate* 9(4): 893–927.

Zeisel, John. 1997. *Resident Housing Preferences: Northside Housing.* Final summary report. Minneapolis: The Minneapolis Public Housing Authority.

About the Author

Edward G. Goetz is associate professor and director of the Urban and Regional Planning Program at the University of Minnesota's Humphrey Institute of Public Affairs. He has published articles on local and regional housing policy in the *Journal of the American Planning Association,* the *Urban Affairs Quarterly,* the *Journal of Urban Affairs,* and *Housing Studies.* He is also the author of *Shelter Burden: Local Politics and Progressive Housing Policy* (Temple University Press, 1993) and *The New Localism: Comparative Urban Politics in a Global Era,* with Susan E. Clarke (Sage Publications, 1993).

Index